T0283333

Antiracism as
Daily Practice

Also by Jennifer Harvey

Raising White Kids
Dear White Christians
Disrupting White Supremacy from Within
Whiteness and Morality

Antiracism as Daily Practice

Refuse Shame,
Change White Communities,
and Help Create a Just World

Jennifer Harvey

ST. MARTIN'S PRESS
NEW YORK

First published in the United States by St. Martin's Press, an imprint of St. Martin's Publishing Group

ANTIRACISM AS DAILY PRACTICE. Copyright © 2024 by Jennifer Harvey. All rights reserved. Printed in the United States of America. For information, address St. Martin's Publishing Group, 120 Broadway, New York, NY 10271.

www.stmartins.com

Designed by Meryl Sussman Levavi

The Library of Congress Cataloging-in-Publication Data is available upon request.

ISBN 978-1-250-28670-3 (hardcover)
ISBN 978-1-250-28671-0 (ebook)

Our books may be purchased in bulk for promotional, educational, or business use. Please contact your local bookseller or the Macmillan Corporate and Premium Sales Department at 1-800-221-7945, extension 5442, or by email at MacmillanSpecialMarkets@macmillan.com.

First Edition: 2024

1 3 5 7 9 10 8 6 4 2

For the community of Union Theological Seminary—
with deepest gratitude;
for the everyday people who keep taking one next step
even though justice comes so slow—in solidarity;
and for the countless movement leaders—past and
present—who keep teaching and showing us and doing
it again and again.
Also for my mom.

Contents

Introduction

"White People, Do Your Own Work"

Ruth Sandhill, who is white, was standing in front of a multi-racial gathering alongside Jackie, who is Black. She was talking about ending racial profiling in her small city. She described the set of demands the group she was part of had been pressing the city council to adopt. She outlined the strategies her group was using.

Just before she wrapped up, Sandhill's tone shifted and she launched into a heartfelt plea to the white folks who were present. She explained why ending racial profiling was important to her as a *white* woman. "None of us should be able to tolerate standing by while our neighbors are being mistreated by *our* police department!" She was passionate and clear.

Sandhill has been an engaged citizen her entire adult life. She's long believed volunteering is important and has a commitment to the common good. But this was different and the moment remarkable. Sandhill is not a trained activist or organizer.

She's not even an extrovert. Sandhill is an accountant who loves Excel spreadsheets and describes herself as "not good at public speaking."

In fact, only a few years prior, Sandhill didn't feel like she knew how to talk about racism with her extended family or even her husband. But after the 2016 presidential election, she felt compelled to do *something*. Still, she was at a loss about how to help. She'd even told folks at an antiracism meeting she tentatively showed up for around this time that she worried it wasn't her place to speak up about what needed to happen in her city. She'd heard white people were supposed to pass the microphone and not take up space.

A significant shift had taken place between then and now. How did that happen?

After the murder of George Floyd, parents in a local public school wanted to do more to ensure the well-being of Black students and other students of color. Lisa Johnston, a white mom, wanted to make antiracist values more explicit and attention to race and racism more prominent in the school's culture and curriculum.

Johnston got energized as she thought about how to move her desires forward at her child's majority white school. But then she listened to the podcast *Nice White Parents*.

Nice White Parents investigates the persistence of racial inequity in public schools. It questions why integration has never resulted in the flourishing of all of our children. The podcast explores this problem through a deep dive into the history of one elementary school in Brooklyn, New York. In the process, it exposes the many ways white parents impede the realization of true equity. One of the most important revelations? That the most well-intentioned ("nice") white parents, time and again, behave in ways that produce the opposite results.

Johnston began to question her own motivations and her skills. She began to worry. What if her efforts to change the school's racial culture led to white backlash? What if parents of color were emotionally harmed because other white parents got angry? Johnston went from feeling galvanized to feeling immobilized.

Taking no action didn't seem better, but her concerns were legitimate. What should she do?

Dr. Dave Smith, who teaches at a midsize university in the western United States, had been growing his understanding of racial inequity and his capacity to do better as a white educator. One day he was walking across campus and bumped into a Black student he recognized. He'd never had the student in class, but had met him before. With dismay, Dr. Smith realized he was pretty confident he knew the student's name, but not 100 percent sure.

Dr. Smith's mind began to churn. Acknowledging students of color by name—especially on a predominantly white campus—mattered for the student's well-being and sense of belonging. Many Black, Latinx, and Asian American students found themselves regularly unacknowledged in this way or even contending with professors who failed to learn to pronounce their names correctly. Worse, almost any Black student could describe situations in which they'd been mistaken for another Black student by white faculty—and how painful that experience was.

The stakes in what seemed like an everyday kind of interaction were high. Dr. Smith was still internally debating whether it was worth the risk of using the wrong name or if it would be better to simply say hello.

Before he'd resolved what to do, the student spoke. "Hi, Dr. Evans!" the student greeted him, smiling. Dr. Smith laughed to himself. "Hello," he responded.

The shared human capacity for error had resolved the dilemma for Dr. Smith—a humorous resolution, even. But he also knew the experience illustrated something serious. The fact that a Black student had mistaken him for a different white professor would not have had the same impact as his misremembering the student's name. He knew the goal had to be to create an environment on campus where justice and belonging was the overwhelming experience of students, faculty, and staff of color, to the point that mundane daily interactions like this one didn't carry such racial risk.

Antiracist environments can be nurtured. What is the role of a white professor in that work?

These three anecdotes are all true (names have been changed). They depict relatively common, everyday challenges white people face as we try to grow our commitment to antiracism. Race and racism create high stakes in all our daily interactions where we live, work, or play.

Meanwhile, high stakes also exist within a civic environment that with each passing day seems to become more tense and fraught with conflicts over racism.

So many of us breathed a sigh of relief back in 2020 when Joe Biden was finally declared the winner of that presidential election. The sighs didn't mean we were all necessarily excited about a Biden presidency. They didn't even correlate consistently with whether we were Democrats or not.

The sighs had to do with how close to the brink our democracy seemed to have come over the prior four years. Someone with authoritarian tendencies, a propensity for corruption, and sympathies for white nationalism had settled into the White House.

Civic life had become exhausting, even frightening to Americans from diverse walks of life and across the political spectrum. The outcome of that 2020 election seemed like it might bring us a little breathing space, time to regroup and return to some semblance of a stable and civil civic life.

But while lots of us were still feeling waves of relief, Ash-Lee Woodard Henderson, an organizer with Stacey Abrams's New Georgia Project (the organization that played an outsize role in turning Georgia blue), implored us differently. "Black people have given everything we've got to create an opening for white people to do their own work in their own communities," she said. "Don't waste that opportunity."

And she was right.

Not only was our relief overblown, but Henderson's clarity and prescience at the time remain descriptive of the now. U.S. democracy continues to struggle. Intense white backlash against Black Lives Matter is ongoing. Efforts to ban books, fearmongering against critical race theory, and takeovers of school boards by those intent on suppressing accurate teaching of U.S. history have roared through the nation. Undercurrents of violence—often threatened, sometimes enacted—swirl throughout the mix.

We're living in really difficult times.

The civic era we're currently navigating was overwhelmingly enabled by white people. Even if they might say they disagreed with the ways the former president disparaged Black people and Latinx communities (not to mention women, people with disabilities, Muslims, and so many others), a majority of white voters found Donald Trump's racial vitriol tolerable enough to pull the lever for him anyway. Many of us were never remotely tempted to do such a thing. But we found ourselves in relationships with white people who had: parents, siblings, neighbors, coworkers, and fellow churchgoers.

Appeals to white nationalism became more explicit the longer Trump was in office—from his use of "very fine people" to refer to the white supremacists who marched in Charlottesville at a rally in which a young white antiracist organizer was killed in 2017 to his infamous "Proud Boys, stand back and stand by" on the debate stage with Joe Biden in 2020. Of course, it was only about six weeks after Henderson insisted white people needed to work among our own that Confederate and Nazi flags flew at the U.S. Capitol.

The insurrection made it irrefutable that racism and white supremacy are thick threads weaving through the forces that continue to imperil our democracy. These forces have been emboldened in local and national contexts and have expanded far beyond Trump's rhetoric and time in office.

Americans from every racial and ethnic group have a role to play in addressing the perils in our civic body. But given the nature of the threats, white Americans have a particular part— people like Ruth Sandhill, Lisa Johnston, and Dr. Dave Smith; people like some of you and people like me.

White people have got to face the racial brokenness that exists in our communities. We need to engage it in consistent and daily ways. We must also understand that participating in racially just changemaking is intrinsically connected not only to a more just future for all but also to our own healing and transformation as white people.

It's not only that "no one is free when others are oppressed," as the Reverend Dr. Martin Luther King Jr. so famously taught us. It's that when I show up, as a white American, alongside Black and Brown neighbors to insist all of our children have access to well-resourced public schools, I'm helping transform the racial shame and guilt that run rampant in white communities into action. It's that a group of white retirees planting themselves in front of a local police station every day at noon—insisting officers who roughed up young organizers who led chants of "No more! Black lives matter!" be held accountable—are embodying a change in the relationship between white people and state violence. Even if they don't "win," they're passing down a different legacy to their grandchildren than the legacies they inherited.

Ash-Lee Woodard Henderson was right. The health of our democracy is tethered to our racial health. On that front, the ball is now squarely in white people's courts.

But here's where it gets trickier.

If white communities enabled the forces trying still to bring democracy to its knees, we've got work to do among our own. *Yes.* Full stop.

But this is a chicken-or-egg problem, because most of us were born in, raised by, and still live in the same white communities in need of the work. Most white people spend a majority of our time in workplaces where white people dominate, in both demographics and decision-making roles. Most of our relationships are with other white people.

The white community has made me who I am. White people have formed and continue to form my thinking because my life remains embedded among them. And my white family has shaped what I know in the first place. How then can I possibly be cognizant of what kind of changes those of us who are white need to make? If I start to develop ideas about what those changes should be, where will I learn *how* to make them?

These are real questions. Answering them feels difficult.

The call for white people to do work in our own communities is as tall an order as it is an urgent one. But there's nothing simple about it. There's no boilerplate, one-size-fits-all set of strategies we can apply and—*poof!*—we're seasoned antiracists. No ten-point plan will quickly generate the racial changes white communities need to make to become the partners in justice communities of color have long needed and deserved. And there's certainly no clean path to becoming better white people, no guaranteed way to avoid all mistakes, complexity, and messiness.

But I'm a believer still. I've watched Sandhill go from feeling too timid to talk about race with her husband to speaking ably in packed city council forums. I've witnessed my own mother break ranks with her church, despite a lifetime of identifying with the same evangelicals who've helped bring democracy to the brink. I've heard young white college students insist, with increasing volume, that they are capable of and ready for involvement in the racially just change Black and Brown students are calling for—this despite not having been taught by their elders how to do that.

White people can learn to show up differently in our own lives and in the world. We can change our communities when and as we do so. I know this to be true with as much certainty as I know that we must.

And that's what this book is about.

1

Where Are We?

The white people who raised me did it in the Denver public schools in the 1970s and '80s, when our district was under a mandate to desegregate. Lots of other families in our neighborhood sent their kids to private schools to avoid busing. This meant I was a racial minority at Stedman Elementary when I climbed on the bus in first grade.

Most of my earliest childhood friends at Stedman were Black girls; I was especially close to Mari, Wendy, and Tyra. My best friend that year was Mollyeka. My mom always got Mollyeka's name wrong at home. "Mom, don't call her Molly!" I'd say. "Her name is Mollyeka."

"That's right. I'm sorry," Mom would respond. "I keep thinking her first name is Molly and her last name is Eka." Mom's apology was sincere. But usually, within days, I'd have to correct her again.

In fourth grade, the bus routes flipped and I started walking to school while the African American and Mexican American kids were bused to my neighborhood. I can still easily picture my white Jewish teacher, Ms. Boss, who had flaming red hair (dyed, I now realize). But I don't remember the classroom itself very well. And the look of the classroom says a great deal about equity and justice when it comes to race and education.

To that end, there couldn't have been a bigger difference between my fifth- and sixth-grade classrooms. When I was in fifth grade, Ms. Brown, who was Black, had a palpable love for all of us. That year shines in my memory as an experience of profound collective community. A kind of messy oneness constituted our identity as a class. But Ms. Brown also made each of us feel like we were uniquely important. I think that's because, to her, we were.

Fifth grade is my last memory of warmth and diversity being bound up together and presumed as a natural part of life. I didn't know it at the time, but being part of a multiracial group with a shared sense of identity that didn't require a second thought—to me, anyway—would never again come with ease. From here on, this would have to be sought out, created, or even fought for and defended. And starting that next year, my classrooms would forever look different from what we'd known in Ms. Brown's class as simply normal.

My sixth-grade teacher was white. Ms. Swenson was older than other teachers I'd had, and though I liked her a lot, she was sterner than any of my earlier teachers. In Ms. Swenson's class, we sat in rows. Every day. The entire year. And the rows were determined by reading level. Two rows of desks for each level, and the first two were placed closest to the teacher's desk. Here's where my *now* friends sat: Julie, Tyler, Greg, Christopher, John, and a few others. All white, in my memory.

I sat there, too. Because I was one of the "good readers."

The kids in the next two rows were a more racially mixed

group. That's where my childhood nemesis sat. Jeff used to tease me relentlessly. One day he sent me over the edge when I walked past where he stood in line after recess and he snorted, "I'll bet Jenny does Minnie Mouse Jazzercise!" I have no idea why, but that did it. I hauled back and punched that boy in the eye as hard as I could; to this day, he's the only person I've ever hit.

But other than Jeff, who was white, I don't remember the kids in the middle rows. They certainly weren't my friends.

In the last two rows, the "worst readers" sat all the way across the room from Ms. Swenson's desk. Lots of Brown kids sat there. Some mostly spoke Spanish. I remember one girl named Consuelo who was very shy, smiled a lot, and seemed nice. I don't remember ever talking to her. There were Black kids in those rows, too. But I wasn't friends with them and I don't remember their names.

The racial tracking that began in late elementary school was a precursor to our being smashed together in middle school hallways that now thrummed with racial tension before we went our separate ways when the bell rang. By the time we hit high school, it was a done deal. At South I remained friends with most of the same white kids I'd grown up with in my neighborhood—the ones who'd also sat in the good reader rows. Only now we had entire classrooms to ourselves. Advanced Placement (AP) trig and calculus, AP English, AP social studies. Check, check, check, check. Aside from one friend who was Native American (Navajo and adopted), one who was Korean American (immigrated when we were all in second grade), and one who was African American, the rest of us in those classes were white.

For some reason, I started to notice this. I'd get an occasional sensation that something was wrong. I had no way to talk or even think about it, really. But I knew something was off and that whatever it was had to do with race.

I'd find myself wondering about Mari and Wendy and Tyra. What had happened to them? Were they at a different high school? Would I ever bump into them at a soccer game?

Why were there almost no Black kids in my "real" classes? I developed some rapport with a few Black students in shop and home economics, and with a couple who were on the soccer team—but it wasn't really friendship. Where did those kids go the rest of the school day?

The strength of my questions ebbed and flowed. But mostly my experience was the same as most white teenagers. Which is to say, not a single adult who was helping to raise, support, and nurture me talked with me about any of this.

So I just noticed. And I knew something was wrong. All by myself.

The white people who raised me also did it in church. Bethel Baptist sat at 1801 South Logan Street. On a slow week, my family of nine could be found there at least three times. Denver's Christian radio station, KWBI, played in our living room day in and day out. Every Saturday morning, James Dobson's voice seeped through the speakers as my siblings and I listened to *Children's Bible Hour* before lacing up our cleats to go play soccer at the local park. Images of Billy Graham adorned our home.

My grammy especially loved Billy Graham. Grammy had been widowed young and never remarried. She'd read and reread the piles of Graham's books she kept stacked on her headboard. When I'd spend the night at her house, I would sometimes find her having fallen fast asleep mid-page, a book drooped down over her sweet face, Graham's image with his dimpled chin and smoldering eyes staring at me off the back cover.

Grammy was also our church pianist. She played every service for decades. She was the preschool Sunday school teacher and, during the week, the director of our church's TUC preschool (from Proverbs 22:6: "Train up a child in the way he should go: and when he is old, he will not depart from it"). All six of my younger siblings went through her Sunday school and preschool classes before they hit first grade.

Bethel was basically the sun around which we orbited. This white evangelical Christianity was more than a belief system or set of moral values. It was my family's formative identity, an ethos and a world, encompassing culture and community. Bethel nurtured the ecosystem through which I came to know and understand myself as a self and to make sense out of my relationships with others.

I have lots of critiques I would make now of this ecosystem. The sexism was everywhere—in my church, women didn't even serve communion, let alone ascend to the pulpit in any official capacity besides choir director. Knowing one was "saved" rested on a traumatically close call—how many times did I sit and give repeated thanks I was born into a Christian family, the dumb luck of such a near miss with eternal damnation making me sweat?

And of course, *Christian* meant Baptist. Catholics, Lutherans, and Methodists certainly weren't included.

My dad told me his conversion story once. In it, he described banging on the door of a Methodist church, soaking wet from the rain on a day when he was feeling depressive despair and on the verge of suicide. No one answered the door.

That was a good thing, Dad told me. "That was the day God saved me from the Methodists."

But despite the troubling parts of this ecosystem, what I knew most deeply because of it was that God so loves the world. God's love for this world was, for me, a fundamental existential framework. I believed it utterly. And I assumed God loving the world meant God so loves the *whole* world. As in, God so loves *all of us*.

I was not prepared, then, for the crisis I would go through when I went off to a predominantly white and conservative evangelical college after high school.

My first year at Westmont College, I volunteered at a local Salvation Army shelter with a student ministry group. I soon found myself spending more and more time talking to families who were unhoused and hungry. Learning about poverty and economic injustice for the first time rattled me. I couldn't believe the suffering. The juxtaposition of such suffering with my own daily life became stark.

At the same time, I was falling in love with the study of theology. I did well and got high grades. Professors reached out, wanting to mentor me. But I sat in my classes of mostly men and the debate turned to questions like, "Can women be leaders in the church?" It started to matter that the same students insisting women couldn't be ordained were unbothered when they whizzed their Mercedes-Benzes past hungry families hunkered down on the streets of Santa Barbara on a Saturday night. The absurdity of this moral position became intolerable.

The longer this went on, the more I found myself realizing the emperor had no clothes and being unwilling to pretend he did. I was noticing contradictions that weren't merely intellectually shattering (though they were). They weren't causing just a faith crisis (though it was quickly becoming that). Rather, all the threads weaving through my understanding of God—threads that held me together as a self, bound me to a community, and rooted me in a world—were being more strained with each passing semester.

Everything changed when, in my third year at Westmont, I was introduced to a form of Christianity rooted in what's called liberation theology. Liberation theology's basic premise is pretty simple: It claims that "God so loves the world" *really does mean* the whole world. God so loves the whole world means God cares about every single part of our lives as humans. This includes caring about human suffering, all of it—including the massive suffering caused by sexism and racism, economic oppression and homophobia, colonialism, and so much more.

The Bible depicts a God who takes sides with the poor and a Jesus who talked about this all the time. But even setting these biblical descriptions aside, if God cares about the suffering caused by profound and pervasive injustice—caused by isms— then by sheer force of logic, God has to be a God of justice.

My trips down to the Salvation Army began to make theological sense. God hated homelessness and the wealth accumulation that turned a blind eye to it. Classroom debates over women's capacity to lead were thrown into sharp relief. I saw them for what they were—straight-up sexism that presumed women were less than.

Then came the day I was introduced to James H. Cone, the father of Black liberation theology. Like other liberation theologians, Cone wrote that God is a God of justice. But he got more explicit. Cone wrote that if God is a God of justice, then God has to be Black, because in the United States, Black people are the oppressed of the oppressed. That's where a God of justice must dwell.

Jesus Christ is Black, too, Cone said. Orthodox Christian belief is that Jesus the Christ was fully human and fully divine. If this is true, it means the Christ—the divine one who is still with us *today*—is who he was *back then*, when he was embodied as a specific human being in a particular time and place. Well, Jesus *was* a working-class Jew who lived under Roman occupation and the oppression of Jewish people. He *lived* a life insisting on dignity for the poor and discarded ("blessed are the poor"!). And he did this so persistently that the powers that be found him a threat too significant to ignore. He was executed by the state. So Jesus the Christ *is* present today amid struggles for the freedom, dignity, and liberation of the poor—for those who are made poor by violent systems and structures of subjugation, including white supremacy. Jesus *is* Black.

Cone didn't only crack open my understanding of "God so loves the world." He handed me an interpretation of my high school experience, shedding light on those confusing questions that haunted me. Cone showed me that structural racism, racial injustice, and white supremacy had been defining features of my short life. He helped me see how they'd infused my education, as well as my church community and its version of Christianity.

Race had already been a central force shaping my life. But from the moment I read *God of the Oppressed,* a switch flipped. Race became a central preoccupation.

Naturally, then, I did what any other economically secure white girl in my situation would do. I gasped with excitement at such newfound clarity, took a deep breath, and announced, "I'm going to Union Theological Seminary to study with Dr. James Cone!"

And that's exactly what I did.

Well, sort of.

That's a story we'll have to come back to.

These are the two stories I usually start with when people ask me, "How did you get passionate about racism?" That's not how the question is always asked, though. Usually people stumble a bit at first while reaching for their words. Maybe they're afraid of offending or being misunderstood. "So, how did you, I mean, when did you become so interested..." Their voice trails off. "You mean," I sometimes try to help, "why do I care about racism when I'm *white*?"

A relieved chuckle often follows. "Well, yeah."

Many kinds of people have asked me this question and for various reasons. But in recent years, when white people ask me how my concern about racism came to be strong enough that working against it and for reparative justice has defined so many of my life choices, I hear some things in the question that are familiar. I hear an ache and a sense of longing.

I recognize these because they're mine, too. It's a longing that began inside of me—as soon as I left my fifth-grade classroom—for what all of our communities could be like. It's an ache because they almost never are.

There are so many white people in touch with a yearning for which we don't have words, for a way of living beyond our national racial brokenness and the constraints systems of racism impose on all our lives. More than a few of us feel the trap of being caught inside white culture—even if we're not sure what "white culture" is. Many Americans long to be part of a community that is rambunctious and flourishing, promiscuous in its diversity and its loving justice–filled energy—all of which are the opposite of what white cultures allow white Americans to experience.

This was true long before the Trump era. But it's become truer since its onset.

In this time in which we are grappling publicly like we never have before over race, identity, who we are as a nation and who we are going to be, I invite you to imagine the possibility that this is the moment in which more of us are ready. We're ready to dig in and go deeper than we've ever gone. We're ready to allow that yearning to help us take a giant leap forward in the liberating journey of changing white communities to realize freedom for all.

When masses of people poured into the streets to protest the killing of George Floyd and Breonna Taylor in the summer of 2020, the multiracial nature of the protests was widely remarked upon. More white people participated than any of us had seen in our lifetimes.

I remember marching through the streets of downtown Des Moines, Iowa, and running into a fellow teacher from my university. This is a white guy I'd worked with for years. He'd always shown me respect when we disagreed over race and reparations. Even when I'd disagreed in turn, I basically liked him. But he was also someone who seemed to find my vocal stances in support of Black Lives Matter over the years a bit—I'm not sure what—unbecoming? naive? overly simplistic?

Now here he was. He was wearing a Black Lives Matter T-shirt he'd obviously made by hand and trying to figure out the chants so he could join in. He was even putting his fist in the air when the Black youth leading the protests called us to do so. He looked awkward and a little uncomfortable. But my coworker gave me a small smile and nod when he saw me. This seemed to me an acknowledgment of our past disagreements and that he was now seeing something different. He knew his participation mattered.

It made me happy to see him there.

This wasn't "performance activism" or "virtue signaling"—these labels we throw around so easily to decry people who aren't really *committed* but just want to *be seen* doing something about racism because it's cool or something. This is not a man at all worried about looking uncool. His presence, like that of so many who'd never gotten into the streets before, was evidence the call for white people to get more involved had for a moment broken through.

Some type of shift in white consciousness has taken place. Historian and antiracist public intellectual Ibram X. Kendi says there "may have never been [before now] such a governing majority that recognizes racism as a big problem." This shift has come about because of persistent and powerful Black organizing and leadership. It's a response to BIPOC-led advocacy in local communities all over the country.

When journalists and commentators saw so many people in the streets, the question of the day became "Is this the start of a national reckoning on race?"[1] And as we now sit looking back at all that has happened in our struggling democracy since 2020, that question remains in the air.

Is it?

My response to that question is not yes. But it also isn't no. What I wanted to say then—what I want to say still—is *we don't know yet.* The next chapter of the story hasn't been written. The fact is, we are the ones, right now, *in this very moment,* who will determine what comes next in this very long American story.

How deeply important. How very humbling.

Those of us who desperately want the answer to be "Yes! Yes, we're in the process of moving through national racial reckoning" get to decide whether we'll help to make it so. This is the moment for us to build on the moral curiosity white people are showing, the awareness that has grown, the buy-in to antiracism that has increased in ourselves and other white people.

But so many of us experiencing these things and feeling a longing for a different racial now and a better racial future have so many questions. Many of these start with "But how?" Or

"Now what?" Or a frustrated admission of "I don't even know what to do!"

Why does it seem so difficult for those of us who are white to figure out our next steps, even if we've read a lot of books and tried to put the voices of people of color at the center of our learning? Some of the reasons have to do with the long-term effects of being socialized as white people. This is a generational phenomenon that's affected white communities in ways we haven't collectively wrestled with enough yet.

Many of these reasons have to do with shame in white lives. Lots of us who feel the injustice of racism in our bones also live with the burn of shame that quickly flares in the wake of such recognition.

Shame is debilitating. It stunts our capacity to take action and do better. Yet we rarely talk about this openly in white antiracism conversations. Shame is also tough to talk about well on social media! Meaningful conversations about shame require a sense of trust and safety. These usually develop only in spaces where relationship-building has been given attention and care.

A different set of reasons for the difficulty has to do with growing tendencies in our public conversations about race, racism, and white people. Amid so much excellent and insightful antiracist teaching we've been offered, we've grabbed on to concepts that have created some behavioral cul-de-sacs. There are stuck points that get in the way of white people moving forward in antiracism.

Of course, some of the reasons have to do with white backlash, accompanied by threats of violence, that has developed to meet the powerful momentum of so many of us pouring into the streets. The intensifying civic climate makes it even more difficult to build trust across racial lines. It makes it harder to summon the courage to take a public stand. It can even seduce us into thinking, *There's just no hope, so why take the risk?*

It might make you mad to hear me acknowledge that it's hard for white people to figure out how to change our lives or know what to do. After all, people's lives are at stake.

But speaking frankly about the various difficulties we encounter is the only way white people can really start to answer the question "Now what?" in concrete terms. We're also going to explore the challenges here, so we can do that. We're going to envision ways white people can develop new habits.

Not only does modifying our racial habits and practices change us, but it enables transformation to happen in the white communities so many of us are part of. And let's be clear. We can't just change individuals. We've got to change communities.

White people can change. I know this to be true because I've lived it. I'm not done, of course. Racism and white supremacy are powerful and dynamic, so my journey is ongoing. I continue to make mistakes and discover even more that I need to learn and do differently.

But even still, the fact remains: I'm not the same white person I was thirty years ago when I showed up at Union Theological Seminary, in all my white entitlement, to "study with Cone" (who hadn't invited me to do that, by the way). Thank god I'm not. To be more specific, thank the many Black and Brown people, and a few white ones, who kept holding me accountable and insisting I learn and grow even when I made a mess.

We don't have to keep allowing the death culture of white supremacy to circumscribe our lives. We can change our relationship to the racist conditions we've inherited. These conditions alienate, separate, and isolate us from our fellow humans. They leave us mistrusted and sometimes despised by communities of color because collectively, and for so long, we've occupied spaces of cultural, institutional, political, and/or emotional dominance and dominion.

We can choose differently.

White people can change.

When I hear Black people insist white people need to do our own work, I hear an invitation to decide to belong. When white people learn to show up and participate in creating conditions in which dignity, freedom, and liberation for Black communities and all communities of color can be fully realized, we're learning to show up to create conditions of dignity, freedom, and liberation for ourselves, too. Because we are all interconnected.

"White people, do work in your own communities."

Ash-Lee Woodard Henderson's words are an invitation to choose life.

My therapist claims grief and love are the same thing. Sometimes it makes me mad when she tells me this. But Buddhist teacher Sharon Salzberg seems to agree. Salzberg says grief is "love without the usual place to land." Salzberg also says that when we are grieving, we are relinquishing the illusion that the past could be different from what it was. And I think those two teachings—about grief and love—are a pretty good place to root a deep conversation.

In some ways, election night of 2016 still plays an outsize role in my memory when I think about white people, racism, and what's going on in the United States, even though it seems like a century ago now.

What a traumatic experience. Like so many others, I'd sat with my family that evening. We assumed history was going to be made, so my then-partner and I had taken our young children with us when we'd voted that day. We'd promised them they could stay up until the election was officially called, even though it was a school night.

It didn't matter that I wasn't a fan of Hillary Clinton. It did matter she was a woman.

But it mattered even more that Trump was an obvious threat. I could see how terrorizing his lying and abusive tendencies would become if amplified through the office of the presidency. I'd watched the impact months of campaigning had on the students of color I worked with every day—African American and Latinx college students, students who were documented and who were not, wealthy students and low-income ones. They knew Trump hated Black and Brown people and white nationalists loved him. The air around all of us became more charged and electrified with danger the longer the campaign season wore on.

So there we sat on election night, with wine and cheese and snacks for the kids, glued to the television.

Then he started to win.

And with each state that turned red, a sense of impending doom made my gut tighten, eyes blink, breath quicken. The television maps got redder. My partner and I got quieter. Neither of us could find the words to explain to our children what was happening. Eventually one of us said quietly, "Kids, it's time to go to bed."

We'd sat holding our older child on the couch when she was only two days old the night Barack Obama had been elected. I'd wept that night and thought, *Wow, this child will never know what it's like to grow up in a country that has never elected a Black president.* Now, only two presidential election nights later, that same child was resisting us angrily. "You promised we could stay up!"

"Yes, we did," we pleaded back. "But we can't keep this promise. This isn't going the way we thought it would. It's going to be a much later night than we realized."

That's what we said.

What I thought was *I'll be damned if I'm going to let you sit and watch something this violent happen.* Plus, I didn't want her to see me lose it.

Our daughter became frantic. "No!" she said. "All my friends are getting to stay up late to watch. I told them I was getting to stay up, too! You're turning me into a liar!" Now she was yelling, beside herself with the injustice of it.

I knew exactly how she felt.

In the terrible days that followed, the depth of white support for Trump cut as deeply as that election night realization that he was winning. Fifty-three percent of white women had voted for him. So had an overwhelming majority of white Christians.[2]

Entanglement with white supremacy has always challenged the vitality of American Christianity. That wasn't news to me. And I know what white women are capable of, not just because I'm one of them. These are communities I've long identified with—albeit in complicated ways.

I wanted nothing more than to place the blame for the beginning of the Trump era at the feet of only the ones who actually voted for him (whether they did it only once or again in 2020). I wanted to be able to say that those of us who knew better than to vote for that man bore no responsibility.

I wanted to yell, "I didn't do it!"

But I couldn't say any of those things. Because they weren't true. And they still aren't. The truth is, I am as connected to the many white people who did as I am insulated from the worst of the racial violence and harm this era has wrought.

Recalling that terrible night elicits the pain, disorientation, and dislocation that unfurled with increasing intensity in the terrible weeks, months, and years that followed. These nightmares continue to envelop us.

But I'm not writing about that night to double down on our

experiences of devastation. I don't want to play light with heart-break or feed despair.

I'm writing about it because we need to relinquish the illusion we can go back to wherever it was or whoever we thought we were before 2016. The past is how we have arrived at this point. There is no undoing it. There is only the question "Now what?"

White people need to grieve. We need to face the grief of who we have been and what our communities have done. This is a necessary part of becoming able to understand and live into Henderson's call to choose life. If grief is love without a place to land, the "Now what?" of this moment is an invitation to learn to build that place.

One of the most important stories in the Christian tradition is about the women who go to the tomb three days after Jesus is executed. These women's names were Mary, Mary, and Salome. They went carrying spices and perfumes that day because they were going to tend to the body. They expected to find a corpse.

Talk about grief. These women had not only just lost someone they loved dearly but had watched him die a gruesome death. They must also have been very afraid. For months they'd hung around in public with a man the state had pronounced guilty and proceeded to kill. The air must have felt electric with danger.

What's so amazing about this story is that these women go anyway. They go through grief and fear. They are willing to bear witness to death and look loss straight in the face.

And because they do, these women become the first people in this story of death to experience new life.

When Mary, Mary, and Salome get to the tomb, a being who turns out to be an angel shows up. He says, "Guess what? Jesus isn't here, because he's alive. And not only is he alive, but you're about to see him." Suddenly the otherwise-always-certain order of things is overturned. The loss and permanency of death turn out not to be so. Mary, Mary, and Salome learn that the life-giving-ness of connection, a vision for the flourishing of all, the sense of possibility despite the current circumstances—all realities they'd known as part of the community Jesus called into existence—aren't gone.

They are still there. Because the ending of the story hasn't yet been written.

You don't have to be religious or believe an actual resurrection happened to access the power in this story. Mary, Mary, and Salome experience resurrection not because they downplayed or minimized catastrophe; not because they averted their eyes or ran away hoping to wait it all out. They dared to look directly at the violence that had irrevocably altered their lives. They risked touching the betrayal they'd just lived through. Then, because they chose to honor their grief by journeying together and standing collectively at the tomb, they came to know new life.

Their walk with grief created a new place for love to land. Just like Sharon Salzberg talks about.

So what might happen if those of us awake to the devastating reality of racism and our own white complicity allowed ourselves to feel? *To grieve?*

What might happen if we understood grief to be a form of love? What if, in allowing ourselves to attend to it, we found ourselves on a journey of creating a place for love to land? To land as justice. To land as equity. As repair. As respect. As redress. As care for the flourishing of all. In our communities. With our neighbors. At our kids' schools. Within our families. In the hearts and lives and futures of all of our children.

Antiracism is the project of building a place for love to land. White communities are the primary construction zones.

My relationship with Christianity and with the complicated family who raised me in it has changed dramatically over the course of my life. I no longer believe in a literal resurrection. And the way I imagine divinity looks nothing like it did back when I sang hymns from the pews while my beloved grammy played the piano up front at Bethel Baptist Church.

But as it turns out, all these years later, I do still believe that God so loves the world. As in the whole world. As in all of us.

So I want to feel and I need to grieve. Because I want to live. I want all of us to live.

The writer and activist adrienne maree brown constantly encourages those of us yearning to grow a world of justice and flourishing. She reminds us that uncertainty is to be expected. It's all breathtakingly new. "We are shaping the future we long for and have not yet experienced," brown writes.[3]

What a relief! These words are an inspiration to keep going when the way feels difficult or unclear. Of course it's difficult and unclear. None of us have ever experienced the kind of world so many of us long to live in.

Yet in the same moment that brown's words are aspirational, they're also declarative: "We are shaping the future we long for." We *are*.

So let us feel this grief and honor our longing for a different future. The time is now to do the slow but possible work of transforming white communities, which is also essential to sustaining American democracy. And we do this by, each of us, taking one next step at a time.

TAKE A NEXT STEP

1. Take a few minutes and, if applicable, think about the white people who raised you. Identify the racial messages and teaching you received. How do these still affect what you

know and don't know now about race and racism? Where do you feel a longing to know more about race or understand racism differently or more fully?

2. Start a "take a next step" log in a notes application on your phone, a journal, or some other place you track things you need to hold on to. As you read this book, jot down thoughts, questions, memories, or ideas related to your own actions and practices. Periodically pause and identify what a next step might be in your local context in regard to some insight that really grabs your attention.

3. Check out "106 Things White People Can Do for Racial Justice" by Corinne Shutack,[4] part of Equality Includes You, which is curated by The Good Men Project. This excellent list of resources continues to be updated. Go back and forth, keeping this diverse list of meaningful actions and resources in conversation with what you learn in this book.

2

Why Is This So Hard?

In the fall of 1994, I headed off to live in New York City, a place I'd never even been as a tourist. As far as I was concerned, there was no point in visiting ahead of time. I just knew I was supposed to go to Union. I'd known ever since I invited myself to go study with Cone.

Union Theological Seminary is the heartbeat of liberation-committed, progressive Christianity. Its faculty are internationally renowned. This school started granting divinity degrees to women in the 1890s, was surveilled by the FBI during the Vietnam War because it was producing so many conscientious objectors, and unapologetically celebrated queer Christians completing PhDs and becoming clergy when doing so was unheard of. Most important to me, it was the place that had invited Dr. James H. Cone to join the faculty after his book *Black Theology and Black Power* rocked the world of Christianity in 1969.

Social justice has gravitas at Union, and racial justice especially so. Situated on the edge of Harlem, Union is marked indelibly by the legacies of Malcolm X and the Black Power Movement. It's also a community with deep ties to the civil rights movement. The Reverend Dr. Martin Luther King Jr. preached six times at the historic Riverside Church next door and delivered his famous sermon against the Vietnam War there only a year before he was assassinated.

Now imagine me, this twenty-something white woman, born and raised in evangelical Christianity, who's undergone a racial justice awakening by reading books while attending a mostly white, wealthy, conservative Christian college. I show up at Union and begin to navigate robustly multiracial hallways and residential buildings. I sit in classrooms with Black, Latinx, and Native American students, many of whom are seasoned activists and most of whom are embedded in ministry within their respective racial/ethnic communities. A number of these students will go on to become some of the most prominent scholars, pastors, and activists in the nation. For example, think of Raphael G. Warnock, pastor of Ebenezer Baptist Church (Dr. King's church) and eventual U.S. senator, but at that point one of Cone's doctoral students.

Here I come. I'm earnest and passionate. I'm thinking things like *God is Black.* Or *Hey! I love the Black Jesus so much!* Sometimes I'm saying these things out loud.

Yep. It was that bad.

I'll never forget raising my hand during a session on diversity in new student orientation and opining about how eager I was to "sit and learn from students of color." I still feel the blush of embarrassment when I remember how, moments later, Michelle Gonzalez Maldonado, a fellow student who is Cuban American and has gone on to have a brilliant scholarly career, raised her hand. She shook her head. She seemed puzzled and annoyed. "I'm not here to be 'learned from,'" she said. I can't remember quite how she put what came next, but it was something about how she wanted and expected to be in intellectually *mutual* learning relationships.

You'd think this early encounter would have chastened me a bit. But I remained remarkably undeterred in my willingness to charge into any situation without first questioning my racial instincts.

I became a reporter for the student newspaper. One day in Bible class, our professor, Phyllis Trible, a white feminist scholar, was lecturing about Moses. She got to a part of the story where Moses's brother and sister get mad because Moses takes a wife from the nation of Cush. Trible said something about their anger having to do with the wife being a Cushite, which would have made her "black." Electricity began to pulse through the room after a Black student raised his hand and asked, "So if your hypothesis is that Moses's siblings were mad because his wife was black, what color are you assuming Moses was?"

I don't remember what Trible said. But even though I was sort of confused by the exchange, I understood my classmate had made some kind of accusation. I could also tell Black students found Trible's response wholly unsatisfying.

I later learned these students were already mad because we had a midterm scheduled on the same day of the soon-to-be-historic Million Man March (1995). A group of Black men had asked Trible if they could be offered a makeup date so they could attend the march. She'd told them no. I heard rumblings that in her denial of their request, she'd described the march as an expression of patriarchy.

The students attended the march anyway. And I just knew I was the right white person to write about all of this for the school paper.

So, after my peers came back from Washington, DC, I got

to work. When one after the other said no, they didn't want to sit for an interview with me, I did what any good white reporter would do. I ignored them and asked again.

They explained they'd made a pact before they'd returned to campus. The experience they'd had was sacred, they said. They'd agreed they wouldn't talk about it with white people; weren't going to put it out there on display for scrutiny within the seminary community.

What did I do when I heard that?

I asked again. "I know, I know, I totally get how you feel, but . . ." I'd said. Then I'd gone on to explain why I could be trusted to share their story. I was confident they just hadn't realized yet that I was on their side—the white person who "got it."

Yep. So cringey.

Then there was the time I got on the elevator with two Black students, one of whom I knew pretty well and the other I did not. The student I knew began to introduce me to the second student. In my eagerness to connect, because I wanted to be friends with Black people so badly, I quickly leaned in and interrupted. I put my hand out to the student I hadn't met yet and said, "Oh yes, I know, you're X," and promptly called the student—who, of course, I didn't really know—the wrong name. Yes, of course, it was the name of a different Black student in our community.

Meanwhile, Cone was clear about his vocational focus. Yes, he was an amazing professor who rigorously taught every single one of the students in his courses. Yes, I did take several of his classes. But Cone was committed to the freedom of Black people. He was intentional about investing his precious time mentoring, advising, and teaching students of color, especially Black students. He knew they would be the next generation of scholars, pastors, and activists and he was committed to the future.

Cone taught me and I learned from him. A lot. But it didn't

matter whether I loved the Black Jesus or not. Cone wasn't there *for me*. It probably took two whole years at Union before the armor of racial entitlement I wore daily began to dissolve enough that this recognition began to sink in.

My early years at Union were some of the most difficult of my life. The white people who raised me hadn't prepared me to handle myself in those classrooms and that community. The segregation that had shaped so much about my life to that point worsened the impact and implications of that lack of preparation.

When I look back, I feel sad about what my lack of readiness meant for the professors and students who had to live and learn with me. I know I extracted energy and insisted on attention that wasn't mine to take. I know I caused harm.

But I also can't help but feel compassion for that young white woman who was me. She hadn't been provided the nurture and support she needed to show up differently. As someone who desperately wanted to get on the right side of racial justice, she lacked mentors and models.

She was someone who didn't want her inherited white identity to be her destiny. But she had no idea what to do about that.

This is not that uncommon in white life.

When students walk into my classes and I tell them we're going to study race and learn about the impact of racism in our shared lives, the response is predictable. For the most part, students of color nod. They're ready. This is particularly true of Black students. The response is something along the lines of "Okay, let's go."

White students' responses couldn't be more different. Their eyes get big. They look like deer in headlights. You can almost hear their thoughts as they start to subtly shake their heads: *No, no, no . . . Um, couldn't we talk about something easier? Like, could we please talk about abortion instead?*

It took me a few years of teaching to understand what was going on. Basically, it's as though these young people walk into a room and are told we're going to do calculus together. Black and Latinx students nod. They've been doing high-level math for years. Their families and communities started teaching them calculus as early as ages three, four, five. By nineteen or twenty, though they have more to learn, they're masters of calculus.

White students, meanwhile, have been taught little more than addition. Their deer-in-headlights panic is real. They know they have no idea how to do calculus, and they're terrified of what's going to happen when they're found out.

Some of them are resistant to learning high-level math. But in my experience, far more of them are worried that their inability to do calculus will expose them as bad people. In recent years, more of them also understand their inability to do calculus might cause their peers harm—cause pain. Honestly, in this they are eons beyond where I was when I would barge into the lives and spaces of students of color at Union like a bull in a china shop. Their awareness is an indication that our culture has improved in this area. But it can also get in the way of their ability and willingness to take the risk of moving into the kinds of discussions and learning that really need to take place.

Our civic realities are making this calculus problem harder. Dr. Rebecca Anderson has been teaching about racism and systemic inequality since she began her work as an educator in feminist ethics nearly twenty years ago. Prior to 2016, students of color overwhelmingly expressed gratitude at how her courses addressed the roots and ongoing expressions of U.S. racism. White students expressed a range of reactions—discomfort, appreciation, defensiveness, transformation. But since 2020, the stressful realities many students of color live with on a daily basis have manifested as frustration and fatigue at having to be in the classroom with white students.

Dr. Anderson knows, from an educational perspective, that white students still need to feel safe and supported to learn about and accept the reality of white supremacy and white privilege. Otherwise they collapse into denial or shame. But many students of color need quite different things: more Black and Brown professors to mentor and teach them, spaces to discuss healing from racialized trauma, support to build coalitions among diverse students of color, and strategies to hold institutions like Dr. Anderson's accountable.

Despite having received countless awards for excellence in teaching over the course of her career, today Dr. Anderson feels like she's simultaneously unable to reach the students she most needs to reach while letting down the very students for whom she wants to be an ally. Today her evaluations range from "too focused on racism" to "not nearly radical enough." "I struggle to create the educational space all of my students need and deserve given the world we're living in right now," she says.

Wherever we may be in our own learning about racism and desire to grow antiracism, and whatever sectors we live or work in, so many of us (of diverse racial and ethnic identities) are contending with challenges very similar to what Dr. Anderson describes.

Layla F. Saad is a writer and teacher who is committed to exploring personal transformation and social change. Saad lives in the Middle East and is particularly focused on the well-being of Black girls and Black women globally. In her book, *Me and White Supremacy,* Saad offers twenty-eight specific lessons to help white people work on becoming "a good ancestor." It's brilliant not only because the step-by-step lessons are powerful, but because invoking ancestry invites the long view. If I imagine antiracism as an invitation to become a good ancestor, I'm recognizing that decisions I make today in a difficult world create a future world very different from—better than—this one. The possibility exists that I might bequeath something incredibly precious not just to the next generation, but to the one after that and the one after that.

What a beautiful invitation.

Such generational framing can also help us better understand what's going on with white people in spaces and places where we're challenged to move constructively into various forms of racial reckoning. Here I want to turn the idea of ancestors around, as it helps us see how the past affects the present. It affects the students in my classes, that young white woman years ago at Union, my coworker in his handmade Black Lives Matter T-shirt struggling to learn chants he now recognizes as important.

White people didn't have good ancestors.

I don't mean that the white people who were our ancestors were only and innately bad humans—as in, "they just weren't good people." Human lives are almost always more complicated than simplistic categories of good and bad.

I'm also not talking about the many of us who have ancestors who specifically engaged in various kinds of racial atrocities. Those people exist in my family, people who were here colonizing and enslaving from the beginning of what would become the origins of the United States. I even know some of these people's names. That's very important, but it constitutes a different kind of conversation about ancestry.

I'm talking about not having had people in our families and communities—parents, grandparents, other white elders—who mentored, nurtured, and supported us to grow justice-sensibilities as part of our basic values formation. My mother didn't get it from her parents, who didn't get it from theirs, who didn't get it . . . On it goes. Until someone intentionally makes a very different choice, we don't and won't begin to hand it down to the next generation.

There are reasons an earnest and eager, Black Jesus–loving white woman showed up *so inappropriately* in those seminary hallways. There are reasons those years became the most difficult of my life. My ancestors didn't pass down what I needed to be a "good" member of that community. I didn't know what walking with others in justice and for justice looked like, especially for me as a white person. I couldn't have known at that point.

The specifics of my time at Union are obviously pretty unique. Most white people don't go to seminary, let alone move across the country, sight unseen, because they want to study Black liberation theology.

But the challenges I ran smack into once I'd realized racism was a huge problem that had affected my entire white life are not unique at all. Neither are the messes I kept making once I realized I wanted to be on the side of justice. Those challenges— and the messes they bring in their wake—pervade white experience as we wake up to the crisis of white supremacy.

We didn't have good ancestors. We didn't get what we needed. And that's why this is so hard.

Getting a better handle on the hard is critical at a time when, across the country, so many white people at once have indicated a stronger awareness of the pervasiveness of racial injustice. Attention to ancestors lets us talk about generational legacies we've inherited and the collective practices we're all embedded in, every single day. It moves us from a focus on individuals to one on communities. This is helpful because the most vexing and perhaps most powerful part of white people's relationship with race is its communal dimensions and has to do with white socialization.

Socialization is everywhere in human life. We get socialized as a woman or a man, an Iowan or a New Yorker, a Harvey or a Patterson. I could paint a picture of what it means to be a third-generation Denver Broncos fan as easily as I can talk about being the great-granddaughter of Bernice Schlessman, whose family settled Cripple Creek, Colorado, in the late 1800s—about whom I imbibed harrowing and inspiring stories while sitting on my great-grandma Schlessman's porch drinking lemonade.

One of these ways of knowing myself as Jen Harvey is relatively benign. Sports team and hometown identity are all tangled up together! The other is much less so. Central to our family origin stories were tales about the strength and grit of (white) women who were, of course, implicated in the displacement of Native peoples in a state that had become Colorado only a few years before my ancestors homesteaded there (my family never shared that part of the story).

But both of these ways of knowing are part of my socialization. Both inform my sense of self and the world. Both connect me to a larger communal identity and a story about who that community is, who *we* are. They tell me how to behave, instill me with values, create traits that run deeper than conscious thought.

Even if I distance myself from some of my inherited identities, my identity still makes sense in reference to a larger communal one. For example, I'm not a third-generation Broncos fan anymore. I'm the Harvey who is now the not-Broncos-fan Denverite, the one who's broken the lineage because I'm raising a fourth generation of not-Broncos-fan children.

Race is in the mix of all of this. Racial socialization is communal. It's about legacies we inherit and generational teachings we pass down. It's about dynamics that go on among us when we sit on one another's porches and drink lemonade or gather around a television to cheer on a football team.

There are many traits we could identify as part and parcel of white socialization. The entitlement that led me to assume I could just "go study with Cone" was a part of my socialization. My expectation that I would be treated as an exception led to my self-assurance that it was okay to ignore the "no, thank you" from my peers. This is a kind of audacity I associate with white socialization.

There's a lot of diversity among white people as well, of course. Geographical origins and class status and gender and a host of other social realities shape what whiteness looks like.

But among the many and diverse traits that characterize our socialization, white silence is pervasive. It's a main reason white people today find it so difficult to start to talk about race, even once we know we need to. And this silence has been accompanied by white passivity in the face of injustice. Passivity learned over time manifests itself as feeling frozen and stuck—not knowing what to do about racism when we see it.

Silence and passivity are the waters in which white communities swim. They create the developmental contexts in which white lives are lived. These waters shape not just *what* white people know about race, but *how* we know it. They inform whether we can talk about it (and with whom), *what it feels like when we try* (usually difficult!), and when and where we feel able to risk it. Where we swim impacts what our bodies understand or miss when racial dynamics are at play in a room, and even how our emotions show up in racial justice work.

These waters are totally different from those in which people of color swim, the developmental contexts in which people of color live their lives. In all their diversity and in ways that vary, communities of color *have* taught and continue to teach race. They model resistance to racism and they strive for justice to and for the next generation. These teachings happen at the family dinner table and in front of the television. They are transmitted through stories passed down and in hopes articulated for the future—sometimes also in the mundane activity of drinking lemonade on the porch.

For communities of color, creating cultures of justice-centered striving has been a necessity of survival and a commitment to a future in which their descendants can thrive. Black communities, for example, have generated knowledge and built on received wisdom in every generation. They've transmitted this knowledge and wisdom in ways that shape the next generation and the one after that. Legacies of resistance to white supremacy are passed down from parent to child. They are threads woven through familial and communal journeys.

In a collective sense, white people don't have any of that. We just don't.

The developmental impact of pervasive white silence and passivity is so formative that when a white person has their "Um, wait, what?!? There's a racial justice crisis in this nation?" moment—for me in my early twenties—or when a whole bunch of white people do—like happened en masse in 2020—we don't know what to do. And most of the time we aren't all that sure how to start to figure it out.

Recognizing the power of white socialization shifts how we understand racism in white lives. In the current climate, antiracist commentary focuses a lot on getting white people to learn new ideas. Changing minds is, of course, critical. But it's just the tip of the iceberg.

Racial socialization means race lives in our bodies.

Long before anyone used words to teach me about racism, I felt the tension of race in my body in those middle school hallways. My body absorbed teachings through the experience of being placed in the rows closest to my teacher's desk—a sense of my body as belonging, being seen, worthy of attention.

There are few white persons among us who haven't learned what race "means" through observing a subtle shift in a white elder's facial expression in some kind of interracial encounter. The people our parents put their bodies close to in a room (or those they avoided), how our parents made eye contact (or not) with a Black child on a playground, the tones they used when they spoke to a Latinx worker at a doctor's office, grocery store, or restaurant—all this informed what our bodies learned to feel and do. The feel of race in the United States shaped our bodily experience long before we developed language for it.

I can learn, intellectually, for example, that white people confusing Black people for each other is a symptom of racism. I can understand this behavior causes Black people harm. But such knowledge and awareness does not help my body feel more at ease if I walk into a room and find myself the only white person among a group of fifty Black people. These kinds of changes develop only when I start putting my body in such rooms more of the time.

Desirable growth and change in our whole personhood requires habitual changes, sustained over time. As humans, we develop through small steps. Learning is scaffolded through the exchange between new ideas and experiences, in which ideas take on life as we try them out. Development involves embodiment—changes in what our bodies know, feel, do. The growth of new neurological pathways is necessary for developmental changes. These are always complex and take time.

We know all of this when it comes to emotional, intellectual, spiritual, and even physical development. It's no less true with racial development.

Racial development is complex and takes time. This claim may evoke frustration. It's a claim that can barely be heard in our public conversation about white people and race because it flies in the face of strong temptations to sort people. We're inclined, these days, to boil down assessments of one another to the overly simplistic question of whether someone is *actually* committed to antiracism or not.

But, though frustrating and hard to hear, the claim is no less true.

Another challenge rests on top of the fact that desirable racial change is a long, slow process. If white socialization is a central culprit, the social structures within which we live make it that much more difficult to intervene for just changes. Why? Because most white Americans live deeply segregated lives, even those of us who live in multiracial places.

It's difficult to undo white socialization when you spend most of your time in white spaces. There are things we can learn and skills we can develop on our own. But, frankly, there are also limits.

Racial segregation makes the transformation of white communities more difficult because we need to shake up and intervene in patterns of white socialization. But if we're living our everyday, ordinary lives in white spaces, we're constantly being resocialized into whiteness.

The obvious answer to this specific challenge is for us as white people to desegregate our lives. But even if that's the obvious answer, it's not a straightforward one. The racial patterns we've developed because we've lived segregated lives are likely to make us messy—even burdensome—when we show up in multiracial spaces. Think me and Union.

Desegregating isn't easy, because segregation is so embedded in the social and economic fabric of American life. Consider that redlining (discrimination in housing), legally practiced until very recently—arguably still practiced in other ways—has shaped virtually every American city. Redlining basically determined who could live where. In turn, public schools, funded through property taxes, came to reflect the same resource disparities and deprivations our neighborhoods do.

There's a familiar refrain among parents: "I need to live where the good schools are." It frames the decision to go along with the historic systems that continue to perpetuate de facto segregation in housing and education as doing what's best for our (often white) kids. It typically also rests on any number of racist and class-biased assumptions.

At the same time, this "good schools" refrain accurately reflects day-to-day dilemmas. These systems challenge all kinds of families, not just white ones, when we try to figure out how to make sure our children attend schools with the ample resources all schools deserve. It can seem impossible to make an individual choice that is also just in a system already so compromised by injustice.

It takes massive commitment, energy, and will to choose against such entrenched, segregating systems. When I begin to morally reckon with racism in a serious way, for example, my first step is not likely to be something as big as moving to a different neighborhood. (And even if it was, in a flash, relocating can become part of the racially complex phenomenon of gentrification.)

The power of segregation doesn't let any of us off the hook. And my point isn't that many of the other steps most of us can easily take to desegregate our lives aren't meaningful places to start. From which libraries I take my kids to what community events I support, there are lots of life choices that help us begin to desegregate (more coming below!).

But it is important to recognize how entrenched generationally inherited segregation and its effects are. There are no quick or one-stop answers for how we change white socialization, because it's not simple to choose against segregation. Meanwhile we need to: The more white children are born into and socialized in exclusively white environments, the more we continue to raise civic actors whose abilities to engage in racially just ways are at best delayed.

Hard things that take time can be done. We do them by taking persistent concrete steps.

We can identify practices to enable substantive shifts to take hold in white lives. Such shifts can generate communal transformation—even if slowly—as the people who make them remain embedded in white families, communities, and relational networks.

We can choose to transfer a majority of the time we spend reading and engaging with various forms of media to engaging with feminists of color—this includes feminist men and other genders of color, too. We can access multimedia that present a vision of a just multiracial democracy where all thrive. A digital media platform like Colorlines is a great place to start. (There's a list of journalists at the end of this chapter, as well as a section of Further Resources at the back of this book.) Reading current events through the analytical framework of BIPOC intellectuals will not only keep you up-to-date on the news. Over time, you'll also start internalizing more racially aware frameworks. These begin to shape how you see and understand other issues on your own.

So do an audit of who you listen to. Opt to fill your time with the many diverse and brilliant people of color who are public commentators, journalists, writers, and activists we can so easily access. Engage their knowledge and wisdom. Read their disagreements with one another. When you don't understand what they're saying or why, or when you don't agree with what some of them are saying—actually, *especially* then—keep reading.

Take a family inventory. Where do you shop? Who cuts your hair? Where do you take your kids to the dentist? What restaurants do you frequent?

Then find ways to move some of your participation in the economy over to Black, Latinx, and other businesses owned and operated by people of color—to as many establishments as you can. Urge others in your life to do so. Get your workplace to do it, too.

This practice not only reallocates resources you're already expending to communities of color. It brings you into more frequent contact with people our white enclaves typically prevent us from being in everyday contact with. It's one way to begin to desegregate your life.

Resist the temptation to just sit there with your feelings. Don't get me wrong: Feelings are important. But even while we're feeling guilty or anxious, we also need to take our actual physical selves to organizations led by people of color who are working for justice. We need to show up in person (assuming the organization welcomes white participation, of course).

Who is working on ending educational and housing segregation in your community? Go help! Who is working on voting access? Plug in!

Notice when we say we're too busy to show up and make a different choice. Maybe I volunteer at my kids' school, do stuff for my neighborhood association, am part of a book club, spend time on Facebook. Can I transfer some of the hours in my week that I am currently investing in the well-being of other white people and invest instead in the justice work people of color are leading all over this nation?

Here again, besides helping with the disproportionate heavy lifting people of color are already doing, this set of habits develops our abilities and shifts our loyalties. We build new relationships in ways that antiracist ideas alone don't make possible. We need to show up and keep showing up. Do what is asked. Listen carefully. Don't speak too much or make suggestions for improvement. If you are uncomfortable being one of only a few white people in that space, stay and stay again.

Make a commitment to reallocate resources to organizations led by women of color—local, regional, national. Donate to women of color running for elected office. I'm not suggesting that women of color are going to "save us," nor should we expect them to. But women of color are often the leaders laying out the most transformative visions for our communities. They are also the most under-resourced by traditional political infrastructures.

So if you're tempted—as I am—to give Facebook shout-outs to Black women in Alabama for defeating someone like Roy Moore in 2017 or to Stacey Abrams for helping flip Georgia blue in 2020 or to someone like my neighbor who ran for our local school board in 2022, you need to go all in. We owe women of color something. We need to give money and knock on doors.

We also need to have Black women's backs as they step up and out into leadership. They take huge risks when they do.

Just look at the onslaught of hate Nikole Hannah-Jones continually receives for the 1619 Project. Images of police in riot gear and blazing fires were used to scare Iowans about what awaited us if gubernatorial candidate Deidre DeJear won. The ad never showed DeJear, but flashed a picture of Representative Cori Bush from Missouri saying "Defund the police" as if these two Black women were interchangeable.

When my neighbor won her bid for school board, she started a group for families committed to equity. Families of color found community and strength there. It was only a few months before the backlash came. Some white parents began to organize. One night they decided to crash and disrupt the group's meetings. In response, my neighbor called on white parents to turn out to show solidarity with the families in the network she'd been growing. We did. And we came with a plan to de-escalate things if we needed to. It all turned out fine. But the message had been sent. Black women leaders will be targeted in our community.

So we need to invest actual time, energy, and resources to support such leaders. We need to be proactive and reliable. Whether that's showing up to a school board meeting, writing letters to our local paper, or displaying support in some other way, we need to show active solidarity.

Finally (for now), there are some white women, white queer folks, and a handful of white feminist men who have been working on antiracism for a long time. Find, follow, and engage them, too. Your learning will speed up if you engage some of the white people who have been on that specific journey for a while.

This strategy has caveats. Be careful who you listen to. Pay attention to who such people are in dialogue with. Vet their credibility by noticing what feminists of color say to and about them. If mostly or only other white people like their work, exercise an abundance of caution. But there are white folks who are obviously in relationships of accountability with people of color. Get with them.

Social change isn't just about hard-core activist demands made in public. Ideas, visions, and values about "race, class, gender, sexuality; about nature, power, climate, the interconnectedness of all things; about compassion, generosity, collectivity, communion; about justice, equality, possibility," build the world we live in. These are collective projects, writes Rebecca Solnit. We don't get there when one person shares a new idea about race, gender, or some such. It begins to matter when "a million [people] integrate [that idea] into how they see and act in the world."[1]

Integrating these new habits into our everyday lives will change what and how we see. They are vital to changing the ways we can act.

My friend Aana has been practicing the kinds of habits described above for a long time. She's committed to learning what she wasn't taught. She also wants to pass down a different legacy to her white son.

That she and her partner, Alison, normalized such habits in their home likely created the conditions that influenced her son's choice of sixth-grade science fair project. The prompt was "What is a real-world problem you are interested in working on?" In answer to this question, Ben wrote: "In our day and age, racism is a very real thing. Part of the problem are implicit biases. The fact is that you can be racially biased without even knowing it."

In response to the follow-up question, "What new (does not exist) solution do you have for your problem?" Ben wrote: "Is there a way we could reverse stereotypes and reduce implicit bias? I want to see if I can show fifth-grade students images that will challenge stereotypes they may have or use."

Initially, Ben's science teacher was on board with this. Racial bias fit the bill. It was a real-world problem, and she said to Aana in an email, she knew it was important. The teacher even proposed a method to help Ben first test for the presence of bias and then for the efficacy of his interventions.

Ben was excited. He started working hard.

Then Aana received some follow-up emails. Ben's teacher started to express concern about other parents' reactions to this project. She asked if they might find a topic with "less risk of misrepresentation." How about obesity or pollution? she wondered.

A researcher herself, with experience designing studies to treat subjects ethically, Aana leaned in. She helped Ben create a permission slip so kids would have to have explicit parental support to participate. They created a questionnaire that could test bias but avoid the word *racism*. She suggested they interview children at a different school to ensure anonymity. She made clear they would engage all children, not just white ones.

In a final email, Aana detailed all the ways they'd designed a method that was "nonthreatening, responsible, and age appropriate." She wanted to be responsive to the teacher's concerns. She was not, however, willing to make Ben give up his idea. He'd arrived at it on his own and by now had invested real time and enthusiasm.

At this point the teacher requested an in-person meeting. Aana and Ben were surprised to arrive and find the assistant principal in attendance. They soon came to understand he was there to squash the project. Students might be harmed, he said. When Aana asked him, "In what way?" he had no answer.

"No matter what constructive proposals we offered to their concerns, they were just against it," Aana later wrote. After going back and forth, Aana eventually told her son they would have to comply. But "I then said [to Ben and in front of both the assistant principal and the teacher] that I felt it was important to put it out there that a significant basis for their decision is fear—not that [racial bias] is not a problem or the project ill-conceived or not feasible . . . they are worried how students and parents will react—fallout. I tried be diplomatic but also honest and strong. I did not raise my voice."

The meeting ended with an angry assistant principal, a stressed teacher, a frustrated parent, and a confused sixth-grader.

Communal white silence is powerful. When we grow skills and try to interrupt white socialization patterns, we will sometimes bump into fear and resistance. Our efforts may not yield the results we seek. But such efforts pass on something different to the next generation even still.

The official outcome to Aana and Ben's experience—Ben had to start his whole project over—felt hard to the whole family. It included hurt feelings and a good bit of parental second-guessing. Aana was shaken for some time. She worried she didn't push hard enough and had let Ben down. She worried she'd pushed too hard and put Ben in an unfair position.

I saw something different. Aana chose to lean into courage, rather than just going along the moment the school got nervous. Her refusal to passively comply boldly modeled a different relationship to race for Ben. We can't know, of course, what the assistant principal and teacher thought about all of this, nor if they integrated the experience in a way that shifted their ideas or actions going forward. But it's reasonable to assume her behavior left an impression on them, too.

This messy story has meaningful transformation in it. It's a good example of what an everyday attempt to break white silence looks like. We create a different legacy through step-by-step choices we make in the places we live, work, play, and learn.

Even when they don't turn out just right.

Ben's science fair took place a few years before a powerful backlash injected the false claim into our public discourse that talking about race in schools is intended to make white children feel bad about themselves. Today, in an environment where teachers and schools are under heightened scrutiny and are truly threatened by such backlash, this same teacher and assistant principal might have squashed such a project even sooner. Fearmongering and hostile political organizing have escalated in civic life.

Such conditions make the need for changes in white communities that much more obvious. But they also make the kind of dialogue and work necessary to grow white people's capacity for racial justice more difficult.

The more stress we are all under, the more difficult it is to work together and build trust. Imagine: If learning calculus is hard on a good day, what about when the day is anything but good? What happens when the school building is on fire? Because that's how things can feel these days.

In 2017, Black Lives Matter cofounder Alicia Garza decided to participate in the Women's March. This was despite criticism of the march by many progressive activists, including many Black women, as well as Garza's own awareness that the march was imperfect.

I highly recommend you read about her choice. One of the things Garza said stays with me these days as an almost constant refrain.

Garza wrote: "Hundreds of thousands of people are trying to figure out what it means to join a movement. If we demonstrate that to be a part of a movement, you must believe that people cannot change, that transformation is not possible . . . we will not win." She went on to remember her own journey to justice activism.

Someone was patient with me. Someone saw that I had something to contribute. Someone stuck with me.

> Someone did the work to increase my commitment.
> Someone taught me how to be accountable. Someone
> opened my eyes to the root causes of the problems we
> face. Someone pushed me to call forward my vision for
> the future. Someone trained me to bring other people
> who are looking for a movement into one.[2]

The slow pace of white learning and the inevitable mistakes made along the way are nearly unbearable when we've lived with uncertainty and instability for so long and the stakes are so high. It's so easy to turn on one another. Our current civic living conditions amplify the temptation to do so and strain our patience for walking with new learners.

But difficulty doesn't change the facts on the ground: This is where we are when it comes to transforming white communities.

There are lots of nuances about who should walk patiently with whom, and when, how, and why—as well as when to stop and say, "No further." And people of color legitimately choose many different ways of relating (or sometimes not relating) to and with white people who are striving to learn justice. I've benefited from different approaches over the course of my life, including from those who chose to not be around me at all because the way my whiteness showed up made it untenable to be patient with me. It's not for me to weigh in on such discernment.

But I do presume to weigh in on what white people committed to antiracism owe other white people—whether we've been on that journey for a long time or are very new.

Garza's words contain so much wisdom. One of the most important experiences of my life was a time when a group of people chose to believe transformation was possible. In that same Union community where I was running around making such a mess, these students decided to stick with me anyway.

A group of students designed a multi-week experience for our community to bear witness to the history of the Middle Passage and its legacies. The experience began with a chapel service commemorating the Middle Passage's horrors. Music with powerful rhythms punctuated by moans played while we sat in a circle around a wooden boat. There were chains inside the boat. Laments were prayed communally. Devastating narratives were read aloud. The experience was incredibly intense. I can only imagine how it must have been for African American students as we sat together—descendants of the perpetrators and the perpetrated against; ancestors who had been the oppressors and ancestors who were wrenched from a homeland and violently subjugated for generations.

The group planned three other services. One was for people of African descent only. It focused on ancestors and communal healing. In parallel, there was another described this way: "A service of confession, repentance, and reparation for those who benefit from white privilege and white supremacy."

The title made me nervous. I went anyway.

The service was powerful. And hard. It made me feel guilty. It gave me other feelings. I didn't know what to do with any of them. It showed me I had serious learning to do. I didn't know what that was.

The final service brought the entire community back together. We didn't come together with an easy sense that everything was now healed and the four services had created interracial unity. We did not sing "We Shall Overcome." We did make individual commitments and wrote them down on pieces of paper. And we collectively recited a litany that rededicated our community to racial truth telling.

All kinds of other programs were offered during the period in which those services were held. One was the chance to sign up for a weekly "white antiracism group." Mary Foulke, a white student acknowledged as an ally and deeply trusted by students of color at Union, would facilitate. One of my individual commitments at the end of that last service was to go ahead and sign up.

Mary had us do things like write out our racial autobiography. For the first time in my life, I was asked to reflect on how I learned about race, what messages I'd been given, and what emotional environments I'd learned these lessons in. I sat with questions about how race informed my relationships with white family members. It was surprising to me how vulnerable and painful it was to talk about such things.

I was supported in getting self-reflective about how my autobiography shaped and formed my perceptions of Black and Brown people, my own morality, and my identity. That left me feeling really vulnerable, too.

Over time I was challenged to learn how to show up differently in a host of spaces in my life—not just when I was around people of color but also, especially, when I was around other white people. We built plans for our own "next steps" in such learning. This included talking through racial incidents we'd experienced to get support to speak up more effectively next time. It included studying up on things we didn't know enough about or understand well enough in terms of racial history. It was our responsibility to become more informed advocates. We constantly reflected on the specific impact being white had on how we experienced racial conversations.

Probably the most important thing was that I had companions. I was *walked with* as I started to see, feel, and notice all of those things. Now, as my senses began to deepen, when I encountered explicit or subtle racism in my everyday, ordinary white life—and actually recognized it—I found myself sharing the experience in that space. By the time I went back out into the world, I'd almost always feel more ready to respond, step up, be brave. I'd go knowing I wasn't doing it alone, and learned that while I still might do it imperfectly, that imperfect attempt was better than not doing it at all.

I don't think I ever apologized to Michelle Gonzalez Maldonado, to the student in the elevator, or to the Black men whom I harangued in my misguided attempt to prove they could trust me. I'm sure at that point I wouldn't have known how.

But later that year when I was again involved in a racist incident on campus—because, of course, I kept screwing up—and again as part of the student newspaper, I made a discovery. I'll spare you the details, but it involved an essay satirizing the robust diversity of our community. Rather than a clever acknowledgment of the challenges diversity can indeed pose that landed clearly in celebration, the satire poked fun at non-native English speakers and caricatured Black students.

I didn't write the essay. I found it objectionable. But as a member of the paper staff, I had foreknowledge of it and didn't find the courage or know-how to stop it from being published.

The piece caused so much hurt, and it was awful to be associated with that. But this time, instead of succumbing to the temptation to ignore, discount, minimize, justify, flee, or flat out just stay in bed until it all blew over (which is what I really wanted to do), I discovered I knew in my body that accountability mattered. And not only that, I discovered I actually longed to be accountable.

Somehow that group had helped me develop to the point that I could feel an emerging soul knowledge that my words and actions mattered. My participation in a community mattered. To put it differently, I had tasted a kind of *belonging* I'd never experienced before and I didn't want to lose it.

It was still really hard to face the consequences of my inaction/ action and take responsibility. But I wrote an open letter to try to do precisely that. I called my coeditor, asking him to do the same. (He was indignant and made clear our relationship was over for good.) Then I headed to campus and put a paper copy of my apology letter in the mailbox of every student.

The hardness of all of those steps was no match for the courage that found me. Though it would have been easier to stay under the covers than show my face on campus and be in conversation with the students whom we'd hurt, I now knew that *belonging* awaited me on the other side of showing up in a posture of accountability.

"White people, do [your] own work in your own communities," says Ash-Lee Woodard Henderson. "Thank you, Mary Foulke and the students of color who trusted you, and, in bestowing that trust, created conditions for me to be companioned," says Jen Harvey.

Alicia Garza believes "transformation is possible."

I believe it is, too. And I want us to believe it together.

TAKE A NEXT STEP

1. Identify an uncomfortable, painful, or otherwise noteworthy racial experience you were part of or observed. List specific characteristics of white racial socialization that were at play in the experience. Name responses, interventions, or "If only I had . . ." thoughts, however large or small, that might have changed the outcome of the story.

2. Listen to National Public Radio's Code Switch every week. Sign up for Colorlines' digital platform. Find at least three journalists of color to read regularly. Yamiche Alcindor, Charles M. Blow, Jamelle Bouie, Errin Haines, and April Ryan are a few great options.

3. Find a list of BIPOC-owned businesses and organizations in your area. Identify several to patronize regularly. Grocery stores, barbershops and hair salons, auto repair shops, dentist offices, clothing stores, and any other place already part of your life routine are places you can choose to support BIPOC enterprises instead.

3

Let's Run Around the Block!

In spring of 2018, I flew to my hometown of Denver, Colorado. I was shocked when I arrived at the house I grew up in and discovered a sign in the front yard. In three different languages it read: "No matter where you are from, we're glad you're our neighbor."

I wasn't shocked by the sign itself. At that point the political climate was such that messages registering dissent and pronouncing a commitment of inclusion weren't unusual. Signs like that were everywhere.

I was shocked by that specific sign in my mom's specific yard because my mom remained as active in the evangelical world as we had been when I'd grown up. And in that world, conservative politics—including those of the Trump variety—were of a piece with born-again salvation. My mom's lawn sign basically screamed to her longtime community: "Hey! There's a traitor living here!"

The only thing more jarring than discovering Mom's sign was

learning that she'd begun opting out of her longtime Conservative Baptist church after the 2016 election. She was now an interloper at a local Lutheran congregation (Evangelical Lutheran Church in America, or ELCA). And *that* was jarring. If my dad thought God saved him from the Methodists, it's no surprise I'd also been taught Lutherans were basically Catholic, which to us meant *not really Christian*. (This is not true, by the way.)

My seventy-five-year-old mother, in other words, had not only lost her political party. She'd also lost her church.

Here's where this gets interesting.

My mother's sign didn't mean she'd left her religious beliefs behind. Her beliefs are still as evangelical as they come. Though she'd do just about anything for her motley group of kids, she'd still get uncomfortably quiet if you started asking her about unwed motherhood at age eighteen, lesbianism, or use of drugs and alcohol. Each of these things violates her worldview in a pretty hard-core way, and all have been part of her children's lives.

At the same time, my mom has always upended the images conjured by the phrase *evangelical woman*.

For starters, Mom was a doctor. She went to medical school in the early 1960s, making her one of only a few women there at the time. My dad claims that while other students sat in class madly scribbling notes, Mom sat in the front row madly knitting. I don't know if this story is true. But if you ever met my mom, you'd realize it easily could be.

My mom also gave birth to seven babies. Having given birth to two babies myself, I can't fathom how she played in a tennis tournament two months before her seventh one was born. Or the fact that she was forty-four when she did so.

Mom gave birth to that baby at 2:07 P.M. on a Wednesday afternoon in early November 1984. By 5:00 P.M. we'd swaddled up our new sibling and Mom had checked herself out of the hospital. We landed at church by 7:00 P.M. that same day where—come hell or high water or childbirth—we *always* spent Wednesday nights.

At church we proudly introduced our baby. It was when the Mexican American kids in Children's Church started laughing that we learned we'd accidentally named our new brother "ham"—as in *jamón*. (It took my parents only another week or so to file the paperwork to officially change my brother's birth certificate from Jamon to Jamin. But it was too late. Poor Jamin. To this day we call him Hambone.)

My mom is the same wherever she goes. She's utterly disinterested in the expectations of others. She wore Birkenstocks years before anyone in the United States knew what they were. She didn't stop even after a patient filed a complaint with Human Resources asserting Dr. Harvey had been seeing patients while wearing "flip-flops."

What's funniest to me is that Birkenstocks put this patient over the edge. Never mind that the Birkenstock-wearing woman doctor had a newborn stowed in her office.

Yes, an actual newborn.

My mom didn't just go right back to church after giving birth. She'd go back to work quickly, too, taking her infant with her. The nurses would care for the newest Harvey while Mom saw patients. She'd duck in, between appointments, to breastfeed. Somehow she never got written up for *that*.

On top of all this, if it wasn't snowing and no kids needed hauling, Mom went about daily life on her beloved Harley-Davidson, a bike she rode until she was almost seventy years old. When I was in high school, she'd don a black leather jacket and zip it tight above the leather chaps my dad had given her as a birthday gift. Just above her heart on the left side, her jacket sported a bright red-and-yellow patch stitched with a *#1* in a large font and text that declared, *Riding for Jesus.*

Now that I'm past the sensitivities of the teenage years, I could go on with stories about how unusual and wonderful my mom is. But that's not why I've shared these here. My mom didn't just have interesting tendencies—though knitting in the front row of your medical school classroom is certainly interesting. She didn't just have a ton of energy that nourished loud and bold living—though she did and still does.

My mom had a propensity to break ranks with the expectations of those who surrounded her. That's what I thought about after I saw her lawn sign. A lifetime of habits lay underneath Mom's ability to make such a risky (for her) public statement. Well-developed muscles of audacity and courage rest underneath Sally's comfort with making a scene. They've developed, over the course of her long life, each time she's thrown others' discomfort to the wind and done her own thing.

It takes a specific kind of strength to stand up for what you know to be true and authentic, especially when doing so means going against the grain of a community in which you are fully immersed, with which you otherwise completely identify, which you love, and in regard to which you have oriented your entire existence. In that sense, my mom's story is a great illustration of a basic principle about racism and antiracism.

There's a direct line between a habit of nonconformity and the ability to stand up against the prevailing posture of one's community. And there's a deep correlation between *that* moral muscle and stamina and a critical capacity necessary for antiracism.

Antiracism is a behavior. It is an embodied practice. It's a set of habits lived out loud and over, and over, again. It's a journey during which we learn to discern when to stay and when to leave. When to lean in and connect and when to make a scene. (There's rarely one right answer.)

Antiracism of the audacity and power necessary for civic transformation is a capacity we develop as we cultivate the audacity and resilience of a woman who, while totally outnumbered in a class full of white men, sits in the front row madly knitting anyway.

White people have a lot to learn about race. We need to learn histories most of us haven't before. We need to learn to recognize racism when it shows up. We need to learn how we benefit from racial injustice and perpetuate it.

There are also values white people need to internalize. Values have to do with what we care about and how we believe things should be. A moral value usually sits at our core, energizing serious commitments that shape our lives. Antiracism is no different.

But a misconception often swirls in spaces where white people are trying to move into antiracism. We tend to perceive our relationship to race—specifically, to *righting* that relationship—as primarily a matter of intellectual understanding and/or moral beliefs. We tend to blame racism as primarily a problem of inadequate cognitive understanding and/or moral conviction.

I'm not splitting semantic hairs. How we frame things matters. When I discovered I needed reading glasses at age forty-five, I quickly realized the shape and size of my frames impacted what I could see. Certain parts of a page would come into focus. Other parts remained blurry.

Just like my ability to read, the frames we use to look at the dilemmas posed by white relationships to race affect what we see or don't see. They affect how we answer important questions or address certain problems. They shape what questions we even ask!

There's quite a bit at stake.

Let's go back to my mom. The stories I shared about her vividly illustrate the gap between moral values and *behaviors* or intellectual proclivities and *actions*. That gap matters in terms of outcomes.

Let's imagine you believe a new parent should have the right to thrive as both a parent and an employee. Imagine you also know intellectually that a parent who wants to remain active at work needs support if they want to sustain a breastfeeding relationship with their baby. It's less than ideal for an infant to be separated from a parent for eight hours at a time in this case.

Lots of us have mindsets or values that affirm some version of these possibilities.

But now imagine having the muscle to translate that knowledge and belief into behavior.

Imagine what it would take to walk into your place of employment with an infant slung over your shoulder. To do so despite organizational norms or policies! Imagine taking it upon yourself to argue for a policy change so that everyone gets access to adequate parental leave.

Is embodying such behaviors synonymous with believing new parents should have the right to take their baby to work? Does merely holding such values accomplish the change in culture necessary for a workplace to become more supportive of new parents? Of course not, and no.

Far fewer of us can imagine actually *doing* what my mom did (let alone doing it in Birkenstocks). That fewer includes me!

A few years ago a white friend shared that when Colin Kaepernick was taking a knee—a protest very much in line with her values—she'd gone to a performance at her hometown's civic center. As the national anthem played, she kept trying to get her body to kneel down. She was shaking. She knew her husband would get mad. She felt the isolation of being the only one to do it. She wrestled internally during the entire time the anthem played. Still her body remained frozen. And then the song was over. She hadn't taken a knee.

A few months later she took part in a protest. In this action, organizers had the entire crowd "die in." This time her body didn't struggle. Despite it being a more vulnerable position, she lay on the ground with hundreds of other people. "But," she told me, "I felt awful about it. Like, what kind of hypocrite am I? I mean, I chickened out when I was going to be the only one."

Turning our beliefs into behavior is a fundamentally different proposition than knowing something is right or having the moral propensity to say so aloud. And the gap between believing new parents should get to do X and being a parent who just does X is the same kind of gap that exists between thinking affirming thoughts about racial justice and embodying antiracist action.

We need to close that gap.

Behaviors bring new realities into the actual, material world we live in. So we need to give explicit attention to habits and skills as we seek to right the relationship between white people and race. We need frames that center behavior. And we need to use those frames every single time.

Before we explore what happens when we center behavior, I want to describe what it looks like when we don't. And I want to talk about collective spaces.

Ash-Lee Woodard Henderson's appeal to white people to do their own work speaks to the importance of transforming white *communities*. The frames we use in collective spaces are especially vital, because they create group or communal culture—in this case, racial culture.

By collective spaces or entities, I mean places where folks are doing something in the world as part of a group. Like the medical practice into which my mom walked carrying an infant. A small business or a college, a PTA or a neighborhood association, a co-op of local artists, a consortium of journalists, a bowling league, a hair salon, a religious organization, or a community center—all of these are collective entities.

We're in a moment in the United States in which so many of these kinds of entities would say they are opposed to racism. There's shared belief in many places that "we" believe people of all racial identities should be treated with respect and access.

It's also not uncommon for organizations to be engaged in antiracism initiatives. The level and quality of the work varies radically, of course. But even in the face of the backlash against Black Lives Matter that has intensified since 2020, corporations, educational institutions, and nonprofit organizations have continued to provide programming to increase awareness of racial injustice.

My university wasn't the only one to implement campus-wide readings of *So, You Want to Talk About Race* by Ijeoma Oluo in the last few years. We did it with a hope of helping white faculty become more able to teach racially and ethnically diverse students well. We want to make antiracism part of our ongoing campus conversations and relationships.

Faith communities all over the country have read *The New Jim Crow* by Michelle Alexander together—a book that exposes the catastrophic ways mass incarceration today functions similarly to enslavement and Jim Crow. Teachers in the public schools have picked up Debby Irving's *Waking Up White*—a memoir by a white educator describing the process of becoming critically aware of the impact of whiteness in her life.

This is all important. But if we overemphasize changing thoughts or beliefs and underemphasize cultivating the habits necessary to grow muscle, predictable tendencies develop in the culture of these spaces.

Here's a big one. Overemphasizing knowledge encourages a tendency toward consumption. An unspoken logic develops that goes something like this: *If I just take one more program or do one more book circle about racial justice, I'm good.* This posture is passive. It can become voyeuristic. It's a kind of outsider-looking-in view in which white people peer into other peoples' lived experiences of harm: "Oh my gosh, racism is so bad! I don't like it!" This stance doesn't require much from the observer.

When we're in this frame of mind, completing a program becomes *the action*. That tendency is reflected in Tre Johnson's June 11, 2020, *Washington Post* article entitled "When Black People Are in Pain, White People Just Join Book Clubs." When Fabiola Cineas, a *Vox* journalist, followed up in 2021 with some of the groups Johnson was talking about, she titled her findings "The Lofty Goals and Short Life of the Antiracist Book Club." She went on to add: "After George Floyd's death, many white Americans formed book clubs. A year later, they're wondering, 'What now?'"

Now, I obviously believe in books—and book groups! Deep conversations about meaningful ideas can cultivate a different consciousness. What's more, such conversations can shape the kinds of relationships that develop among those who engage them, and these relationships can carry forward beyond the group experience itself.

Take one parent feeling like there's something not quite right about the way their child's school is teaching about George Washington. That parent pulls together a group with other parents—some of whom have the same feeling, others who've never thought about it. Suppose that group engages with a thinker who offers language to explain that feeling. Let them begin to understand the reasons race-conscious, morally complex history lessons are vital for all children's well-being. Build group consciousness and parental relationships around all of *that* and you have the potential to change a whole school building.

Changed consciousness and relationships matter. Battles against race-conscious teaching are being waged all over the country. You've no doubt heard the trumped-up charges deployed against critical race theory (CRT) in school districts. CRT is a body of legal thought that articulates how advances in civil rights have always benefited people of all races. It's not anti-white. It assesses the ways race and law interact. Plus, it's not only that CRT doesn't argue what its opponents say it does. CRT *isn't taught in K–12 education!* (I didn't encounter CRT until I was working on a graduate degree!)

Maybe you've heard about teachers who put up Black Lives Matter signs in their classrooms and who were censured or even suspended. I've known teachers who have been required to take their signs down.

White parents have overwhelmed school board meetings. They've insisted on their right to review what educators teach about race and to place limits on what's taught in U.S. history classes. Candidates for school boards have been put forth by right-wing organizations to attempt to pass such measures into local law.

Those book group parents who've built relationships in the process of deepening their racial literacy have the potential to be a constituency. They'll be prepared to support teachers if or when they become targets. Even in this difficult climate, they are more easily galvanized because they've become invested in racial truth. They have the potential to be every bit as powerful as those who would attempt to turn our education systems back.

But their new ideas aren't transformative on their own. That school won't change unless these ideas are activated. The school board won't be influenced if parents don't act publicly and do it together.

We need to close the gap between values and behavior with as much intention as possible. Remember my mom and my baby brother?

Sometimes we also overemphasize the changing of minds and underemphasize the changing of behavior when we ask at our workplaces or a school, "But how can I [we] convince the *entire* group to care about racial justice? How do we get *everyone* on board?"

We should always be thinking about how to reach more people. But the primary question isn't, "How do we change Kathy's mind?" The question is, "What actions do we need to take to implement racial equity?" The question is, "How do we transform X to get closer to making racially just outcomes a reality here?"

Of course we should support Kathy in reaching a new understanding. We need to stick with her—"companion her," the way Alicia Garza calls us to. But we also need to move ahead whether Kathy's ready or not. The goal is policies and practices that make justice, equity, and antiracism characterize our various interactions and the structures of a place.

If we make progress on the real goal, we begin to change an entity's culture. When we do that, Kathy's ability to cause harm to Black and Brown people or their interests is reduced, regardless of what she thinks.

Plus something else could happen. As Kathy experiences a workplace in which justice, equity, and antiracism are increasingly part of the air we're all breathing, she might eventually begin to think a bit differently, too. Maybe she starts to behave differently.

But again, even if she doesn't—antiracist shifts need not wait on convincing Kathy.

There's another insidious tendency that can develop when we underfocus on behavior.

For seven full years after joining the faculty where I work, I'd find myself thinking, *Why don't they hire more faculty of color?* I'd point my finger at this ambiguous *they* in self-righteous moral outrage—all the while cashing my monthly paycheck.

I knew my *values.* I was confident in my *knowledge* and *analysis.* So . . . *I* was good. Surely, then, racial disparities in our faculty demographics were someone else's responsibility!

Then at some point, it hit me: *Oh, wait a second! I'm on the faculty here. . . . Who do I think "they" is?!*

Yikes.

It's not that I'd done nothing to take action for justice prior to that point at my university. I'd taught about racism in classes, spoken up about it in some committee meetings, and brought in speakers to talk about social change. Nor did realizing *I* was the *they* mean I suddenly had all the power, strategy, or solutions to change faculty demographics overnight. I still don't.

But intense investment in my analysis and values actually allowed me to stay pretty comfortable with the presence of racial inequity because I could take solace in my great thoughts and deep moral convictions. This focus offered me a comparatively comfortable place to stand when what I most needed was to feel intensely uncomfortable.

Such a dynamic would have been less likely if my frames had more consistently centered behavior. Upon arrival, I would have begun to look for and ask where, how, and with whom I was going to take action in response to my values. I would have gotten to work right away.

It's so easy for those of us who are white to take unjustifiable solace in a false belief that even though racism is here in this community or expressed by a coworker or through a policy "over there," we're not implicated, because we know or believe better. White apathy shapes group culture with ease. This happens even in organizations that have public declarations about or programming on race and antiracism!

A climate in which racial equity and justice are being robustly pursued in measurable and concrete ways doesn't magically grow when people's minds change.

Back when I was at Union, I took a course on public speaking. Each week we had to memorize and recite a piece in front of everyone in the class. The professor worked with us in real time to loosen and strengthen our speaking voices as we did so.

So, for example, I would recite a short section from my favorite Indigo Girls song. The professor had me do it while flapping my arms up and down, shaking my head back and forth with my mouth wide open. The point is to free up the body and voice and break through inhibition.

Talk about vulnerability! Brené Brown would love it. I hated it. (Okay, I loved it a little.)

The class bonded because we were doing such vulnerable stuff together. But our bond was jeopardized partway through the semester when one of my classmates, who was Black, recited a poem. Our professor, as he began to work with Scott, started referring to the poem as a "rap."

This poem was most assuredly not a rap.

The longer Scott was up there, the more times the word *rap* came out of Professor Seaver's mouth. The more times it did, the squirmier I got.

I'd learned enough about racism by this point to know how regularly Black cultural forms are unknown and misunderstood by white people. We often reduce such forms into simplistic, inaccurate categories. All spoken word or poetry is rap. Every Black choir performance is gospel. Every meal made by a Black chef is soul food.

Right before our eyes, my classmate was being reduced to a one-dimensional person—a caricature, even. His poetic recitation could be heard as a rap only because he was Black and the listener was white.

I watched Scott's face for a sign of unease. I waited for him to correct our professor. But he never did, and I couldn't tell what he thought or felt.

By the end of class, I felt like I'd participated in something gross. I was simultaneously terrified to do anything about it, knew I had to do something, and had no idea what that was.

After a couple of nights of restless sleep and countless conversations with friends, I reached out to Scott. I had prepared a speech.

"I don't know if it bothered you, but I was really bothered when Professor Seaver called your poem a rap. I'm not telling you to ask you what I should do. Since it made *me* uncomfortable, I feel like I need to talk to him. But I also realize this could put you in a weird position. So I'm not exactly asking for your permission, but I do feel like I need to make sure you'd be okay with that."

My palms were sweaty. I talked way too fast.

Scott looked at me. "Go ahead. Talk to him," he said. "Just please be clear with him I didn't ask you to come and you're not speaking for me. If you can do that, go for it."

Of course I secretly wished Scott would tell me not to say anything. But now I'd created a situation where I couldn't opt out. So I made an appointment. After another sleepless night, I sat down with Professor Seaver and told him what I'd noticed and why it had upset me.

My palms were sweaty. I talked way too fast.

As it turned out, we had a good conversation. He listened and understood. He was glad I had brought it to his attention. He also deftly brought the incident up in class the following week and explained he'd made a mistake because of his own white limitations. He apologized to the whole class. He did this without singling Scott out or seemingly making it weird for him. (Maybe he also talked to Scott one-on-one before that. I'm not sure.)

This was the first time in my life I enacted a behavior that meaningfully responded to a specific racist incident I was part of. Looking back, I have to say it felt much harder than it seems like it should have. Nonetheless, this was a big growth step for me.

I learned I could do a particular kind of hard thing despite how nervous race still made me.

I learned I wouldn't die from doing that hard thing.

I learned it even felt good to follow all the way through and do the hard thing.

I experienced a chance for a more meaningful relationship with Scott because I didn't stay silent.

I came through it all a slightly different person.

Taking action nurtured my muscles for next time. Remember the feedback loop?

The time I'd spent in the white antiracism group I'd been part of during that communal Middle Passage remembrance had been significant. We'd centered behavior in that group. We'd worked to name and practice habits that enable action:

- I'd grown the habit of checking in with my feelings when something racial or racist was going on and paying attention to them—feeling discomfort in my body.
- I'd developed a practice of talking about racial incidents with people I not only trusted but who were following their own antiracist journeys, too.
- I'd spent time with others wrestling with scenarios and talking about how to activate moral commitments in certain situations and relationships—envisioning the *how*.

All of these habits helped me grow new muscles I hadn't had only a year before.

On top of that, engaging with others in these ways had brought a network of relationships into my life. I had people to rely on for support and accountability when I needed to act.

All of this was vital for becoming able to *just do it* (at least this time; my failure to recognize I had an active role to play in hiring more faculty of color when I joined my university ten years later is a reminder that the challenge is ongoing).

I would never have engaged my professor if embodied learning, support, and accountability hadn't become part of my life prior to this incident. New behaviors in human life—especially behaviors that are difficult—require a whole bunch of smaller habits and consistent practices before they become possible.

We met Ruth Sandhill, the introverted accountant, in the introduction when she spoke at an end-of-year celebration in her city where justice efforts of various local organizations were being spotlighted. The celebration was intended to strengthen connections among various advocacy groups. It was also to introduce their work to more people in the hope of generating financial support and growing the list of folks who might be persuaded to take a step closer into action themselves.

Sandhill's role was powerful because of the love for her neighbors that shone through as she shared her passion and commitment to ending racial profiling. It was striking because when she had first shown up at her local SURJ—Showing Up for Racial Justice—chapter only a few years prior, she'd come with a lot of guilt about not having gotten involved before that point. Yet despite being troubled by the impact Trump's policies were having in her city—the reason she'd shown up now—she had no confidence she had something meaningful to contribute.

Still, Sandhill told the people who were strangers to her that first meeting that she'd decided to consistently attend SURJ meetings for a while. She was going to see if she could figure some things out.

SURJ is a national organization, with local chapters all over the country. Its mission is to get more white people off the sidelines and into active struggle against white supremacy.

Sandhill created a habit: consistently attend twice-a-month SURJ meetings. This habit soon turned into a next step. A need arose, and she offered to keep the financial books. That step drew on expertise she already had. But this step turned into other experiences and skills. Sandhill got to know people whose lives were directly affected by racial profiling. Her learning deepened in dialogues and educational sessions where white work, in active partnership with BIPOC communities, was the focus.

Another need emerged. There was an opening for a liaison—someone from SURJ who would attend strategic action planning against profiling being led by Black leaders. Sandhill found it easy to say yes. As that group prepared for city council meetings and needed white citizens to show up and speak, Sandhill found it impossible to say no—even though she was nervous.

The depth of her commitment grew yet again as Ruth took one next step at a time.

Soon Sandhill began to have conversations with her husband she hadn't before. "I'm going to be out again on Wednesday. You'll have to eat dinner without me."

"Again? Why is this group so important to you?" Tom Sandhill would ask.

"We live here, Tom. We're responsible to stand with our neighbors. And I'm learning I can actually have an impact instead of just feeling bad about the state of everything. The next time a police officer beats or kills a Black or Latinx person, I won't be just sitting here, berating myself that I've never been part of trying to help do something about it."

Then? "Tom, we need more people at the city council meeting tonight. Will you come with me? You don't have to say anything. Plus I think you'd love getting to connect with all these groups of people we've not had relationships with before—who live in our city, too."

Conversations about racial justice and local politics became an increasing part of the Sandhills' family life. And the next thing Tom Sandhill knew? He was offering his IT expertise to under-resourced Black organizations in their community, building new relationships himself, learning that his everyday expertise could have an impact, too.

Growing white capacity for antiracist behavior is not dissimilar to what it takes to become a runner. You begin where you are. You take a run around the block. You probably walk part of the way the first, second, or even third time you go. After that, you string together several times around the block in a row. You start to do this multiple times a week. Even when it's hot. Even when you don't feel like it. And you find people to run with you, especially as the distances get longer.

One of the most well-attended meetings of my Des Moines SURJ chapter is called "Talking to Family and Friends." It's a session on navigating difficult racial justice conversations with friends and family.

We offer this teach-in every year as the winter holidays approach. We invite attendees to proactively think through exchanges we're likely to have with family members or guests who'll show up at holiday dinner tables and parties.

We present scenarios and even invite participants to share actual experiences in which someone at a gathering says or does something racist. We discuss various strategies of interruption, engagement, and response. Sometimes we act these out so we can literally practice finding our words. Here are a few possible responses:

- "What you said just now about Black Lives Matter being violent made me really uncomfortable, especially because I know it isn't true. Can we find a way to talk about why you think this?"
- "I don't know if you realized it, but the term you just used to refer to immigrants dehumanizes people in need. I don't want any of us to use words like that when we're together."
- "I can't exactly answer that, but I'd love the chance to think about it. Let me find a couple of resources to help me better explain what I'm trying to say, and then we can talk again later. For now, can we pause this conversation so we don't engage in stereotyping or deepen our bias without knowing more of the facts?"

Interrupting racism can feel hard at first. Lots of us stumble the first time we say such things aloud. At Des Moines SURJ we normalize how awkward this can feel. We remind each other that the more we do it, the better at it we get.

We notice that having such vulnerable but authentic conversations deepens our relationships with one another. This is especially important: We become more likely to interrupt and challenge racism when we're in white spaces, when we can feel and envision a crew of people cheering us on from afar—and holding us accountable with honesty, support, and a "how'd it go?" when we get back.

There they are again. Those parts that mattered in my own first group experience in which *righting* the relationship of white people to race was the goal: feelings, conversations, strategies, support, and accountability.

This is how we can build moral muscle in collective spaces. We design gatherings not to just talk about running. We actually go on training runs together!

Such personal and interpersonal skills building is not only about individualistic transformation. Ruth Sandhill certainly developed the capacity to talk about racism in her personal and familial relationships by getting involved with SURJ. But the anti-racist habits she began to practice also drew her into collective strategic organizing.

Alicia Garza differentiates activism and organizing. Activism can be done by anyone, anytime, in any number of ways. Garza gives an example of a beloved relative who is a peace activist. "[S]he's, you know, engaged in many different organizations . . . she gives money to this, that, and the other thing . . . when she goes out and walks her dogs, she wears this . . . cardboard sign, right. That it's like about peace and not, you know, stopping war." Garza says activism is when you let someone know where you stand on something.

Organizing is different. Organizing "is driven by a strategy to impact somebody who can give you what you want. . . . Organizing requires an analysis of power. It requires an analysis of the political landscape, and it also requires a plan to win. How do we get from here to there?"[1]

We need both.

Activism leads that teacher to put up her Black Lives Matter sign. When she's told to take it down, we need dozens and dozens of families to organize for her. First, to give her support. Then to get as many students as possible—especially white ones—to wear Black Lives Matter T-shirts to school on the same day, many days in a row. So many students that they can't possibly all be expelled.

If that teacher loses her job, we need dozens and dozens of families—especially the white ones—to show up at the administrations offices and say, "We won't have this."

And also . . . we must do all of this together. Organizing helps us figure out how to do that.

In the same essay where Rebecca Solnit talks about how the world changes when millions of us integrate new ideas and act on our values around race, class, gender, justice, the possibility of equality (and more), she describes something else as well.[2] Parts of the population in the United States and Europe, she says, are currently "moving backward, trying to take up residence in the wreckage of white supremacy and patriarchy."[3] We need to change conditions so those actors invested in white supremacy and patriarchy and queer-hatred don't hold disproportionate power.

Those kinds of changes require us to be involved with one another. It's vital we work together because it's more than yelling or banning books at school boards. There's violence in the air. It's a kidnapping plot against a governor. The husband of the speaker of the House of Representatives battered in a home invasion. Gunshots into lawmakers' homes in New Mexico. Portions of our population have fallen prey to conspiracy theories and QAnon.

In 2023, one of my friends in the Midwest agreed to give a talk on white antiracism for a local community group. My friend is a hardworking educator. She works tirelessly and loves her students. When she presented on Zoom outside of school hours, she gave permission to be recorded. But she hadn't anticipated the recording being downloaded by a nefarious actor. Her words were clipped out of context. They were spread widely online through a white nationalist network. She received so much hate mail in her email inbox her school had to shut down her account. And then she was doxed—her personal information, including her home address, was publicly released.

The experience was terrifying. Horrifying.

But this educator had long been deeply invested in her local relationships. She was active with others, organizing to change conditions in her local context. So as soon as she was doxed, those folks activated those organizing skills and dispositions. Members of her community, among whom she is beloved, parked outside her home in four-hour shifts twenty-four hours a day for a full week—until the threats had died down—so she wouldn't go through that experience alone.

Solnit says that for those of us trying to build a more just world in these frightening times, "the real work is not to convert those who hate us but to change the world so that haters don't hold disproportionate power and so that others are not sucked into the nightmare."[4]

She's right. But the work is also to build connections with one another so we can create networks of safety and support as we go.

* * *

Let's make action the center of our frames.

When we collectively name the goal as behavioral transformation, *because antiracism is a behavior,* we keep questions of habits and practices squarely on the table.

Such clarity shapes an entity's racial culture. Behaviorally focused questions—"So what?" and "Now what?"—become familiar and habitual. The more behavioral questions are experienced as the default, the more we grow racial cultures in which reflective inquiry on how to make antiracism concrete becomes part of the ecosystem.

Let's go back to the example of a faith community sharing the intellectually transformative experience of reading *The New Jim Crow.* If the frame is behavior, that experience won't end when the book does. Instead, that community turns the last page poised to ask, "Now that we are differently aware of this crisis, how can we become part of work to end this catastrophic injustice in Black life?" Such a question may mean individual reflection on next steps people can take within their varied spheres of influence (see chapter 9). It might mean group inquiry into congregational relationship-building with Black-led organizations already engaged in criminal justice reform in the local community (see chapter 10).

Also, we know criminal justice is a part of civic life where antiblack rhetoric and policy show up persistently. Tropes of "Black criminality" run amok in white relational networks—among white people we work with, live near, or *even worship with.* A commitment to disrupting such tropes is the least we owe in response to the incredible gift Michelle Alexander gives in this book.

As they finish it, that book group can role-play talking about what they learned. They can list concrete strategies to interrupt the racism that masks as "law and order" speak in polite white conversation because so many of us hear those conversations in white spaces. Members of the group could write an op-ed together for the local newspaper, making their newfound knowledge and the commitments it inspired public in their local context. Such actions build our sense of a group identity. They help us get better at using our words and explaining things most of us haven't spoken publicly about before.

Then, if participants need to, they can talk yet again about why some or all of this seems difficult or leaves them feeling vulnerable.

So many white people show up for Des Moines's SURJ's "Talking to Family and Friends" meeting not only because family networks are a place so many of us encounter racism, but because so many of us find such encounters stressful. For many of us, when Uncle Joe, Grandma, a beloved neighbor, or any other white person we have a relational stake in being connected to says or does something racist, an inner dialogue begins to take place. *I have to do something*, we say to ourselves. This might mean sweaty palms, an adrenaline rush, heart pounding—reactions manifested in our bodies.

It's critical we create spaces for white people to acknowledge, face, and work through the hard feelings that come up when we imagine challenging family and friends; to better understand why it feels hard; and to hear that it won't remain as hard, or at least not as hard in the same way once we begin to do it. Finding it hard doesn't mean you are a bad white person; it just means you—like most of us—were socialized by other white people. The question for all of us is, "What do we do with that?" And that's a question our collective programming can help with.

Role-plays and other embodied experiences in our programming create space to process emotional and even physical reactions.

We need to grow new muscles. And we can. We need to

develop stamina. And we can. We need to become more agile. And we absolutely can.

Donna Carding, a middle-aged white woman, became determined to get better at interrupting conversations in which white folks say things that have racist innuendos. She realized she'd get stuck, and thus stay quiet, when she didn't know *how* to counter a racial assumption. Sometimes she wouldn't even know how to prove a racist stereotype was being inserted into the conversation.

Determined to change her behavior, Carding began to practice one simple line: "Oh, I'm sorry, are you assuming I'm white?"

"I wouldn't shop at a Target in *that* part of town. Why are they putting it *there*?" says a neighbor in a casual conversation about a new development. Carding responds, "Oh, I'm sorry, are you assuming I'm white?"

"Have you noticed our boss seems more interested in making our company look good by being PC than in hiring actually qualified people?" says a coworker annoyed by diversity efforts. Carding: "Oh, I'm sorry, are you assuming I'm white?"

"You know, I'm a public schools person. But with all those families moving into Davenport from Chicago, and the issues they're bringing here, I can see why private schools feel attractive." Carding: "Oh, I'm sorry, are you assuming I'm white?"

Sometimes Carding's simple question would be met with a confused look. Sometimes it caused embarrassment. Every time it helped her disentangle from a racially coded conversation that set her up to endorse views she did not share. Over time, she found she felt less and less nervous about uttering that question. Some of the conversations that resulted from the disorientation caused by her unexpected response were even productive.

So, whatever it is: Pick a strategy and an approach to help you turn your ideas and values into behaviors. Doing this will make you stronger and will have an increasingly significant impact on your life and in your relationships.

I have a beautiful double-knitted blanket. It's old. It's warm. It's colorful. It's very heavy—in translation, that means *cozy*. Its value can't be quantified, because someone made it for me.

That someone was my mom.

It's not the blanket she made while knitting madly in the front row of a medical school classroom. But every time I snuggle up in it, I feel wrapped up in her audacity all the same.

What we *do* in the world—how we act and behave—becomes the legacy we leave the next generation, just like that old hand-knitted blanket. Every time we bridge the gap and go from sitting quietly at a table while racism is being spoken to saying, "I'm not okay with what's being said"—even if we don't know what's going to happen next—we don't just change ourselves. We don't just change that room. We change the realm of possibilities others alongside us and those coming behind us have within their grasp, too. We begin to hand down something that has rarely been bequeathed by white people to the next generation. We practice, as Layla F. Saad might put it, "becoming good ancestors."

Before long, if we stick with it, we may find we've also started knitting full-length cozy blankets in places where women are absolutely not supposed to be madly knitting. And they'll be the sorts of creations we pass down to the next generation, too.

TAKE A NEXT STEP

1. Identify or imagine a racial incident or situation. Visualize yourself moving through it without taking action (for example, not speaking up). Imagine how your body and heart

feel after you leave the situation not having acted. Now visualize that same incident and taking action (for example, speaking up). Imagine how your body and heart feel after you do so.

2. Look at your volunteer or other nonwork and nonfamily commitments over the next three, six, and twelve months. Figure out a time commitment to make to a local community effort on racial justice, or identify a place to join a local initiative where your time and energy support the well-being of people of color. You might have to say no to something else! Put it in your calendar. Take a friend or family member with you.

3. Join an antiracism group—or a group that has signaled racial equity and inclusion values in some way—at your workplace. Ask these questions there: What measurable outcomes are we seeking? What structures are we creating to assess whether we're achieving them? If no such group exists, start one.

4

The Freedom of a Ruined Party

I have extended family in Mississippi. They're on a branch of our family tree that connects through my grammy. My great-aunt Kay, Grammy's sister, made her way south with her husband when she was young. There she and my great-uncle Syl spawned what became three or four generations of southerners on our tree. This branch is as white and evangelical as mine was.

I didn't know this part of our family well growing up because we didn't see them often. But Grammy took me to visit once for a family wedding. It was a great trip. I had my first plane ride, got Grammy to myself, and played with a whole bunch of second cousins around the ages of my siblings and me, kids who'd existed only in my imagination before that trip.

Somewhere in there, I made the connection between the civil rights movement and the fact that Mississippi—a place I'd now been to—was *in the South*. I became fascinated. My family had been there! In the months and then years that followed, I'd go through phases of badgering the adults in my life with questions.

Did Aunt Kay make her maid ride in the back seat when she drove her home after her work at my relatives' house? Did the adults send their kids to segregated schools—even though they knew segregation was wrong (they knew it was wrong, right)? Did the kids obey and drink out of the "white" water fountains? What did they think about that?! And—a question that came much later—what did my great-uncle, who was a dean at the University of Mississippi, do when James Meredith tried to integrate Ole Miss? Where was he exactly the night of September 30, 1962, as white people began to riot, destroy property, and set fires all to try to stop Meredith from enrolling?

I was never satisfied with the answers. Even when I was a kid, they struck me as vague and left me unsettled. I don't remember a single conversation in which my adults spoke to the heart of what I was trying to understand. I now realize I was asking about my family's level of complicity (a word I didn't know yet) in something I assumed we *all* knew was terrible.

"Well, it would have been uncomfortable for everyone at that time—including the maid—for a Black and white woman to sit together in the front of a car. That doesn't mean your aunt agreed with how things were," I remember Mom saying. "Okay, well, Uncle Syl sure didn't believe segregation was right and wanted everyone to have a good education. He didn't like the way things were."

I can't remember what Grammy said about the schools or drinking fountains. She probably shook her head about how sad it was the South had been like that and insinuated everyone "had to do it."

I'm also sure she believed that was true.

There was a moment one time, again back at Union, when

the vagueness of what I'd been told growing up smashed into the concreteness of what my family's behavior meant for others. I was getting to know someone who would become a friend. He was a Black student who *actually* was there to study with James Cone and who'd participated in the Million Man March.

We were standing at the library checkout counter chatting and I learned he was from Taylorsville, Mississippi, and had extended family in Oxford. This was the same town my extended family lived in.

This encounter abruptly exposed the distortions in my family's self-perception (so common in white families) as nice people. As soon as my would-be friend Sylvester Johnson said, "I have family in Oxford," the human stakes in "Well, he didn't like it, but . . ." were laid bare. I experienced a rush of shame. There was so much I didn't know about my family's engagement with civil rights. The rush combined with a sick feeling in my gut as I recognized what I could surmise given my elders' evasive answers and what all of that meant in terms of real consequences for families like Sylvester's.

It was a moment that was both awful and clarifying.

Fast-forward. In the same season my mom had planted her lawn sign, Mom and I kept finding ourselves talking about the national racial climate. We were in contention about whether there was a through line between the white evangelical cultures my parents had raised us in and the 2016 election. Mom did not see a through line. She felt betrayed by her community's role in Trump's election. I absolutely saw a through line. I felt betrayed by her insistence that such behavior was something new or aberrant.

We were having such a conversation one evening when Mom told me a story I'd never heard. She said during the civil rights movement, Uncle Syl had introduced a motion to desegregate his church. He was a deacon—a church leader who is not ordained—and a highly respected figure in his congregation. He brought his motion to the board of deacons.

Why had I never heard this before? How had it never occurred to me that, of course, my family's church would have also been segregated?

My childhood fascination returned. I began to pepper my mom with questions.

How did Uncle Syl do it? Did he do it alone or did he organize with others? Given his status as a respected pillar, was there a reckoning? Did his community see the light?

The answers that came were as vague as the ones I'd received as a kid. Mom didn't really know how he did it. She didn't know why he'd taken the risk, nor whether it was just him or if others were involved. She didn't know how his family—which included her first cousins, people she did know well growing up—felt about it.

She did know the motion had failed. The leaders of the church voted no. Their community would remain segregated.

It was here I asked the fateful question, "So then what happened?"

Mom kind of shrugged. Then nothing. That was it. That was the story.

Translation: The motion failed, my family let it be, and they stayed. My family stayed in a church that had now explicitly said white supremacy was consistent with Christianity. They raised their children and some of their grandchildren there. They prayed and broke bread with other whites there. They listened to Protestant-length sermons that ostensibly proclaimed the word of God there. Week in and week out.

They stayed.

I'm a little conflicted about putting this family story in print. That's not because we shouldn't air white laundry. We need to talk openly about what happens in our families and communities (see chapter 8).

I'm hesitant because my point isn't to call out this part of my family. These are folks I still don't know very well and about whom there's a lot I don't know. But it is *my* experience as someone from a separate branch of the same tree, someone who engaged with my family's stories while drinking lemonade on the porch. I was shaped by the family culture they reflect.

But also I'm not pointing at this branch as if they were unique and different. They weren't. In fact, *that's the point.* This story encapsulates what is normal in so many white families and in our communal culture. Notice the white silence—from not throwing a loud and massive fit after a motion to desegregate fails (quietly staying?) to no one's speaking about or passing down this story at all.

I was almost fifty years old before I learned about a living, breathing, direct encounter with the moral demands of civil rights only two generations above me, something that happened when my own mother was very much alive. This, despite my known interest in talking about race in my family. Despite being someone who had asked a lot of questions for decades.

White silence is powerful.

Notice, too, the generational inheritance visible in this story. Regardless of the geographical origins of our families, versions of this account are present in so many white American families. *What did your great-aunt do when they built the interstate through the center of the Black neighborhood in her city eighty years ago? How did Grandpa respond when Black people were complaining they couldn't get loans and mortgages? How did your parents decide which public school to live near, and what did they think about Black parents raising frustrations about inequitable funding?*

Answer: "They didn't like the way things were." But probably, mostly, they stayed, too.

I've since learned there are serious relational breaks in this part of our family. I've heard rumors that the breaks have to do with race. Descendants feel either betrayed by or loyal to the prior generation. Those who feel loyal are thus defensive (and angry in return) when anger is expressed by those who feel betrayed. Fractures all around.

But whatever the next generation of my family has done in response to what they saw, the fact remains, the elders modeled staying. They demonstrated in their living that *you do not, ultimately, break ranks*.

Entangled in the decision to stay is a value passed down from generation to generation. White cohesion reigns supreme. Even when it depends on tolerating racism.

And it's this last part I want us to see.

Racism exists in concrete form within white-on-white interactions. It's in our relationships. It's literally present in our relational bonds.

It might be easy to see how this would be the case in a space like my mom's church, an evangelical one that makes no apology for opposing efforts for racial justice and is mostly on board with the white Christian nationalism that's been catalyzing since 2015. It's harder to recognize in the liberal church up the street that can't agree to put up a sign, let alone generate financial support, for Black Lives Matter or won't move its Sunday service to the streets to take part in the same-time-as-our-services rally where people are raging about ICE caging babies at the border because doing so would be controversial in the congregation.

Racism flows through the connections in these more cautious, careful white spaces, too. There are so many ways to quietly stay.

We don't usually think of racism as an element in the glue connecting us to our white families and members of our community. And, just to be clear, my next claim here *isn't* going to be "you have to totally break up with your family." There's not a one-size-fits-all answer to the nearly ubiquitous question among white people moving into antiracist commitment: "So what *do* I do about my family?" We're going to explore this question later (see chapter 8).

Rather, recognizing that cohesion is overvalued in white-on-white relationships and racism is embedded in them reveals an added dimension to antiracism as behavior—namely, practices and habits that challenge racism put us in postures of direct dissent with our own people. And there's nothing easy about that.

Patricia J. Williams is a legal scholar who works in critical race theory and feminism, and is known for her ability to bring her deep understanding of the law into accessible public discussion. She wrote words I repeat like a mantra when I'm trying to summon the courage to challenge some manifestation of racism (though we're now better at replacing *nonracist* with *antiracist*). She writes: "The hard work of a nonracist sensibility is the boundary crossing, from safe circle into wilderness: the testing of boundary, the consecration of sacrilege. It is the willingness to spoil a good party and break an encompassing circle, to travel from the safe to the unsafe."[1]

Repeating this mantra doesn't always work.

But Williams's words capture the fortitude that transforming white communities requires. For white people, it's about ruining a party our own people have been throwing all along. It's uniquely hard to be a whistleblower or a scene thrower when you're in a place with people you like or love or with whom you're included as some sort of "we" as the good times roll.

Yes, white people didn't get the ancestors we needed. But it's not only that. When we hit that "Oh wait, what? Racism is a crisis?" moment, walking into antiracist commitment requires us to be willing to clash with the people we are closest to. We're not breaking ranks with abstract systems from a distance. We're breaking ranks with people we know. With the cultures that shaped us. With people who love us.

Justice-oriented actions and commitments around race typically keep people of color aligned with their familial and communal networks. But the same actions and commitments typically require white people to disrupt those networks.

(Also, when those of us who are white summon the courage to clash and potentially rupture those relationships, we don't really have an obvious place to go when we get kicked out. We can't just drop into community with people of color. What group of students of color would have wanted messy me hanging around with them at Union? Few. And for obvious reasons. But the isolation facing white people who strive to move into antiracism is real. This is why it matters for white people to build relationships with one another on antiracist ground. We'll talk about this more in chapter 7.)

If my great-uncle had been unwilling to give up on his push for desegregation of his church, if he'd chosen momentum toward justice and morality over white cohesion, one of several things might have happened. He would have kept on pushing and eventually been successful. Some whites would have left, and those relationships would have been broken. But desegregation would have passed. Or he would have had to make an increasingly large scene as he kept choosing justice-momentum. Eventually he'd have been shown the door. Or it would have become clear at some point that no change was coming. If justice-momentum continued to matter most to him, he would have left and taken his descendants with him. In any of these scenarios, the party, such as it was, would have been ruined.

Obviously, none of these scenarios happened.

It's devastating to watch people choose white connection over justice again and again and again. The consequences of these generational habits are catastrophic. There is profound grief in this—wastelands created because every choice to stay was also a choice to refuse a place for the love of humanity to be actualized.

Acknowledging the consequences that awaited my great-uncle and his family had he broken ranks does not excuse his choices. Full stop.

Acknowledging that such choices bring real consequences at the level of our intimate relationships is a step toward helping us respond to racial communal pressures. It's a way to gain some traction and leverage over them.

There's an analogous experience here to that of LGBTQ+ people. Queer people, collectively, understand that staying in the closet or denying our sexual orientation or gender identity is death-dealing. Complicity with cultures that value heterosexuality and won't acknowledge transgender or gender nonconforming people erodes, corrodes, and destroys the self.

Those of us who are queer know this at some level. We often know it early in our lives.

But coming out requires us to confront familial and communal rejection. And that's tough, even if we suspect joy, freedom, and the liberation of claiming our full self might lay on the other side of such a choice. Even if we have reason to imagine a different kind of connection and community is possible.

I have a young child who is nonbinary and uses they/them pronouns. They once asked me why all the nonbinary people they knew were so much older than them. They were lamenting the lack of kids their age who used they/them pronouns. I found myself suggesting it can take people a while to figure out who they are when those they are closest to are telling them who they are—and are wrong. Pressures from family make it hard for us to feel and find, let alone fully embody, our selfhood.

The second thing I said was that when someone *does* figure it out, it takes a ton of courage to come on out and say it, claim it, make it known. It just does.

Coming out takes courage. It is risky. It challenges family culture. And the threat of disconnection from the very relationships through which we've come to know ourselves and on which we may still rely for all kinds of things is serious.

This is one of the most difficult truths in Ash-Lee Woodard Henderson's call for white people to do our work. But this same truth also contains potent seeds. These seeds can grow similar kinds of plants and flowers—deeply rooted and beautiful—to those LGBTQ+ people grow when we choose to seek liberation and freedom anyway. Watering such seeds, even when it's difficult, is necessary for creating the kinds of communities in which all of us, and perhaps U.S. democracy itself, can begin to flourish. For throwing the kinds of parties where everyone is welcome and we experience the joy of dancing with all kinds of beautifully different people.

Fourth grade was a whole new world. It was the first year I got to walk to school. Each morning I'd stand out in front of my house and watch as my best friend, Rachel, would start out as a tiny blob and slowly grow into a full-size ten-year-old as she walked down Tennessee Avenue from her house to mine. I'd meet up with her and off we'd go to Washington Park Elementary, three more blocks away.

That year we had homework! I was diligent about mine. This wasn't so much a conscious decision; it just hadn't occurred to me (yet) that *not* following rules was an option. So the first time I forgot my homework I felt a pit wrench open in my gut and my mouth go dry. I dragged my now vacuous, parched body to Ms. Boss's desk. "I forgot my homework," I sobbed, trying to explain that I'd done it but forgotten to put it in my backpack.

Before I could get the story out, Ms. Boss threw back her head and laughed. She turned to the entire class. "Jenny just told me she forgot her homework. And I want you to know I can laugh because Jenny *always* does her homework." She went on to say something like she wished she could say the same for the whole class. I have my doubts about where that declaration landed on the continuum of teacher-appropriate practices, but my sweaty palms began to dry, and the adrenaline induced by near catastrophe evaporated.

Finally, fourth grade brought Gifted and Talented (G/T) into my life.

I was aware that Rachel and a couple other friends had been placed in G/T because they'd started leaving class on Friday afternoons. Then one day, I was pulled out of class to take a test. I killed it on the memory part. But my mind went blank when they set a sheet of paper with a dozen large circles on it in front of me. I was supposed to turn the circles into something unique and inventive. A clock? Too obvious. Connect several to make a caterpillar? Minimal effort. I didn't know what to do with those stupid circles.

When I didn't get into G/T, I didn't think much about it or care. The notion of G/T was a total abstraction to me.

But Ms. Boss apparently did care. At some point, I became

vaguely aware of adult murmurings about trying to get me into G/T. Then one day, Ms. Boss waved me over to her desk. She was smiling big. "Good news! You get to start G/T next week!" She handed me a note to give to my mom.

I peeked at the note on my walk home. *Well, Sally, we did it!* it began.

I'm not sure who *we* referred to. She might have meant she and I had done it. Maybe I'd shown enough aptitude on the right kind of thing that she'd finally convinced the G/T gate-keepers to let me in. Maybe she meant she and some other staff person(s) had lobbied and succeeded.

But probably she meant she and my mom had done it. This would have been an understandable presumption—that there was a *we* made up of the two of them, who shared an investment in this outcome. That's what all parents want, isn't it? For our individual kid(s) to access the maximum resources? The most opportunities? Such aims are woven deep into the fabric of economically secure white cultures. We know it's our job as parents to make sure our kids "get the most" they can. (We don't describe it that way, of course. We just call it "good parenting.")

But if that's who Ms. Boss meant by *we*, she was mistaken. My mom couldn't have cared less about my getting into G/T. I'd be surprised if she knew efforts were being made on my behalf. I'm confident she had nothing to do with them.

Well, Sally, we did it! Jenny's going to start G/T. I handed my mom the note. After reading it, Mom's response was something along the lines of "humph." My mom thought kids who were already thriving in school were *not* the ones who needed more resources shoveled into their buckets. My mom was opposed to programs like G/T on principle, and she was specifically against putting kids like me into them.

I hadn't before, but Mom's reaction made me now care very

much. So I was relieved as I watched her initial resistance, bordering on disdain, melt into sigh-filled resignation over the course of the evening.

In other words, she didn't say no.

A week later, off I went to my first G/T. I quickly came to love it.

Two things happened right away. First, word came that the G/T program was bringing the reel-to-reel, animated, full-length Technicolor film adaptation of *The Hobbit* (1977) to our school. The G/T kids would get a special Friday-afternoon viewing. Second, the entire school had begun one of those General Mills box top programs, the one where kids bring in points cut from food packaging and the school exchanges these for cash to buy supplies.

Apparently, someone in the decision-making chain realized *The Hobbit* could be a perfect way to incentivize students to bring in more box tops. So shortly after the General Mills initiative got underway, an announcement came. A tiny handful of kids who collected the most points would win a big prize. They'd get to join the G/T kids for *The Hobbit*.

From today's vantage point, I can't imagine why any educator thought this was a good idea. To nine-year-old me, it all made perfect sense.

Here's what I knew: Rachel was going to get to see *The Hobbit*, my other closest friend Julie was going, too, and I was going to be there with the both of them. I couldn't wait.

Translation: A small number of other (mostly white and economically secure[2]) kids were going to get to see *The Hobbit*. A bunch of kids deemed "not gifted and talented," as well as those who didn't collect those box tops, were not. That second set of kids would also have to live with the significant excitement buzzing among and on behalf of those of us who were.

When my mom learned about this plan, she lost her mind.

I remember explaining the competition to Mom after school. I assumed she'd be as excited as I was. Instead, her eyes grew wide. She became agitated. "Wait. You mean they're spending *school money* on *The Hobbit* and only a *few kids* get to see it?" Agitated turned into irate.

Next thing I knew she'd barreled down to school. Hair flying. Birkenstocks on feet. No makeup. I can still picture her standing in front of Ms. Boss's desk. "This is ridiculous! Why isn't everybody included? We're going to reward kids *for being put in G/T*?!? What about kids who can't collect box tops? You're not using taxpayers' money and leaving kids out!"

I felt tiny against the classroom wall. My mom was going toe-to-toe with the same teacher who'd laughed when I forgot my homework and invested effort to get me into G/T. I was horrified and embarrassed.

To top it all off, Mom won. A few days later we learned *The Hobbit* would be a celebration of the entire school's collective box top efforts. Instead of sitting in a special small room watching *The Hobbit* (with snacks) on a Friday afternoon while everyone else had to stay in class and do boring schoolwork, we'd *all* watch *The Hobbit* in the auditorium (no mention of snacks), the only place with enough room for everyone.

Rachel didn't speak to me for a week. She was furious her special treat's specialness had been snatched away. To use her words, "It's all your mom's fault!" I was to be shunned for proximity.

Party ruined.

My mom didn't have a carefully formulated, structural analysis of school systems—though she certainly understood programs like G/T exacerbated inequity and believed this was immoral. But she had the thing that was the make-or-break: *she was willing to spoil a good party*. The audacious habits she'd practiced in her life had grown muscles that kicked in powerfully when it was time to commit the sort of sacrilege that ruined a party someone was throwing not only on her behalf . . . but on behalf of her kid.

This family story couldn't be more different than the one involving my great-uncle and his church. Nor could its generational effects.

Breaking ranks is terrifying. In the moment, it's often loud and messy. But ultimately it's an action rooted in love that literally makes new life and new worlds possible.

As much as I rued the day *The Hobbit* thing went down, this memory is important to me. So many unspoken norms allow racism, in different forms, to go unchecked and to be politely or quietly tolerated in predominantly white networks. How many "good" white (and economically privileged) parents—people who believed themselves to value fairness—gave a nod to *The Hobbit* plan?

It's just so easy to go along.

Disruption will end some relationships. It will change all of them. But, wherever on the relational continuum such choices land, they will, over time, transform our communities. Disrupting the status quo changes the ethos of what is allowed to happen, what is treated as acceptable, what no longer happens because it has been repeatedly treated as intolerable.

We need some productive instability in white-on-white networks. That's how new ways of being stand a chance to grow.

But it matters that we acknowledge behaving in these ways requires fortitude. When I can't see *why* I struggle to do something that's important to me, it's easy to assume something's wrong with me, feel isolated and alone, and then . . . well, give up.

In contrast, "Oh, wait! It makes sense it feels this way! It's because . . ." is like a magic formula. Clarity about what's going on is a powerful boost for taking steps in a direction I want to go so I can grow.

Like lots of white people, when I first began to grapple seriously with racism, I took a deep dive into white guilt. To top it off, because I knew white guilt did nothing for people of color, I also beat myself up about wallowing in it (while continuing to wallow).

Then I learned in my white antiracism group at Union that white guilt was normal! It's a developmentally predictable response to perceiving yourself as someone who values justice but starts recognizing how much you're benefiting from unjust systems and at the expense of others.

That clarity aided me in interpreting my own experience. I could talk about what was happening. I could test strategies to work through it. Instead of just feeling guilty because there weren't more faculty of color teaching at our seminary, I could join students of color as they pressured decision-makers to change that reality. Instead of simply grieving police violence against Black and Latinx people in NYC, I could encourage people in the church where I worked to take a stand, or I could advocate that we offer free use of our building to those organizing against police violence.

I learned taking action metabolized white guilt.

Interpretive leverage made me more likely to keep going. The more I understood how the larger systems and patterns acted on me, the more resilient I became against narratives that I was just a lousy, incapable human—narratives that actually did keep me stuck. I started to see I could make choices about how I interacted with systems. I became more able to make those choices.

Also, when we recognize relational risk is on the table for white people, we realize other relationships are particularly important in offering support for these actions. What a difference it might have made if my great-uncle had had other white people in his life who were engaged in similar efforts in their own communal spaces. If he'd been in contact with Black organizers and thus known there were people waiting on the other side when the party was ruined, he might have found the courage to go ahead and muck it up.

My mom had blazed into Ms. Boss's classroom solo, except for her mortified ten-year-old. To be fair, she might say Jesus was a primary support for her party-ruinous behavior (that's a whole different book). But my mom had long built relationships with families in the low-income and predominantly people of color neighborhoods near our church. It probably mattered that the kids most at risk of being left out of *The Hobbit* were a lot like the kids who laughed that we'd named our brother Ham. These were actual people to her, not just statistics. When the human costs of racism become part of our own relationships, we tend to become more willing to disrupt it in other ones.

The cognitive dissonance I experienced when I began to develop friendships with Sylvester and other Black and Brown people changed my own disposition for risk-taking. Real relationships with people affected by what "my white people" did gave me fewer places to hide from myself. I couldn't make up stories about whether my actions mattered or not.

(A quick word here. It's dicey when white people publicly talk about friendships with people of color. Suspicion is warranted. It's not uncommon for white people to claim people of color as friends, when the person being claimed would not describe the relationship that way.

Also, I'm not suggesting friendships with people of color make us less racist nor that we should just go "find a Black friend"! I'm narrowly pointing to the human phenomenon in which we become more invested when someone we care about is harmed.)

Relationships with people I can call on when I need support matter, too. People who are similarly growing habits and practices in their lives as well. I think of it like this: "Who do I have on speed dial who will get it right away when I need a dose of courage or feedback on some party-ruinous activity?"

These kinds of relationships don't happen by accident. We need to make it a practice to create them, and spend time and energy nurturing them.

In the early 2000s, several hundred queer Christians gathered for a conference called Witness Our Welcome (WOW). It was the first large interdenominational LGBTQ+ gathering of its kind. So there was significant excitement in the air.

During the opening session, one of the leaders walked us through a "who is in the room" icebreaker. "Stand up if you're from Arizona!" "Stand up if you love cats!" We'd all applaud to acknowledge one another.

More serious social identities began to be welcomed into the space. "Stand up if you're Methodist!" (Applause.) "Stand up if you're trans!" (Applause.) Then something went awry.

The icebreaker was wrapping up, but no welcome had been called out for people of color. So just before the emcee stepped away, several people yelled from the floor: "Stand up if you're a person of color!"

The leader paused briefly at the microphone. Then she leaned in: "Yes, stand up if you're a person of color!" People of color stood up. (Applause.)

Just then a white man quipped loudly from the floor, "What color?" (A microsecond of stunned silence.)

The moderator ignored the quip, and we moved on.

Thirty-six hours later, during the opening announcements, Tolonda Henderson (they/them), a Black person who was a participant in the gathering—not on the formal program—was standing on the platform. The emcee said something like "Tolonda would like to address us before we move on this morning."

Henderson stepped to the podium.

They began to revisit what had happened two nights before. Henderson described how painful it was to have all these other identities called out for celebration, but to have racial identity omitted. The man's comment, which had felt like such disparagement, had added significantly to that pain. Equally bad was the fact the moderator had moved us along and had failed to address this incident in the moment.

Henderson went on to say how excited they'd been when they first saw the conference program. All these phenomenal queer Christian leaders were in the speaking lineup. It was incredibly racially diverse. But when Henderson had walked into the conference, they were shocked. The actual attendees were more than 90 percent white.

Henderson was pointing out the failure of the planning team to do outreach beyond entrenched white church networks. They were naming how existing racial divides in the LGBTQ+ movement were also present in the church. Such divides persist when racial justice is not given serious attention and understood to be central to queer lives. To Henderson this just looked like another white queer gathering. And then the *anti-welcome* confirmed it. It all felt devastating when they'd come expecting to belong.

When Henderson was done speaking, if I recall correctly, some of us stood up and clapped.

I vividly remember, in the moment of that first interruption from the floor, feeling respect. *Wow!* I thought. *I didn't know you could just yell out and interrupt like that!* I vividly remember being shocked by the white man's loud retort. But in response to Tolonda Henderson's address, I remember being in total awe. I couldn't believe the courage this person had just displayed, speaking the truth with such clarity (and in front of so many people). They had totally disrupted business as usual. The gathering would not be the same.

The emcee came back to the microphone as Henderson started to leave the stage. Then the emcee moved on into the morning announcements and called us into the day's opening worship service.

The precise details of all that happened and what came next are fuzzy in my recall of this twenty-plus-year-old story. And at the time, I wasn't even aware of all that was going on behind the scenes.

I missed the part where several white men began to storm out of the gathering when Henderson took the microphone. And where Melanie Morrison, a respected white lesbian activist in the space with a long track record of antiracism, walked over to try to block them, pointing and mouthing the words "you sit back down."

I missed the part where other white people followed Henderson out after they spoke, just to argue with Henderson and insist that their interpretation of what had happened was "wrong." I wouldn't learn until meeting Henderson more than twenty years later that they'd gone to the conference leadership multiple times after that painful opening night to try to get on that platform. I did not know that the first response they'd been given was "there's a panel on race on Saturday afternoon; we can talk about it then if you want."

"It took a lot of energy to get the little bit of time on the main stage I eventually got," Henderson told me. They also shared something else I hadn't noticed that first night. That "as soon as that white man yelled out, a bunch of people of color who had stood up when the emcee had said, 'Yes, stand up if you're a person of color!' sat back down because they immediately felt unsafe."

I definitely missed the part where people of color left in protest after the emcee moved us on ahead into worship right after Henderson spoke. They were angry it had taken thirty-six hours for the incident to be addressed, that it was squeezed in between announcements and worship, and that we were now moving forward—relegating this to the one "diversity panel" to be held "later today" (which, it just so happened, Morrison was scheduled to facilitate).

What I did not miss, however, was what the leaders who put themselves in the thick of what happened helped create during our remaining time at the conference. That experience changed my life.

A small multiracial group that included Henderson and Morrison had begun to strategize as this incident began to unfold. They stepped into a kind of community-authorized leadership role. They set up spaces for people of color to convene, talk about their needs, anger, and hurt—name their vision for LGBTQ+-affirming work in the church. They set up spaces for those of us who were white, too. I remember being in space with all these queer white people, who had experience in antiracism. They were teaching us and facilitating discussion as many of us tried to make sense of what was going on and figure out what was being asked of us going forward.

Black queer theologian and activist Irene Monroe later wrote to name those asks:

For WOW 2003 [the next WOW] to be racially responsible it must ask itself these three questions:

1. What will be the theological and spiritual fallout for WOW 2003 should it not engage in antiracist work?
2. What might be the ways WOW 2003 can incorporate antiracist work as a priority in all developmental stages of the conference?
3. And, what spiritual practices or ritual or liturgies should WOW 2003 develop in order to strengthen its commitment in doing antiracist work?

Many years later I learned that Henderson had sought Morrison out after having been told they could wait for the panel on diversity to address the incident that had taken place on opening night. Morrison shared Henderson's anger at what a tokenizing response that was. "What do you need?" Morrison asked. Henderson responded, "I want you to go with me." Together they'd gone again to the committee to again insist, "Tolonda needs a place in a plenary session in order to address the entire gathering."

New things grew because of what Henderson had courageously done. And by the time the "diversity panel" happened, Morrison knew she had to directly address the white participants. "I don't ever again want to hear any white queer people talk about homophobia in the Black church. We know not of what we speak!" Morrison said. She also told us that there was no such thing as *the* LGBT community. Racism and other isms had to be a constant focus if our movement was to become "more just, more diverse, more complex, more colorful, more deviant, and more outrageous in the ways it transgresses the status quo." She asked us what our churches and organizations would look like if we cared as passionately about eliminating racism as we do about eliminating homophobia.

I vividly remember thinking, *Wow! I didn't know a white person could say things like that!*

But we can.

Sometimes we literally just need to stand up, like Henderson did. We need to say as loudly and bravely as we can: "Stop! This whole damn party as it's been planned and is playing out just needs to stop." And sometimes we need to step up, like Morrison did, willing to help organize the chaos that may erupt after the party is ruined to figure out with as much integrity as possible where we must go from there.

Fortitude isn't the only experience in this whole white-on-white relationships situation. Here comes the freedom and liberation part!

There's more to Patricia J. Williams's wisdom in regard to race, law, and public life. After describing what an antiracist sensibility requires, Williams closes with a breathtaking claim: "the transgression is dizzyingly intense, [it's] a reminder of what it is to be alive."

And she's right.

Have you ever been to an LGBTQ+ pride event? These are some of the most colorful, beautifully unconstrained, and ridiculously gorgeous parties there are.

Protest still always bubbles under the surface and through the air at pride. Queer celebrations have their historical origins in resistance. Pride celebrations are *dizzyingly intense* because they are born of people who have chosen to transgress and, as a result of such transgression, have become *fully alive*. Through choosing themselves. Through choosing one another in the process of saying no to death-dealing systems.

Still in grief and devastation after the massacre at Club Q

in Colorado Springs in 2022, Chase Strangio—a lawyer and a transgender rights activist—wrote about the joy transgender people create.[3] "Our embodiment is resistance. . . . We build connections to ourselves and others. . . . As artist Carlos Motta wrote in 2016 . . . 'We build dissenting forms of living. We construct futures that resist the suffocating norms of the mainstream.' Our queerness, as Motta wrote, 'is an unstoppable force powered by dreams of survival.' And so is our joy."

Being a white person moving into antiracism is not the same thing as being a queer person. Erasure, rejection, and violence—especially within marginalized parts of the queer community, the trans community, and especially the community of queer and trans people of color—remain ever-present threats. There is no corollary to the risks many queer people endure just to survive.

But there are resonances. And it's this potential for joy, life, and liberation that I want white people to see, feel, touch.

Radical wholeness comes when we push back against systems and cultures that require conformity to oppressive stories about who we are. We find freedom when we reject practices designed to keep our identity bound up in racial silence and oppression. And also, we discover there are others who are choosing rank-breaking wholeness. They become *our people*.

The refusal to comply with the everyday norms in our white families and other communal spaces that demand loyalty with racism in exchange for inclusion opens portals. It makes a kind of liberation possible.

White antiracism is the work of building dissenting forms of living and loving. It's probably the queerest journey I've ever chosen.

I felt dizzy in those messy, chaotic spaces carved out after Henderson, Morrison, and others made sure we all stopped. I felt fully alive. I knew something meaningful was happening. I was part of a communal creation. I met people I am still in relationship with. And I learned things that changed my racial understanding—and thus my life—in the most welcome of ways.

The worlds of possibility my mom opened with her *Hobbit* protest still resonate in my body. They vibrate there still because I experienced the life-giving nature of refusal, the creative power released by not just going along.

This is such a contrast to what my body came to know through possibilities denied—a smothering, a misdirection every time an adult said, "They didn't like the way things were," in response to my searing and truth-seeking questions. Death knells to new worlds that sounded every time my ancestors made the choice to stay in the white world as it was and then handed that world on to me.

What a difference one choice by one ancestor can make.

Sharon Salzberg describes the process of grief as relinquishing the illusion that the past could have been other than it was. I experience grief every time I reflect on the racial legacies I have inherited.

But we need to face and tell the truth of our white inheritances. We need to summon the courage like those women did back at that tomb, and stare it right in the face. Because when we tell the truth about the past and how it shapes the present, we can begin to process racial grief.

When we break ranks, we open space for radically different selves to be born and make radical transgression more possible for others as well. Violating the agreements of whiteness is dizzyingly intense. It's a reminder of what it is to be alive. And that's because it is a way of actually choosing life.

TAKE A NEXT STEP

1. Make a list of specific behaviors that support white cohesion in a communal space you are part of. Brainstorm counter-strategies to disrupt the racial bonding that keeps cohesion stable. Even a question as simple as "Did you mean to say what it sounds like you said?" can be an effective start if you aren't sure what to say or do.

2. Do an inventory of your relationships. Who in your life can challenge and cheerlead you when it comes to antiracism? Identify concrete ways to prioritize and invest in these relationships in order to strengthen them. Tell these people you want to grow racial courage with them.

3. Pick up one of the many recently published how-to workbooks on everyday practices for antiracism (see Further Resources at the back of this book). Find at least three people to work through the book with. Encourage one another to stick with new habits. Make them measurable. Strategize with one another when actions seem hard.

5

Beyond White Fragility

Okay, it's time to talk about feelings.

I want to tell you about a time I needed to cry—to wail, actually. But suspicion of white emotions in our public conversations about race almost stopped me from doing so.

After about ten years of teaching, I moved into the leadership of the Crew Scholars Program. Crew is an academic excellence and leadership development program for students of color at Drake University, where I taught. My role meant an overwhelming majority of my work hours in a given week was spent in spaces mostly with people of color or those deeply engaged in initiatives focused on the well-being of people of color. Over time, my sustained immersion in these relationships reshaped how and what I saw when I looked out into the world. It shifted my embodied sense of race, my experience of my own whiteness in our campus community.

It also transformed how I felt racial violence.

For example, when Donald Trump first ran for president, I was in consistent proximity to the suffering his rhetoric and hatred unleashed. Through my relationships with students, I felt the human impact of high-volume hate speech filling the civic airwaves, directed at Black people, Mexican people, Muslims, and so many others, and of images of physically aggressive treatment of such folks at his rallies. Early versions of what became a white Christian nationalist tsunami were largely treated as a legitimate part of our political discourse—even by folks who found it repugnant. This treatment added to the devastating impact on students. Crew scholars were living and learning among peers who mostly didn't acknowledge these noxious effects and might calmly debate (again, even if they ultimately rejected it) or even embrace this hate cloud.

While that campaign was in full swing, we also went through yet another season in which it felt as if every week or so, we saw horrifying footage of a Black person being killed by police. A hashtag of someone's name would then flood our collective consciousness. And somewhere in the mix would be news of another failure to prosecute anyone for a different killing we'd all watched take place.

Grief, rage, and, frankly, terror began to seep into and overwhelm the Crew community. This was on top of the day in, day out impact the national racial climate had long since been having.

On campus, I was students' primary formal support person. I was responsible for tending not just to their academic thriving but to their emotional well-being, physical safety, and mental health as well. Students might knock on my office door at any time of day needing to come in and process what was going on. To rage. Sometimes to cry.

Our weekly class became a space of painful churning. Students articulated devastating questions. How do you make sense of being a target in a country that's supposedly home? How do you build a life when antiblack violence occupies such a level of normalcy? How do you function in predominantly white spaces when awareness that your humanity is fundamentally unrecognized is a moment-by-moment one—almost an onslaught?

To top it off, one student had a parent who'd been killed by police a few years before he came to college. Another had a brother arrested on questionable allegations who was being prosecuted during this time. Virtually all Crew students had experienced unprovoked (by them!) contact with police and/or other public safety officials. Or they had relatives whose lives had been chewed up by the criminal justice system.

I held my breath every time they arrived for our Thursday-night class. I kept holding it each time they left.

I held space for their experiences as best I could. I didn't pretend to have answers. I was distraught because they deserved answers.

It was a season of death. And fear. And grief. And there was no end in sight.

(It still is such a season.)

Then one day, I was on the phone with one of my best friends, the Reverend Dr. Melanie L. Harris, who is a Black woman, a brilliant scholar, and a mom. We've been friends for decades. And we were talking about all that was happening to Black people. Melanie was sharing her experience of the season. I was listening. Eventually, I shared a bit about my students and how I was walking with them.

She listened for a minute and then Melanie interrupted. "Jen, you know it's okay to cry, right? Go ahead. You need to let it out."

Her words stopped me in my tracks. I felt pain well up in my body—the despair and devastation I'd been carrying for weeks. My distress was there not because of my own personal experience but because of my love for and relationships with these young people. But wait. That means it was in fact there because of my personal experience. It was there because as I'd held space for despair and devastation, I'd experienced a kind of suffering. Even though I'm white.

When Melanie said these words, my brain started to argue with my body. "It's not okay for you to cry. You have no right." "Wail? Nonsense. This isn't about you! How inappropriate. You're a white woman parent of two white children. Your lives are *not* at risk from police. You're not going to cry on the phone while a Black mother (friend or not) with a Black son who *is* at risk holds space for your tears."

"Oh, no, I'm okay," I said.

"Jen, release it," Melanie said again.

And then it broke. Pain and anger turned into sobs. Sobs turned into wails. I remember dropping my forehead onto my desk while I grieved aloud and said over and over, "It's all too much."

"Yes. It is," Melanie said. "It's all too much."

Here's what I learned. I was carrying rage and grief, and probably a whole lot of other things. But my posture of "I'm a white person who knows this isn't about me" meant I was disconnecting from my own experience. Building a wall around my heart.

The pain I was experiencing was vicarious. But it was still pain. And I was cutting myself off from human parts of me that desperately needed to process it.

Metabolizing that pain was crucial to keeping me on a path of anything approximating wellness, let alone allowing me to support my students in healthy ways. Instead, I'd been turning my actual lived experience into an abstract perspective, an intellectual assessment of the situation. Acting as if I had no skin in the game.

And honestly? That's one of the whitest things you can do.

It was my embrace of prevalent interpretations of the concept of white fragility that almost prevented me from doing what any human being needs to do when living under violent conditions. Emotions are necessary to be in meaningful relationships with others—including with people whose well-being is threatened by those violent conditions; including with ourselves.

Thank god for Reverend Dr. Melanie L. Harris—contemplative practitioner, eco-womanist scholar, friend, and that day, pastor.

It's time we start talking about white feelings.

I quit using the term *white privilege* in 2013. This was a little late, actually. I remember womanist theologian Dr. Delores S. Williams challenging her students at Union to reconsider it back in the 1990s. We should think twice about the implications of using a word with such positive connotations—*privilege*—to talk about such an evil reality, she told us.

But I didn't stop using it until the day after George Zimmerman was exonerated for killing Trayvon Martin. In the wake of that atrocity, I was overwhelmed by the way so many white people described what had happened.

"This is the epitome of white privilege!" my Facebook feed declared.

Wait, I thought. *We're going to use the same term we use to describe being able to buy a Band-Aid that matches your skin tone to talk about the predatory stalking and murder of a teenager?*

Given the cold-blooded killing by Zimmerman and then his exoneration, white privilege was antiseptic. It pointed at something in an intellectual mode. The category was woefully inadequate to capture the thing it was pointing to.

White privilege is an important concept. It describes one of the results of the entanglements of white bodies with white supremacy.[1] But some time ago it started to be used as a kind of one-stop-shop concept. It started to function as *the* answer to what is, in fact, a living and multilayered question.

Question: What's the flip side of racism's denial of access to people of color? Answer: overaccess for white people (i.e., white privilege). But white privilege doesn't begin to and can't explain the entirety of racism's impact on those of us who are white. White privilege is *an* answer to only one specific and tiny thing. When it becomes *the* talking point response to every manifestation of racism, the nuanced and exploratory conversations we need to have shrivel up. They become flat and one-dimensional.

After Trayvon Martin was killed, the response that "this is the epitome of white privilege!" prevented those of us who are white from grappling with the devastating and irrefutable reality of the loss of this child to his family and community. It got in the way of engaging deeply with the terror once again inflicted upon Black people everywhere in the wake of that loss. It offered an end run around the need for us to *tarry*, as philosopher George Yancy calls it, with the reality that a vile ethos of racial profiling pervades all white spaces. Harm and violence can be unleashed on Black and Brown people at any moment in the same spaces where white folks, meanwhile, just keep living our everyday lives.

The only appropriate response to the killing of Trayvon Martin was to rend our garments and pour into the streets.

"The trick is not to flee," says Yancy, "but to have the foundations of one's white being challenged, to lose one's sense of white self-certainty. . . . The process of tarrying encourages forms of courageous listening, humility, and the capacity to be touched, to be shaken." White people need to learn to endure the gravity of being entangled in a social and psychic web of white racism, Yancy writes.[2]

We need to be shaken.

It is grave to be a white person caught in such a deadly violent story. Who am I that I dare move through my day-to-day life unshaken in a world in which Tamir Rice is dead—killed in 2014 at the age of twelve, the same age (at the time of this writing) as my beloved and very much alive child? How do I make sense of my life as someone who considers the age of twenty-six the point at which endless possibility, a whole new life, and a gorgeous community engulfed me when I came out as queer—the same age, twenty-six, at which Breonna Taylor (beloved daughter and so much more) was shot to death while sleeping in her bed?

Indeed. Those of us who yearn to walk a path of justice-seeking alongside people of color with enough faithfulness that we help change our local communities are ourselves transformed by that experience, and pass something different down to our children . . . well . . . we only stand a chance at such transformation if we *are shaken.*

If we are to do any of the things Yancy is sure we need to do, we're going to have *to feel.* Lobbing easy concepts as explanatory answers at any and every racial incident is precisely the opposite of that.

Social justice educator Robin DiAngelo coined the term *white fragility* to help us recognize certain behavior patterns. When discussions about racism come up, white people get angry. We divert attention, emotionally break down, evade the topic in any number of ways. We can't take it!

Fragility specifically conjures a deadly history of white

women's tears. White women have long deployed cries of victim-hood against Black men in ways that fed cultures of lynching. A modern-day version of this legacy transpired in New York City the same day a police officer murdered George Floyd in Minne-apolis. Amy Cooper (white) began to shriek and cry—lying as she called 911—in response to Christian Cooper (Black) asking her to leash her dog, which was running around a sensitive bird habitat in Central Park.

Tears weaponized.

White fragility specifically indicts tears that flow in spaces where we've gathered to try to get better at antiracism and eq-uity. Take diversity trainings in a workplace, for example. Black women talk about the racism they contend with every day, in-cluding in spaces they share with white women and often at white women's hands. White women begin to cry. Maybe it's a pity cry: "oh, *I feel* so bad you've felt hurt." Often, it's a victim cry: "*I've been attacked* by how upset you are by this. Stop being so angry." Whatever the specific version, white feelings become the center of the concern and take the attention.

The language of fragility has caught on in a big way. But its overuse short-circuits the ability of white people to tarry. "Don't be fragile" has become a stand-in for not having any emotional response to racism if you're white.

And that's a problem. How are we supposed to engage in anti-racism as a building project for love if we can't face and touch our grief?

I've seen white men in organizations who resist or shut down attempts to create critical, transformational policy for racial re-pair and justice described as doing so because they're fragile.

An aggressive use of power (even if subtle) gets lobbed into the same container used to describe something weak or breakable.

This disorients us.

When we're talking about recalcitrant use of power, the motives or emotional state of the person wielding it doesn't matter. It's time to build some kind of coalition to challenge such recalcitrance and insist on organizational change.

I've heard the behavior of white women in supervisory roles attributed to fragility when they won't take Black and Brown employees seriously or treat women of color badly.

No. A more apt description for such behavior is racial bullying or hostile intransigence. These descriptions are not only more accurate; they're also more likely to help us engage with clear policy and grievance responses in support of employee well-being and supervisor accountability.

White people have always been insulated (by privilege!) from looking at racism. Fragility is merely a symptom of that. It's evidence we haven't gotten ourselves in shape and developed the emotional and moral stamina to keep at it when antiracist commitment gets hard.

Fragility is not *innate* to being white.

We don't have to stay fragile.

Unfortunately, you don't have to listen very long in our public conversations to hear "white fragility" used to insinuate this is just "how white people are."

"White people don't show up against racism *because of* white fragility." The statement sounds like a diagnosis. It explains why white people are the way we are.

But this diagnosis can't take us anywhere.

I've heard white folks, in antiracism spaces they've actually sought out, begin to struggle with the new knowledge they've been offered. This is a *perfectly reasonable stage* of any meaningful growth process. But then they'll dismiss or disparage their own learning by saying aloud, "Well, I guess this is just my white fragility talking," and they'll back off. This invocation of fragility is humbler than the finger-pointing kind. But it doesn't short-circuit growth any less.

What happens when we say, instead, "White people don't show up against racism because of white fragility *and* white people *have developed* white fragility because we've never shown up against racism." When we pair these ideas, we make it clear that there are active processes at work in our lives. As my friend Debby Irving has described it, such a pairing makes clear both that, indeed, whiteness traps us in vicious cycles, and that we can also set virtuous cycles in motion when we practice showing up and staying.

This more complete statement doesn't offer easy answers. But it opens into possibility. It thus has movement in it—we could choose differently. We can ask, "How do we do that?"

Also, at this point in its public usage, that first statement, "White people don't show up against racism because of white fragility," rests on a foundation of shame. This is a dynamic we have far too much of in our public racial discourse right now—and specifically when white people weaponize a flattened notion of white fragility against other white people (we're coming back to that in chapter 7).

Shame is the feeling that we're *innately* unworthy. That our entire selfhood is fundamentally flawed or bad.

Shame is different from guilt. Guilt is the feeling one has done or participated in something wrong or bad. Notice the distinction: *is* wrong versus *has done* wrong.

Guilt does make you feel bad. But when you have participated in something wrong, agency still exists. You can make amends. Try to repair. Guilt can be transformed—one of the primary ways is through action.

But there's little agency in shame. There's nowhere to go when *you* are the thing that's wrong.

There's an even more serious misuse of fragility that goes back to my opening story—namely, its use to shut down virtually any expression of white emotionality. This dynamic in our civic racial conversation makes it very difficult to talk about the reality that waking up to the horrors of racism actually calls for a full-throated emotional response.

White people need to feel.

We need to grieve.

We need to get angry.

And sometimes, we may even need to cry.

I wasn't being flippant earlier when I described cutting myself off and intellectualizing my experience of suffering in proximity to racial violence as a totally *white* thing to do. It really was.

Kenneth Jones and Tema Okun developed the concept of *white supremacy culture* to talk about the beliefs and practices that have developed over time to make it more possible for white people to maintain control and dominance. These attributes include, for example, an emphasis on perfectionism instead of an appreciation of learning through risk-taking and mistakes. A sense of urgency is an attribute that leads us to move fast for expediency's sake rather than engaging in slower, democratic forms of decision-making. Individualism is a trait that emerges when competition is valued above collaboration.

There are others.

These characteristics emerged through the historical forces of white supremacy, extractive capitalism, and colonial-settler structures as the United States was being built. As Okun puts it, the practices that enabled dispossession of Native people, enslavement of African people, and an economic system that worked only for elites were made possible by disconnecting and dividing people. This included severing relations between white people and Black people, Indigenous people, and other people of color (BIPOC); separating BIPOC people from one another; and disconnecting and dividing white people from one another, the earth, nonhuman creatures, relationship with land, and even ourselves.[3]

We can see these various phenomena at work in one small glimpse of U.S. history. When groups of people immigrated from Europe, they were met with racist imagery, discourse, and other kinds of ethnic "policing." *How the Irish Became White* by Noel Ignatiev describes the profound discrimination the Irish experienced upon their arrival to the United States in the 1850s. They were depicted in newspaper cartoons in ways similar to the disparaging ways Black people were depicted. They were referred to by the N-word. They were pitted against other European immigrant groups.

Over time, many Irish gave up their ethnic distinctiveness to escape such treatment. Folks changed their last names. They quit participating in religious, cultural, and other communal practices that marked them as Irish. They began to actively participate in racism against Black people.

Because they had light skin, the Irish were able to assimilate into whiteness. They became "white Americans." But this was a costly trade-off. Access to the benefits white supremacy gave people deemed white came in exchange for giving up your ethnic identity, not to mention your collective bargaining power.

Similar histories exist for many European groups. A capitalist economy in the process of industrializing put pressures on immigrant communities to take on the cultural characteristics needed for a compliant, controllable workforce. The details of this history are too far afield for our focus. But the general arc was that ethnic groups whose cultures tended to celebrate embodiment—music, dance, public displays of emotion, community—were coerced out of such rambunctious collective cultural expressions. These were tamped down to emulate white Anglo-Saxon communal forms more acceptable to a wealthy white ownership class (who were also the employers).

Remnants of this assimilation history exist today in familiar jokes or stereotypes. For example, white people can't dance. Or white churches are quiet and stiff (in contrast to, for example, emotional and movement-filled Black churches). Or the joke I just heard this week on Anderson Cooper's podcast, *All There Is*, which is a look at grief. Cooper begins to cry and says something like "I'm a WASP! I'm not supposed to have feelings."

When I rejected the expression of grief that day in my office, I thought I was being a good white *antiracist* person. What I was actually doing was being a good *white* person. Numbing instead of feeling. Severing body and heart from mind. Denying my interconnectedness with young people I loved.

Suppressing emotions doesn't help us resist racism. That form of disconnect is a product of racist histories and a consequence of en-culturation into systems ensuring racial and economic dominance.

There's more.

From W. E. B. Du Bois to James Baldwin to Ella Baker to Toni Morrison—Black activists, scholars, writers, artists have long insisted the fight against racism is about white people's freedom, too. We need to develop a deep awareness in our soul that we're not fighting white supremacy for others, nor on their behalf.

From a strictly practical perspective, challenging racism for someone else is patronizing. Standing on such ground quickly leads to behaviors likely to cause more harm than good. It's also a posture that feeds into white superiority complexes: the conscious or unconscious assumption that we're somehow more capable or morally superior.

But another reason it's important we see our stake in ending racism is simply because it's true. Racism has damaged and cost white people, too.

During the same period of my life in which I began reading James Cone and reckoning with the ways systemic oppression had shaped my life, I went to Guatemala and El Salvador. For three months I studied civic and political realities in Central America. This included a hard look at the role of the U.S. government in training and funding death squads who committed atrocities against the poorest of the poor. I listened to mothers describe how their children and husbands had been "disappeared." I learned about ways the U.S. church had supported this colonial/imperial violence.

I shared all of this with my parents. About white supremacy. U.S. militarism. Racism in the church. My anger that U.S. Christians cared more about Bill Clinton's affair with Gennifer Flowers than about humans tortured by U.S.-funded militias.

My parents hung in there with me for a bit, even when they weren't quite sure what to do with me. But, one day, I crossed a line.

I was talking to my dad. He was asking questions. He was trying, with love, to wrap his mind around what was going on with me. But then I said something about how white supremacy and military violence meant I wasn't going to say the Pledge of Allegiance anymore.

My prior-to-this-point curious, calm dad exploded. His face got red. He started to shake. I remember his finger pointing in my face. "You know what? If you hate it here so much," he said, "why don't you go live in Guatemala?"

I was stunned. As his response sunk in, devastated. I felt the rage emanating from his shaking body in my own body. I wasn't physically afraid of him, but I was physically and emotionally shaken in turn.

Something cracked in our relationship.

More than twenty years ago, in *Learning to Be White,* Thandeka described the process of being racialized as white as a form of racial abuse. A child playing happily across racial lines is disparaged one day for such human behavior. She's told "no more will you have your Black friend here or go to their house." An Italian American teenager is stopped while riding a bike through a Black neighborhood where his school friends live. A police officer tells him he shouldn't be there, escorts him home, and warns him never to cross that line again.

Children learn how to be white through familial and communal discipline, Thandeka argues. Such learning deploys shame. It embeds three deeply damaging experiences that are particularly harmful given children's developmental vulnerability. These are:

1. Your belonging to this family/community is contingent. In other words, you can be excised, which also means you are loved *conditionally.*
2. You're not good enough. Innate unworthiness gets exposed in such racial disciplinary moments.
3. Whiteness, including the racism it's entangled with, is a primary source of connection to your community. Given your age, you have to become "white" in order to survive.

In the process of racialization, your humanity becomes malformed and mangled.

Thandeka invented a game. She was trying to understand dynamics she kept bumping into in encounters with white people who were showing interest in developing racially just ways of being in the world that felt strange to her. She posed a challenge to these people. "For one week use the descriptor 'white' anytime you refer to yourselves or another white person." She soon discovered no one could see the game through. They all quit—usually in less than a day.

As she seeks to understand why, Thandeka finds that the racial shame from those childhood experiences remains alive, persistent, and powerful in white life. It rushes to the surface when her subjects are required to use *white*.

Racial abuse may be too strong. At the time, this phrase generated dissent. So did the perception by some that Thandeka's work seemed to want us to feel sorry for white people.

Also, there have been shifts in *how* white people are racialized. Racial discipline for Thandeka's subjects, who grew up in the 1950s and '60s, came for crossing racial lines. Today such discipline is as likely to happen when a white child begins to notice and name difference. White parents, uncomfortable with how to handle race-conscious talk, might respond: "It doesn't matter he's Black! We're all the same underneath our skin." Depending on the circumstances, this response might range from a calm "we just treat everyone the same" to a disciplinary "shush—it's not polite to talk about that." It can happen when a child's been taught "we value equality," but when a grandparent makes a racist comment, she watches her parents say nothing; she also feels a subtle or not-so-subtle pressure to stay silent herself for the sake of avoiding family conflict. It can happen in other ways, too, such as when a white teenager experiences a school full of racial tension—even though the school mantra is "we value diversity"—and none of the adults who are otherwise trustworthy acknowledge or talk about this with them.

White racial identity develops through the process of being taught how to behave in regard to both racial difference and injustice. In any of these scenarios, white youth internalize moral and cognitive dissonance. And, because we depend on our families for survival at developmentally vulnerable stages, and messages around race, racism, and whiteness invoke the possibility that our belonging, belovedness, or worth might be withdrawn if we are dissonant with our families, shame hovers all around white racial experience.

My experience with my dad offers a firsthand account of how white supremacy can damage white relationships between parent and child. But something more also took place in that exchange.

My dad is a very intellectually engaged human. His response to me was not aligned with his analytical disposition.

I believe the something more had to do with Thandeka's findings about shame. I suspect the ways I pressed on the question of complicity around family and religion triggered a shame reaction in my father—but it came out as rage.

This strikes me as important. If a white parent can respond to their child in this way because the shame of complicity they feel is so intolerable ("I will not look. So get out!"), imagine what unprocessed shame does to the white capacity to stay present and open when people of color press on it.

Not so long ago, when another incident of deadly and hate-imbued gun violence erupted in the United States, a friend said to me, "We are drowning in shame."

Shame impairs humans' abilities to connect in authentic and holistic ways. Racial shame destroys the white ability to connect in humane ways with Black people and other people of color. It damages connection in white familial relationships. It interrupts internal cohesion and alignment within the white self.

Real costs.

My dad may remember this exchange differently or not at all. But that experience remains painful to me to this day. When he hit a limit in his ability to look at racial complicity with me, it didn't manifest as "You're wrong! I disagree!" The limit manifested as excision: "Get out!" His investment in not looking was deeper than his investment in me.

Real costs.

I think about the fractured branches of my family tree. Generational rage over their elders' lack of engagement with civil rights led some of my great-uncle's children and grandchildren to estrangement from his generation and one another. Or the trust breached every time my elders told me, "They didn't like the way things were," but I knew I wasn't getting the whole story.

We lose authentic connection with every white lie. The damage done by white supremacy, in and through interpersonal relationships, emanates from and overlaps with systemic, structural, and historic processes.

I used to be close to someone who grew up with the last name Roberts. In her thirties, after her grandfather's death, she learned she was actually Italian American. Her paternal grandfather had immigrated. His last name had been Russo. He'd changed it when he'd severed ties with his large family so as to dissolve into the sea of whiteness. She had second cousins she'd never met. Her father had aunts, uncles, and first cousins she never knew existed. They'd both been cut off from a large family tree, not to mention from any meaningful tie to their culture.

This same person had always struggled with how disconnected her own dad seemed from her. She wondered whether the withholding required for her grandfather to keep such a huge secret from his children and spouse had impaired his connection and this inability to connect had been passed on to her dad—affecting her in turn. She wondered if her dad's impaired ability had also affected her parents' marriage. Her mother always seemed deeply lonely and struggled with alcoholism over the years.

Real costs.

There are also economic costs. Most white people have economic interests more aligned with Black people and other communities of color than we do with wealthy elites.

In *The Sum of Us: What Racism Costs Everyone and How We Can Prosper Together,* Heather McGhee makes a compelling case that the collapse of unions, inadequate access to health care, and the loss of access to homeownership are directly linked to white people's investment in racism. We take actions against our own interests because of it. (She also provides inspiring real-life examples of the possibilities we create when we come together in multiracial coalitions.)

McGhee's specific argument is that an investment in racism has compelled whites to trade public goods for private goods only the wealthy can actually afford.

One of the most visceral examples she gives is the white choice to destroy public swimming pools rather than have them desegregated. Before the civil rights era, "pools were the pride of their communities, monuments to what public investment could do. . . . Then came the desegregation orders. The pools would need to be open to everyone. But these communities found a loophole. They could close them for everyone. Drain them. Fill them with concrete. Shutter their parks departments entirely. And so they did."[4]

Jonathan Metzl documents something similar in *Dying of Whiteness.* White communities most in need of universal health care vehemently reject it because the thought of Black communities "getting government welfare" is so objectionable. These communities end up sicker because they can't afford insurance. Metzl finds anti-Black and anti-Brown views at the heart of resistance to robustly funding public education, even though we all suffer when schools are inadequately resourced. And an investment in racism sits at the core of this country's inability to get reasonable gun laws passed. Powerful white rhetoric about the need to protect family, home, and nation from menacing darker hordes keeps some of us clinging to guns, while white men are dying from suicide, through use of a firearm kept at home, at astronomical rates.

Real costs: Racial resentment led us to act against our own well-being. White Americans destroy things that are basic to our quality of life, too, over and over again.

Chris Crass, a cofounder of the national Showing Up for Racial Justice (SURJ), always describes SURJ as rooted in the tradition of Anne and Carl Braden. The Bradens were white organizers in the South during the civil rights movement. They insistently described the struggle against racism as about white people's freedom and liberation, too.

In an interview a few years ago, Crass was asked about the stakes for white people in working for justice. He explained,

> "White supremacy does incredible damage to the imagination, to the heart, to the values, to the sense of self of white people." European indentured servants were forming families, forming friendships, forming communities with enslaved Africans, with indigenous people. Laws were enacted to prevent people coming together, there were rewards for white people to only align with the ruling class . . . there was punishment for

people of color (POC) and punishment for white people who stepped out of that white racist world view.[5]

Real costs.

Resmaa Menakem argues that white supremacy is best understood as a form of racial trauma. In *My Grandmother's Hands: Racialized Trauma and the Pathway to Mending Our Hearts and Bodies,* Menakem—who is a somatic healer based in Minneapolis—illustrates how white supremacy and colonial-settler violence enacted trauma on *all* the bodies implicated in these histories.

The violence of white supremacy ensnares the perpetrators in ways that are of course distinct from those who are victimized and subjugated but are themselves deeply damaging and debilitating.[6] The historical origins of white supremacy were the original traumatizing events. (Consider the violence required to fracture relationships, as Crass describes.) But the ongoing generational violence required to sustain white supremacy perpetuates this trauma. And—like all trauma—racial trauma lives in the body and gets passed down when it goes unhealed.

There are remarkable resonances between Menakem's claims and Thandeka's. Menakem, too, is clear that white supremacy cannot be healed through the intellect alone.[7] We're going to have to deal with our bodies. We are going to have to process pain. We're going to have to feel.

Some of my most exciting moments as a teacher are when white students get upset. This happens when we tarry with a book like Waziyatawin's *What Does Justice Look Like?* Waziyatawin provides a devastatingly detailed history of the state we call Minnesota. She keeps the Lakotas' experience relentlessly at the center.

Engaging with the actual story of Minnesota leaves my students deeply shaken—especially the midwesterners.

The history horrifies them. The fact their teachers and parents lied about or hid the history makes them angry. They feel their white Minnesotan identities caught in the gravity of the social and psychic web of racism. The disorientation is profound. They don't know what to do.

I've had white students blurt out in class, "How am I going to go home over spring break?" Sometimes they erupt in tears as they say it.

Beverly Harrison (someone I studied with at Union) was an audacious white lesbian Christian ethicist whose life's work was devoted to challenging patriarchy, sexism and homophobia, racism, and economic injustice. Harrison insisted on the importance of bodies and the significance of the feelings we experience in them. She wrote: "When we cannot feel, literally, we lose our connection to the world."

Harrison celebrated anger. "Anger is a mode of connectedness to others and it is always a vivid form of caring," she wrote. "Anger is—and it always is—a sign of some resistance in ourselves to the moral quality of the social relations in which we are immersed."

This perception of feelings is why I get excited when white students start to get pissed off. Something amazing is potentially at work when their feelings bubble up.

As we grow to care about the social relations in which we are embedded, accessing the part of us that can feel enraged is vital. These forces have affected us all so intimately. Anger is a move from intellectual observation to embodied care about our own lives and the lives of our fellow humans.

Anger is a sign some part of our own humanity is still intact.

It's also a sign our humanity is being activated. As Harrison put it, "Where anger arises, there the energy to act is present."[8]

School districts all over the country began banning books in 2021. In Iowa, a group of mostly white women got really angry about this. Ann Lohry-Smith, a mom deeply committed to public education, dove in and started educating herself about what was happening. She became very active in school board meetings. She galvanized this emerging group of women to raise a fuss.

When the book bans began to pass, the women stayed angry and would not be deterred. Ann died unexpectedly in 2022. The grief left in the wake of her passing furthered these women's determination to ensure people in their mostly white county had "unhindered access to books, with characters that reflect the diversity and complexity of the world around them"[9] despite what the bans did.

Their motto? "We Read Banned Books. We Want You to Read Them Too."

I met members of this scrappy group of women wearing matching T-shirts at a public library in a tiny rural town during Black History Month. There, a young white librarian, who was also angry, had decided she would host an event for youth. The Black Lives Matter sign the library had put on display many months before had gotten some pushback in the community, so the librarian knew she might get more pushback now. But her team forged ahead.

She invited children and families in her community to gather, browse books by Black authors, and have a community conversation about race and racism. She called up Annie's Foundation and invited them to come, too. They did. And they brought with them stacks of books, copies of Jason Reynolds and Ibram X. Kendi's *Stamped (for Kids): Racism, Antiracism, and You.* They gave them away to anyone—kid, parent, grandparent—who wanted one.

The event was great. It opened a space for connection. People talked with one another about their commitments, they shared their feelings about the politics tearing through their schools, and they spoke their desires to keep learning and help change the course of things in Iowa. They left feeling less alone and more galvanized.

What a powerful everyday example of what anger can do. It can be deployed to give us courage to do what we can where we are in the places we already know. It can be used to build connection instead of keeping us isolated or tearing us apart.

But my favorite part about that small-town library event was that it brought attention to hard truths, in the context of community, into the lives of youth in that little town. I loved that it was unapologetically focused on kids of all ages, even really young ones. The choice to showcase stories about our shared racial legacy as Americans was a choice to invest in the *humanity* of those young people. It was a move counter to the tendencies and pressures to try to insulate young white Americans, have them look away, pressure them to stay numb. It was an event full of *feeling* and *emotion.*

I shared a story in my last book about my young white child, who created a sign that read "Black Lives Matter." On her sign, she wrote in green and red marker: "Stop killing them." Below that she wrote: "People who are Blak [sic] are" and then listed the names of her aunt and cousins.

Discovering that sign was a painful parental moment. I realized my child was living with a broken heart. She was aching from racism's deadliness. I grieved this but also wanted that for her.

We're living in a world in which our neighbors, coworkers, students, friends, and sometimes family members are being brutalized. People live with a constant awareness, and the trauma that comes with it, that in the most mundane of daily encounters they might experience violence at any time. Fellow human beings who eat, sleep, love, give birth, cry, and more, just like I do. Fellow humans who have created gorgeous and courageous legacies of artistic creativity, intellectual brilliance, moral persistence, spiritual wisdom, and so much more. These are legacies innately invaluable in their own right and that have offered so much to this nation and the world.

What a devastating cost to white people that unmetabolized shame and unacknowledged grief prevent connection. What a tragedy that we deny ourselves the possibility of authentic relationship with such vibrant and gorgeous human beings and communities. What possibilities would emerge if we begin to feel that cost?

My daughter's sign was a written version of weeping and wailing. Not in a million years, and *even if she'd cried actual tears that day*, would I have told her, "Knock it off."

When my white students cry, I never tell them to stop. I ask us to wait and make space and time for it. I feel in their tears the emergence of a reckoning that is *necessary*. Their grief or rage is welcome as they tarry with their own history.

There is a chasm of meaningful difference between manipulative, dangerous tears and tears that signify authentic feeling.

White fragility is indeed a part of our problem. But it isn't *the* problem. And one-stop-shop overuse and flattened misuse of this concept are posing a bigger problem still to the necessarily messy and emotional work of white antiracism.

* * *

About a year before the pandemic began, a white woman came up to me after a speaking event in Washington. She looked exhausted and stressed. She was upset. She began to talk to me about the antiracism organizing she'd been doing. I could tell from the little I heard her say that she was plugged in with real organizations doing good racial justice work in her area. She was on the journey that seemed deep and committed.

But she was also a mess. She said she had a question. Then as she spoke, she started to cry.

I wasn't quite sure what was going on or what she thought she might gain from a conversation with me. As I started to ask more, however, she suddenly shut down. She stiffened up as abruptly as she'd walked up to me. Her tone got crisp. She said, "Sorry! What am I doing? I don't get to be exhausted. *This isn't about me!* I don't know why I'm crying. I'm so embarrassed."

"No, no, no! Let it out, oh white stranger!" is what I wanted to say as I watched her do the precise thing I'd done a year or two before that day in my office. "You need to release it."

But I didn't say any of those things. I didn't quite know how to say them. I also, admittedly, didn't really try. Even as a flash of desire went through me to invite her emotion in, I felt afraid someone might overhear and accuse me of coddling white fragility. So when she stopped, I didn't push. Our short exchange came to an end.

I regret my response that day. Were I to have the chance again, I'd want to push past my worry about being perceived as coddling and hold space to see what might grow from the shaking that George Yancy says is so necessary and was so obviously going on in her case.

Today I hope I'd gently lean in and see if she would take the risk to not shut down—somewhat like when the Reverend Dr. Melanie Harris leaned in and stopped me. "You need to release it."

White emotionality is complicated. Yes.

We must be careful about when, where, and with whom we release it. I still don't go running to Melanie as my first go-to if or when I feel grief-rage. And I'm not encouraging white readers to run around and just let the tears flow whenever and wherever they are.

But we can show responsible care with our emotion. Of course, expressing white emotion (tears, anger, or anything else for that matter) isn't appropriate in a situation where we're in multiracial space and BIPOC people risk sharing their experiences. The only right response then is to listen—and do so no matter the tone in which experiences are shared. To tarry with what is shared.

White emotionality can easily place a burden on people of color that is not theirs to bear—even if the emerging grief-rage *is* authentic.

But being responsible for our emotional expressions is not the same thing as never crying.

We need lots of words to get at the beast of racism and to identify white participation in it.

But always, as we grow our vocabularies, we need to be wary of latching on to simplistic answers.

Because mostly, right now, we need to heed Yancy's challenging invitation to be shaken. Can we find ways to be open to feeling in the ways tarrying both requires and generates? Intellectual understanding alone will never get us where we need to go. But grief and rage, processed in healthy ways, while we move through deeper and deeper head knowledge, just might.

It's time to create spaces for white feelings.

TAKE A NEXT STEP

1. Write down how you felt in 2020 when the killings of Breonna Taylor and George Floyd were so present in our collective consciousness. What did you do with those feelings? Visualize getting in touch with your anger and feeling your heart break over racism. What happens when you do this?

2. Find a friend who is trying to grow their racial understanding and commitment to antiracist behavior. Set up a time for an intentional conversation about what the reflection exercise in the first question made you aware of. Notice if such connective dialogue elicits other yearnings for racial healing.

3. Get engaged with some kind of therapeutic process. This isn't a touchy-feely suggestion! Maybe it's therapy. Maybe it's a group space where processing the emotional impact of systemic oppression is welcomed. Maybe it's a somatic healing course (see chapter 7 and the Further Resources at the back of this book).

6

Finding Our Way Through Paradox

In May of 2020, Gayle King interviewed filmmaker Ava DuVernay after DuVernay's miniseries *When They See Us* had generated such powerful public engagement that she created a platform to carry that momentum forward. Her ongoing education initiative, ARRAY 101, "amplif[ies] storytelling by Black artists, people of color and women directors of all kinds."

The interview took place right after the Amy Cooper incident in Central Park. After the two women talk about that incident for a bit, King asks DuVernay, "So what action can white people who see themselves as allies, what can they do?"

To this DuVernay responds,

> I really feel strongly that that's not a question that people who are not white should answer. You know, we take on the emotional labor of racism. And it is not our job to explain to white folk how to fix their broken selves in

> this context, right? Because there's a brokenness there. . . .
> There are many educated Caucasian [*sic*] folk who are
> talking to each other about it. They need to continue to
> do that, so that we can save our energy for survival and
> thriving.[1]

I didn't see this interview when it aired. I looked it up after a white woman who was part of a multiracial workshop I facilitated brought it up during a group discussion.

The woman had described the exchange—though she didn't share, and didn't seem to have really heard, the entirety of DuVernay's comment. Then she said, "I just want to know what I need to be doing. I'm not sure how I'm supposed to learn or know what I don't know? I wish DuVernay had been willing to say *something*."

And there we were.

One comment dropped our group right into the middle of one of the paradoxes that abound in white antiracism.

I feel tension increasing in my body as I write this scenario down on a page. Maybe you feel some tension reading it.

I find myself needing to resist the temptation to not immediately write (preferably in all capital letters): It's not any person of color's job to educate us.

And then just end the chapter.

But maybe this isn't the first point in this book where tension emerged. Remember the story about my white public speaking professor who referred to my Black classmate's poem as a rap and how I stumbled my way into a response? As I wrote that story, I imagined someone might read it and go, "Wow, Jen, that's some serious white savior shit going on right there."

Or maybe worries about saviorism came up in response to the story about my mom and *The Hobbit*.

I don't know if the term *white savior* had been coined back when I sat down with my professor (though we surely had plenty of Sandra Bullock and Kevin Costner movies). But I'd be claiming a kind of purity I'm not sure is possible if I insisted I didn't feel proud of myself after that intervention. I did try to be conscious and remind myself I wasn't doing something *for* my classmate. But human motives are rarely pure.

The culture that's developed around white antiracism has elevated a set of standards against which white behaviors and motivations are measured, and they can be pretty exacting. Plenty of my own actions over the years haven't lived up to them. It may be that my experience with my Union professor is one of these.

I shared a story in *Raising White Kids* about my young nephew, who is Black. When he was about five or six, he was playing with a group of children when one of the white kids made a derogatory comment about his skin. Another white kid immediately jumped in and said, "Hey! That's racist!"

I wrote about my nephew's experience of that interaction, along with my curiosity about how the parents of the second white kid approached the subject of race. I wanted to illustrate that white children can learn to challenge racism from much younger ages than white adults typically presume they can.

But I've noticed a shift over time when I share that story. With increasing frequency, white people respond with concern that the second white kid was acting like a white savior. "Should that kid have stepped in like that?" they'll ask. "Was it his place to define what that moment meant?" "Shouldn't he have waited for your nephew to respond first?"

White saviorism gets about as much airtime as fragility does of late. A lot of white anxiety swirls around it.

Racism affects white people and people of color differently. The large collective project we might refer to as white antiracism assumes different roles, responsibilities, and behaviors are needed of us. Teaching white folks in clear and specific ways can reshape both what we know and what we do.

An emphasis on the different roles and responsibilities in shared justice struggle goes back to at least the civil rights movement. Ella Baker, one of the founders of the Student Nonviolent Coordinating Committee (SNCC), was perhaps the first activist to separate folks into distinct racial groups when she sent white SNCC organizers to organize in white communities.

Baker knew white people were more likely to listen to white people, and that the changes needed in white communities were different from those needed among Black people. She also knew white activists' interactions with Black people were sometimes condescending and carried other forms of presumed white superiority.

The goal of freedom and liberation for all remained overarching and shared. The movement was one movement. But Baker's methods emphasized that *differentiation* was also legitimate—working *together* by white activists working primarily among white folks, Black activists working primarily among Black folks in the multiracial organization that was SNCC.

So a philosophy endorsing particular attention to white folks isn't new. But the power of Black-led antiracism organizing combined with the urgency of our civic crisis has catalyzed a public conversation around white people and race in ways that are new.

Our civic crisis has created a particular kind of intensity in antiracism spaces. This intensity has generated lots of directive coaching. It's almost like those of us engaged with questions about white roles have collectively authored a Wikipedia page. The page is full of community-authorized lists of "white people dos and don'ts."

The clarity and focus of this collective project have been fantastic and necessary. Vital, even. Books like this one sit squarely within the confines of this project.

But the emotional and intellectual intensity of the conversation can be overwhelming.

For example, are white people supposed to speak up about racism? (Yes.) Or are we supposed to "pass the mic" to people of color and stop taking up so much space? (Also yes.)

Are we supposed to step in to make our neighborhoods and workplaces more inclusive? Or does that mean we're being patronizing and playing the white savior? (Yes, and it depends.)

We're not supposed to get emotional, because it's not about us. Right? (Right, that's white fragility—see chapter 5!) But wait, we've got to stop being apathetic and untouched by racism's violence. (Yep. Absolutely—see chapter 5 again!)

We've never experienced being the targets of racism, so we need to listen to and learn from people of color, right? White people can't fix this. We can't know what we don't know. (Yes.) But we've got to stop expecting people of color to educate us and instead *do our own work*. (There it is. One of the truths DuVernay articulated in her response to King.)

Also, since white people are responsible for white supremacy, we're responsible for ending it. Racism is a white problem. (This is getting complicated.)

And oh my god, what if I say or do something wrong? What happens when I totally miss the mark while trying to pull off these complicated responsibilities well? Will my reputation be ruined on social media? Will I be canceled at the PTA?

(Maybe I should just stay out of this altogether.)

See how this can go?

The more visible the urgency of effective work for justice has become, the more fraught the issues we're all dealing with have gotten. The reality is most of us don't yet have the experience to skillfully navigate dynamics as challenging as those captured in the questions above.

Racial transformation is slow, long-haul work. The changes we need to make, the habits and skills we need to grow, and the sensibilities and dispositions we need to develop don't happen overnight.

That's not an argument for moving slowly. Frankly, it's the opposite.

But still. When large-scale culture shifts get boiled down to lists of dos and don'ts we try to apply quickly and easily, there can be unintended consequences.

One consequence can be impediments to the complex and layered societal work many of our organizations are trying to do. Another is that barriers to relationships can be increased and become more locked in. Checklists, quickly applied, fuel our tendencies to put one another in boxes based on one-dimensional assessments.

Like so many others in recent years, Jeff Bolden's large environmental nonprofit organization has invested significant energy, time, and staff capacity to address equity and justice issues both inside and outside the organization. Bolden is a sixty-year-old white guy. He's very progressive and has been engaged in social change work—especially around climate—for more than thirty years. He's also humble, curious, earnest, and a great listener. He's fully on board with his organization's commitments.

But Bolden says, "The pace of trainings, expectations, and change has been frenetic and almost panicked. So many of the trainings have been unskillfully carried out." One effect of this has been a fair amount of confusion and shame among the staff.

Recently, Bolden took part in a team retreat. It was "wonderful, one of the better and more enjoyable in my career. . . . Our young staff are incredibly smart, capable, and passionate, and remind me of how fired up I was at that age."

Bolden had enjoyed a number of conversations with two young women of color about their careers. At the end of the three days together, the team was sitting in a circle reflecting on the experience. When it was their turn, the women looked at Bolden and another older colleague and said, "The biggest surprise was that the old . . . I mean, old*er* staff are amazing! I thought they . . . well I don't know what I thought, but they have so much experience and really get it! We didn't expect that! I know we don't have a formal mentor program in the organization, but I learned so much from them this week and would love to spend more time with them in the future."

Bolden's response was to be "touched because the feeling was very mutual." "But" he admitted, "I was also conflicted and more than a little hurt."

The incident helped him put into words part of his recent experience. "Approaching age sixty, I am frequently treated like I'm an oddity and automatically someone who is out of touch. . . . On my drive home I realized that many of our young staff are projecting an awful lot of inaccurate beliefs about the older staff. They see us as politically conservative, un-woke old farts that get in the way of their progress. . . . My organization needs their passion and energy *and* also needs us old-timers with decades of practical experience. In many ways, my organization is giving the power to young staff who want to burn the whole place down and shunt the older staff to the side."

A really well-facilitated retreat, in this case, may have created precisely the opening necessary for the kind of relationship-building so many of our organizations need—interracial but also intergenerational. I genuinely hope so.

But the tensions so evident in Bolden's experience are the sort those of us committed to creating a just world need to figure out how to navigate. And lists of dos and don'ts on their own simply aren't up to the task.

We need more practice navigating tension. Because complicated tensions do show up when you're white and trying to stand up again racism.

Like, for example, white people need to find our own stakes and get outraged at what white supremacy has done in our lives. Well, we already explored how we short-circuit that process when a simplistic "don't be fragile!" tamps it down.

Like, what happens when fears of white saviorism take on such an outsize role that we're willing to interrogate and second-guess a *six-year-old* who interrupts racial bullying?

Like, are pure motivations and impeccable skills necessary before I step up and address the kind of racism I bore witness to in my public speaking class? If so, what does such purity even look like?

There are few directives in our lists of dos and don'ts that can just be applied across the board.

"Pass the mic!" sits near the top of the list when we start talking about white behaviors. Even if you don't know quite what you're supposed to do, no longer presuming it's always you who needs to be doing the talking seems straightforward. "Don't take the microphone from people of color."

But we can't just follow this "don't" in all circumstances. Why?

Well, in some cases, talking less actually strengthens racism. Right alongside "pass the mic" sits an *equally true* instruction: "Speak up!" There are times when stepping up to the mic is a form of solidarity.

Let's try a more complex example. Let's imagine I work for an organization in which structural racism is embedded in various ways. Let's say I've learned I need to center the voices and experiences of Black and Brown people. I recognize the white tendency to swoop in and take over.

If I just go applying any one item on our list of dos and don'ts, I'm likely to walk on over to underrepresented and overworked faculty and staff of color where I teach and say something like, "Hey! See all the racism here. Let's go tackle it!" Or "I know all this racism is hurting you. How can I support you while you do something about it?"

That approach is replete with tokenizing behavior. It places labor on my coworkers' backs without their consent. It forgets the part where racism is a white problem and white people's responsibility to address and redress.

Okay, so should I do the opposite? Am I supposed to go, "Oh, hey! I see all this racism here . . . and over here and over there!"? And "I've learned racism is a white people problem. OKAY! Here's what we white people are going to do." (Rolls up sleeves.) Off I go to create some initiative or solution.

Nope. Failing to consult those concerned can easily make conditions worse for faculty of color or put staff of color at risk of backlash. Also, in my insulation, I'm certain to understand the problems inadequately. The likelihood I will design "solutions" that make things worse is high.

Lists of dos and don'ts can be incredibly helpful for moving white folks.

But.

And.

And.

And.

The same lists so helpful in their specificity are risky. Human living always unfolds in complex situations and environments.

If antiracism and systemic change could be put into a simple formula, generations of Black and Brown organizing would have brought this entire system crashing down a very long time ago. The problem here is not with the lists themselves, any more than the problem was Ava DuVernay not giving an answer to the woman in my workshop. The problem emerges when we treat antiracism as something we do by following a set of step-by-step instructions.

Our lists of white antiracism dos and don'ts *are* really complex. They *are* full of paradoxes.

But some of our most powerful and meaningful ways of living as human beings are found as we figure out how to live with integrity amid paradoxes.

I would say it's important to participate in political processes in the United States of America, for example. I vote regularly. I even have strong feelings about the outcomes of elections.

I suspect you might, too.

At the same time, I never forget that this nation-state is a colonial-settler, white supremacist entity. The land we live on is made up of territories that Native tribes did not cede to the U.S. government or, if they did, only ceded through coercive, violent historical realities. This is Indigenous people's land. And I know who the founding white fathers were. Most of them were enslavers. Those who weren't made compromises about enslavement, worked with enslavers, and/or accrued wealth generated by the enslaving economy that built this nation—South and North. These are the same men who set up our political system. All of this is inherent in the origins and identity of this nation-state.

Still, I vote. Every time.

That's a paradox.

Many of us decrying the ongoing threats being waged against the Constitution in our political environment are equally clear that the scaffolding on which the Constitution was built is innately flawed. Yet, again, we still want to protect it.

Paradox.

During the 2020 election cycle, many racial justice activists struggled with how much energy to put into securing Trump's defeat once it was clear the nominee for the Democrats would be Biden. A strong contingent of #BlackLivesMatter activists and Latinx community organizers didn't believe Biden would deliver on a meaningful racial justice vision.

During this public conversation, activist Bree Newsome—who famously climbed the flagpole outside the South Carolina statehouse and took down the Confederate flag in 2015—insisted on the *both/and*. We *both* work to elect Biden, she said, because presidential leadership shapes the conditions under which we organize. *And* we continue to organize relentlessly, because a Biden presidency wouldn't bring the justice agenda we need and deserve.

The paradoxes inherent in our dos and don'ts are appropriate. They reflect something about the nature of white supremacy. White supremacy is dynamic and malleable. Its systems are complex, savvy, and powerful.

White supremacy has so permeated the environments in which we imagine antiracist ways of being that it lays before us options for which there are rarely perfect or correct responses. Mono-dimensional approaches like my hypothetical workplace example are likely to play out in racially harmful ways.

In this civic era, when so many more white people have shown moral curiosity, awareness, and buy-in to antiracism, there's a lot of possibility for transformation and change. It's worth spending some energy, then, to attend to the kind of culture and conversation we're growing around it.

Our dos and don'ts aren't a recipe or a map. They're more like guidelines or, better, landmarks that point in a direction. We can emphasize that growing our ability to discern is *itself* a major component of antiracist journey. We can practice the "do" of ongoing reflection. This is different from trying to memorize a rule we think—if we just follow it to a tee—will ensure we always get things "right."

We need to remember antiracism is full of paradox.

Remember the woman I described in chapter 5 who came up to me starting to ask about staying with antiracism for the long haul? She was experiencing exhaustion from being stretched too thin. When she shut down because she remembered she wasn't supposed to be fragile, she didn't just short-circuit her grief. By trying to avoid white fragility, by ignoring her own limits, she was actually running in the direction of saviorism.

I've observed members of my own local community do something similar. We wake up to the recognition of who we've been racially. We begin to feel the shame of it, find zeal to make up for lost time, presume human limitations should be dismissed as fragility, and a false belief gets activated. The belief is "we white antiracists are going to fix historic legacies of white supremacy single-handedly and tomorrow." Never mind that people of color have obviously been working at this for generations.

When we create a vibe that positions us as poised to save the day, we move into antiracist practices in a white heat that flares big and bright, but burns out quickly. Stacey and David started a White People Against Racism (WPAR) group in their midsize city a few years back. Their goal was to connect white members of their faith community with folks active in other civic and educational bodies, and organize them to support justice projects Latinx and Black communities were working on.

It went great at first. Within the course of a year, WPAR became recognized as a viable partner in antiracism in the community. They became recognized as white folks who were doing their own work and would actually show up if you called on them for support.

But pretty soon a couple of group members—because they were excited and the needs were indeed great—started saying yes to everything. They would commit WPAR to every project, fundraiser, or event that got on their radar. They would cajole the group into adding another task to their plate. WPAR did not develop a process for *how* they were going to make such decisions. So when Pauly and Beth would come to meetings and say, "We have this on the fifteenth, and then the week of the twenty-seventh we need to . . . ," other members would say okay. But it quickly became more than fifteen people could meaningfully support.

A group that had been, for a time, experienced by communities of color as reliable in allyship soon became yet another white disappointment. WPAR would be named as a partner for an event, but only two or three people would show up. The same three were doing everything. The group began to shrink because members who stayed eventually got burned out and just quit, or quit because a culture in which the constant refrain of "you're not doing enough; if you're committed, you'll say yes to this one more thing" became more pervasive than they could withstand.

WPAR dissolved only two years after being born.

This is an important lesson. The culture of antiracism we need to grow is one that values communal exploration about how we individually prioritize and collectively collaborate. White people do need to stretch beyond our current habits and comfort zones. We do need to increase our commitment, as Alicia Garza might describe it. But we also need to build new practices and habits that are sustainable as we do so we stay engaged for the long haul (see chapter 9). And we also need to build the relationships that sustain our commitment, and these take time if they are going to get deep.

Another tough paradox exists in the directive to center the voices of people of color. Yes, we must consistently practice doing this. But we also have to consistently remind one another that people of color never speak in one voice! Black people don't all agree with one another. Latinx communities are incredibly diverse. There is no such thing as a "person of color perspective."

Some Native people believe land acknowledgments are important. If we don't at least identify and name the first peoples of the land on which we gather or work, we participate in brazen erasure. For other Native people, land acknowledgments feel like an empty performance. Active solidarity, which includes finding ways to cede the land back, is the only authentic action.

I began to use the term *Latinx* several years ago because the young people I work with use it. For them, Latinx is not only gender inclusive but an umbrella that creates space under which the incredible diversity of Latinx communities can be present. Then I read a piece by a Latino commentator who vehemently claimed the term *Latinx* was a white academic elitist invention. I was especially vulnerable to this critique, given my identities, so he convinced me I'd been wrong to use it. Not long thereafter, I wrote a post on Facebook and in it used the term *Latino/a*. A colleague who is an activist and educator wrote in my comment thread: "I'm going to challenge you to please use the terminology 'Latinx' next time. It's a far more inclusive way to refer to us."

Those of us who are white need to build our capacity to engage with such differing viewpoints. If we don't, the "do" of centering those voices immobilizes us the moment BIPOC people don't agree about what direction something should go!

We need to risk being authentic enough to listen deeply. I need to understand why different Latino/a/x peoples have the stance they do, assess my context, and then, still in humility, go ahead and speak and act anyway.

The same is true with so many other things communities of color disagree about. One of the toughest can be when such communities don't agree about what they think white people should be doing! This is not an uncommon experience when priorities are being set, policies are being pursued, or activist groups are organizing in attempts to grow racial justice—especially in local communities. What role should white people play? Taking the lead in order to bear more labor, or stepping back in more quiet forms of support? Making decisions because people of color shouldn't have to figure out what white folks should be doing? Or only acting when called upon? For any number of reasons and in any number of contexts, people of color may not agree on the role of white people.

No one is just going to give us the right answers. There rarely is only one. But the option to not engage and participate is always the wrong one.

Finally, fears of doing it wrong can easily become excuses for staying on the sidelines. This is especially true given the anxieties around white saviorism. But there are meaningful differences between taking action in solidarity and playing the white savior. We can learn these.

White saviorism tends to proceed from charity or pity. When something racist happens, saviors tend to hyperfocus on people of color. They are more likely to engage people of color privately, after the fact. "I'm so sorry that happened to you." Little to no real risk is taken by the white person.

Attempts rooted in solidarity focus on the racist action, statement, or practice and its effects instead. They name or engage the person(s) or policy causing harm. They are more likely to be public. If there's been a specific incident, a solidarity response is more likely to be enacted when the event happens. Or if it's later, it's made among (at least) the same group in which the initial transgression transpired—so everyone sees the correction. Some kind of social, economic, or political capital is risked by the white person.

That second white kid in the story about the six-year-olds was concerned about my nephew's well-being. His focus was on the behavior. He said, "Hey, that's racist!" because he wanted the behavior to stop. He addressed the white child who said the racist thing. The challenge was public. His action risked six-year-old social capital.

Here are a few more distinctions worth thinking about:

- White saviorism assumes people of color cannot act and speak for themselves.
- In solidarity-striving, white people know people of color can and do act and speak for themselves—constantly. But they act anyway because people of color have said white people need to speak up.
- White saviorism assumes white people or white cultures have innate traits that can add value to people of color's identities or experiences.
- Solidarity-informed action is rooted in clarity that people

of color are not innately in need of anything we have to offer specifically as white people. Rather, people of color need our persistent, faithful partnership to eradicate racism from the environments, institutions, coworkers, and every other thing people of color encounter in day-to-day living.

We should *always* try to mobilize around people of color's stated needs and strategies when we challenge complex supremacist structures, policies, and cultures in institutions and civic spaces. Many times this means slowing down.

But even with all self-reflective caution in the world, people of color still won't all necessarily agree that the second white kid, my mom with *The Hobbit,* or I at Union did the right thing. Not every person in a particular situation wants or needs a specific kind of intervention. There is no one-size-fits-all form of advocacy. Developing the resilience to live with that *truth* is another characteristic we want to grow in white antiracist culture.

As we're trying to grow justice at our jobs, in our schools, wherever we are trying to take action, we need to collaboratively assess the context and do the hard work of creating strategic multiracial relationships so we can do that better and better.

Some of the conditions that help us honor paradox and navigate nuance were present among the group I was standing with in a church that day the comment about Ava DuVernay was made.

Before I write another word about that, I want to notice that when frustration is one of the feelings we experience in our antiracism yearnings—and I've certainly felt it—*especially* if it emerges because we don't get what we want from people of color—we need to remind one another that white supremacy's legacies are the appropriate target. White people who came before us, who had ample opportunity to create a different story and legacy, are responsible. Our own failure to put in the effort to learn what we could have before now is responsible.

Okay. Caveats on the table, I understood why this woman felt like she doesn't know what to do (see chapter 1).

I couldn't tell if her desire to learn from DuVernay was drawing on her awareness that we're supposed to center BIPOC experiences or if she was articulating a more common white stuck feeling. But the multiracial and multiethnic community present that day began immediately to engage with and explore what she'd said.

"The thing is," Jeffrey Chin, a man of Asian descent, responded, "there are times I'm too tired and don't want to answer white questions. They're the same questions over and over—I can predict them." Chin went on to describe his commitment to equity work. He said he believed we need to do it together across racial and ethnic lines, even when our levels of experience and knowledge are very different. We all always have more to learn. Our collective future depends on us finding ways to be patient, to be open, and to teach and share with one another, he explained. "But I still get really tired of the same questions."

Monica Framer, a Black woman, was acknowledged by the group as one of their primary leaders. This group had been working together for more than a couple of years by the point we shared space, not just in their church but in externally facing ways in their small city. It was Framer who'd insisted the group begin discussing how whiteness complicated their work as a diverse community.

As the dialogue unfolded, Framer initially echoed Chin. She emphasized how much heavy lifting it was to be committed to the local Black community but *also* be constantly expected to respond to white needs, asks, and desires to learn.

"We need to build real relationships with one another," she said in response to the white woman. Framer went on to describe how predominantly white local groups ask her to come to their table, sit on their boards, or otherwise move in their direction. They want her knowledge to inform what they're doing. She said she appreciated their expanding awareness that people of color's needs and agenda should inform their equity commitments.

But Framer went on to say, "That's still a really one-way relationship." She went on to tell the group how disheartening it was to never see the same white people who want her to come to their spaces in places where Black people convene. She told the white people in the church group—people she addressed as her friends and her community—that she wished she saw more of them in Black spaces, too.

"If I'm in relationship with you, and we've already invested in each other that way," she said, "I'm much more able to tell you what I need or need differently from you. I begin to actually even *want* to have that exchange with you." She gestured toward the white people in the space.

In contrast, when it's just questions that get asked in one direction without mutually shared vulnerability, or outside of a context of a meaningful connection—"well then," she said, "it feels like I'm just being asked to do things for you. And I'm already doing too much." By *meaningful connection*, she meant cases where someone (a white someone) has shown they're willing to get out of their racial comfort zone and come to Black space instead. She pointed out that a couple of white people in her community did do this, and it had profoundly changed her relationship with them.

The group hypothesized that white people don't go to people of color's spaces more often because long-term segregated living means such spaces feel uncomfortable.

In recent years I've increasingly heard white students claim they don't participate in the events of students of color out of respect for their understanding that people of color need their own spaces. This claim appears to honor one of the dos of antiracism. But this explanation gets offered even when people of color haven't said that's the need, and sometimes even when a welcome has been explicit. It's become a cover for white people not getting out of our comfort zones.

The group talked at length about what being unwilling to stretch and go out of your comfort zone signals, and what it does for connection when you are—and do so consistently. Things shift when there's real exchange in the context of mutual relationship. More and deeper learning happens when we're in spaces where discomfort is part of the experience. When white people get out of our enclaves, our questions shift. We learn new things about ourselves we can't learn from books.

At one point Framer told the group: "The other thing is: You can't just ask me what you need to do. Sometimes I don't know, either. But when we're in real relationship, we can figure that out together."

This made so much sense to me. It's true in human life more broadly. In real relationships, we learn how to be with each other. We come to better understand each other's needs. We become more able to respond.

As awareness of the exhaustion and trauma of Black people has increased in recent years, I've seen raging debates on Facebook about whether or not, and especially when visible acts of violence take place, white people should reach out to the Black people in their lives to "check on them." Does offering to drop off a meal to a coworker who still has to show up and get through the workday right after learning about the killing of Tyre Nichols feel like a kindness or a patronizing intrusion? Does not making any such offer feel like one's humanity is being ignored or one's privacy respected? How we show care for one another can be a real dilemma as we all continue to live in such death-dealing systems. The more we have prioritized time spent really coming to know one another, the better we will be able to discern how to live out such humanizing acts of kindness.

I noticed that day the woman who raised the initial question hung in there. She listened. She, too, engaged further. She demonstrated that she heard the correction and redirection she was offered. It seemed likely this was possible because relationships existed among that group of people already.

So much of the collective project of white antiracism is happening in abstract realms, in the world of ideas, on social media, and more. Such spaces can get us to a point.

But it's also true there's no substitute for relationships and community. With others, in collective space, is often the where, when, and how of learning the wisdom of discernment. We can try things and get redirected. We integrate experiences into our bodies that we can't really know only through the intellect.

We learn the most about what our neighbors, coworkers, fellow churchgoers, and, sometimes, family members and friends need from us in relationship. Relationships help us develop the ability to sense whether it's a moment to pass or pick up the microphone. And, in relationship, people are more likely to be willing to say what they need—assuming they have reason to trust they're going to be heard and responded to in a meaningful way.

It was wonderful to watch a multiracial group of people engage in a connective exploration of the comment the white woman dropped into the room that day. They did so in ways that were honest. What I mean by this is that nobody tried to let the woman who made the comment off the hook. But they also did so in ways that honored one another's humanity. Their postures of engagement left them poised to continue into deeper and more justice-infused relationships of mutual learning and collaborative action with one another.

When we know paradox is endemic to the relationship between white people and racial justice, we can respond in ways that honor it. Let's go back to the example I shared earlier about my workplace. What does *both/and* movement look like in a workplace or organization where structural racism is embedded and you, as a white person, want to do something about it?

First, let's recognize the challenges:

- Existing racism makes it more difficult to get antiracism momentum going.
- Such an environment makes it especially important that people of color *not* be tasked with figuring out solutions or bringing white people up to speed in any antiracism work.
- A lack of trust already likely exists, making cross-racial consulting and collaboration both more difficult and that much more important. Relationship-building is tough and vital, so it must consistently be prioritized in formal and informal ways.

Second, how might you toggle back and forth between paradoxical dos and don'ts as a white person seeking to move into action for justice in such a space?

- *Study the system.* What components of organizational culture are implicated and how?
- *Do your homework.* Read up on efforts in similar organizations to learn about opportunities, risks, things to avoid, and

potential models for success. Find out if other attempts at redressing the issue(s) have been made here before. (It's always good to assume people of color have already thought about and even worked on a problem.)

- *Collaborate with others.* Find others to share your research and desire to create constructive interventions. A collaborator could be a white person and/or a person of color. The likelihood of trust, or of being able to grow it, is very important.

- *Consult with others.* Engage with people of color to directly share what you're noticing, what you want to do, and what homework you've done without feeling entitled to their buy-in. Transparency matters.

  o Find out if folks have concerns and/or want to be part of your efforts and/or want to be uninvolved (even insulated) from the initiative.

  o Be reliable in following through on those asks.

- *Strategize with possible collaborators.* Find a decision-maker likely to be open or persuadable who also has some power and influence to affect others.

- *Prepare your possible actions.* Initiatives invested in resourcing the well-being of people of color create white backlash. Share information proactively with white people able to run interference when backlash comes. Have a plan for how you will both educate and respond to those who create backlash in ways that minimize its effects.

- *Reflect with curiosity and humility.* Create a feedback loop between what you're doing and the perspectives people of color have on what you're doing. Returning to check in is an ongoing practice. Relationship-building is a constant.

  o You might learn your attempt is misguided and find yourself redirected.

o You might do such strong work that people for whom it felt too dangerous before now feel more willing and able to step in and speak up and take on more formal leadership.

We met Dr. Dave Smith in the introduction. He'd been working to create a more antiracist environment on his campus for some time when he encountered the student whose name he wasn't sure he remembered. He and a colleague helped pull together a small group of faculty who cared about the university's racial environment.

Dr. Smith and his colleague made sure faculty of color knew about the small group and were clearly invited to be part of it. They also were careful to not unduly pressure them to participate. Not surprising, given the campus demographics and climate, the group was initially all white.

The group began to identify specific places racial inequity was present. They strategized ways they could have an impact in a large, complex system. There was a lot they weren't in charge of. But they were determined to find ways to use their power nonetheless.

The group launched an emergency scholarship fund for students of color and first-generation students. The institution hadn't prioritized fundraising for such students. But Dr. Smith's group knew financial hardship often got in the way of degree completion.

They wrote an open letter to the incoming university president. They described why a racially inclusive campus mattered to everyone and to the educational mission of the school. They detailed many of the issues they knew students, staff, and faculty of color faced. In cases where they shared specific experiences that might be traceable to a particular member of the campus community, they were careful to get permission first.

The group identified specific areas in which they expected the president to exercise leadership. They offered to be constructive partners. Then they passed the letter around and secured more than a hundred signatures from across campus. They presented the letter in person before the new president's administration even got underway.

They embarked on a third, more complicated campaign to create colleague-to-colleague peer pressure to hire more faculty of color. This project required doing research on best practices for inclusive hiring processes. They reached out and sat down with every search committee beginning to hire for the next academic year. They presented what they'd learned and urged their colleagues to implement these best practices.

All these efforts required them to learn more about how racism and barriers to access operated in the everyday structures of work and life at their school. They also had to get better talking about this. And their efforts—especially around hiring—required them to build skills and support one another as they talked about race directly with their mostly white colleagues, many of whom were not initially receptive.

Over time their efforts took root. The scholarship fund began to grow as others got excited about it. Upper-level leadership began to see this group as a constituency and to consult as it created structures and invested more resources in inclusion efforts.

The group had to navigate more challenging paradoxes as they kept working. For example, even if you succeed in hiring more faculty of color, you have to attend to the environment people are being hired into.

Faculty of color at predominantly white institutions often

do more uncompensated labor than their counterparts, a practice known as identity-based labor. (It affects white women, LGBTQ+ people, and people with disabilities as well.) Students of color seek such faculty out for support in ways they don't seek out white faculty. These dynamics happen in business and other organizational environments, too. Faculty of color often find themselves assigned to diversity committees, whether they're interested in such work or not. On top of all this, student evaluations—which lots of schools use to evaluate faculty—are well known to be conduits for various kinds of student bias.

These additional layers of work go unrecognized in most official channels of evaluation. This means they don't get "counted" when it comes to salary increases or promotions. Meanwhile, this additional labor takes time, energy, and focus away from writing and publishing—areas where official evaluation is rigorous. This phenomenon can create a disastrous equation when it comes to faculty of color's well-being, as well as producing racial disparities in rates of promotion.

Dr. Smith's group decided to advocate for processes to formally recognize identity-based labor. They knew they needed to challenge how student evaluations were used if they were serious about growing an antiracist environment. But such efforts required even more careful consulting. They needed to talk and keep communicating with faculty who knew from firsthand experience that these systems of evaluation needed to be changed. They also had to collaborate and strategize about how to ensure faculty of color coming up for evaluation and promotion weren't harmed by the backlash these efforts were sure to unleash, at least initially.

They moved slowly. They worked first to build alliances with other faculty and to meet informally with decision-makers who had the power to change the evaluation processes, long before their efforts were made public.

They've had some successes. In annual faculty reviews, the university now asks: "Have you done any added work that hasn't been asked about here?" This provides a formal opportunity for acknowledgment of identity-based labor. The committees that do evaluation have been educated about the body of evidence that demonstrates student evaluations are conduits for bias. The group helped initiate work to get a staffed office for diversity and equity efforts established.

This work has required many rounds of dialogue. Lots of both/and movement: leading as white faculty, collaborating with faculty of color, sitting back to listen and respond and move differently.

We can grow white antiracist cultures able to support ongoing discernment of the tensions created by both/ands and to nurture creative responses to them. If racism is nuanced and complex, our capacities and responses need to be just as dynamic and complex.

We can learn to be humble, but also courageous. We can assume we always have more to learn and things we do not understand, while assuming we *can* learn and are responsible to exercise the capacities we develop as we do. We can grow the number of contexts in which we take part in multiracial community and connection, even while we keep doing our own white work, too.

So to that end, I want to add some items to our Wikipedia page:

- Don't: assume you can just follow any list of dos and don'ts like you follow the recipe on the back of a cake mix.
- Do: embrace the challenge of acknowledging and walking with paradox.

- Do: move slowly enough to listen, reflect, and discern.
- Don't: wait until the path is so clear and perfect—or your motive so incandescently pure—that you never move at all.
- Do: seek others, build relationships, prioritize connections with people who share your antiracist values.

At the end of the day there's no either/or answer to the question "Do I need to pass the mic or do I need to speak up?"

The answer is always YES.

TAKE A NEXT STEP

1. Revisit a time you took an action in response to racism and it didn't turn out the way you wanted it to. Walk back through that experience with the notion of paradox in mind. Would a more nuanced framework have changed how you experienced or behaved? How so?

2. Explore Ava DuVernay's ARRAY 101 resource, which was created to support people moving into social justice engagement. Use it to plan and host a film event in a space where you live, work, or play.

3. Find people. Find people. Find people. Join an existing multiracial group in which active discussion of and attention to what people in the group need and expect from one another is part of the group culture as it engages in justice work in its local community. Or create one of your own (for example, maybe a few people who show up for an ARRAY 101 event want to keep going). Keep participating with others.

7

Accountability as Belonging

My childhood was full of certainty. When my motley group of siblings and I encountered the complexities of teenage life, we had ready access to boiled-down, clear-cut responses. Feeling depressed or anxious? "Cheer up. (Pray, too.)" An eighteen-year-old daughter (two of them eventually) finding herself pregnant? The message to the rest of the kids: "Immoral. Don't do that." If a fifteen-year-old manifests signs of alcoholism and addiction, the explanation is "bad choices." The response: "Drinking's illegal, so stop." No matter the experience, there was a rigid and crisp answer. Nuance or ambiguity was never allowed.

I learned young what precisely to believe and how to stand unwaveringly in it. I knew who the enemy was. I knew any truth that mattered (we called them doctrines) could be shrunk to the size of a five-point list and tucked in my back pocket. I knew that if doubt or uncertainty did show up, I could whip that list out at a moment's notice and it would keep me safe: from temptation, from hell, and—just like my dad—from the Methodists.

There was no art in that religious world, only answers. There were no questions to explore, only Bible verses to apply. There was no discernment or perspectives: People were saved or unsaved, good or bad, faithful or unfaithful. The lines were stark. Everyone was on one side or the other.

This is what the world of fundamentalism looks and feels like.

A few other characteristics hang out in fundamentalist spaces, too. There was a strong emphasis on purity and a fondness for purity tests to clarify which side of the line someone was on. There was also a deep investment in shame. Not an acknowledgment that shame is something we experience as humans sometimes, but a use of shame, a valuing of it, a worldview that assumed we should be ashamed: So, get yourself on the right side of the line! (Or, if you're already there, use it to try to pull others over and/or expel them from your life if they won't come.)

Fundamentalism. Purity. Shame. Three bedfellows in communities or cultures that get invested in certitude.

And they don't only show up in the world of religion. They've shown up in the culture of white antiracism.

In July 2022 Richie Reseda, founder of Question Culture, a media collective that houses projects devoted to feminism and abolitionism, was a guest on Prentis Hemphill's podcast *Finding Our Way*. (Side note: *Finding Our Way* is sheer brilliance. I can't recommend enough that you listen to it. See Further Resources at the back of this book.) Both of these Black Lives Matter activists, who work on healing and transformative justice, were exploring the question of harm. Specifically, they were exploring how we handle harm when it's committed by those of us engaged in justice work.

The premise of their conversation was that every single one of us causes harm at some point. Their concern was the way shame shows up in movements. Reseda was specifically explaining what happens when we choose to throw shame at others in response to harm—or bring it in and direct it at ourselves. When we do this, our movements for social change and our justice-seeking communities remain bought into the same systems of patriarchy, white supremacy, and other forms of oppression we're seeking to dismantle, he said.

All of these systems would have us throw one another away, *other* one another, reject and expel the "thing" (who is really a person) that we (supposedly) are not. Shame operates on this same logic. It's about being innately unworthy.

During their conversation, Reseda described shame as a toxin—literally a neurotoxin. He explained: "Shame disables us from being our most creative, our most accountable, our most honest, most loving, our most accepting."[1] He compared the effect of shame to a situation in which a tense verbal conflict is underway and then someone pulls out a gun. Instantly the entire situation changes.

When shame gets introduced into a challenging conversation or disagreement, that situation also changes immediately and dramatically. Shame triggers the "fight, flight, or freeze" mode. It impedes the person who's caused the harm from being able to genuinely ask, as Reseda puts it, "Oh, that hurt you? What I did?" Rather than leaning into learning that can enable us to take responsibility for ways we've fallen short, help us do better, and facilitate repair and healing, shame prevents accountability. It makes transformative justice impossible.

For example, when Whoopi Goldberg made antisemitic

comments on *The View* in 2022, ABC suspended her for seven days. I remember reading people's reactions. Among progressives, the main discussion was whether Goldberg had been banished for long enough for it to count as really being held accountable.

Reseda had a totally different take. What did suspension do for Jewish people? What kind of transformation came by silencing Goldberg? Reseda's answer: not a thing.[2] This was a missed opportunity for a collective conversation about antisemitism. The many of us who might hold ideas similar to those Goldberg expressed might have learned something if ABC had used this incident to support such a conversation. That's what actual accountability requires and what transformative justice would have looked like.

Reseda described ABC's version of accountability as merely performative activism. Nothing and no one changed. It just made the network look good. ("We're properly shaming this person, so you don't shame us," is how Reseda described the strategy.)

Reseda went on to say that collectively, we're facing a powerful question right now as to whether those of us claiming to care about justice actually believe people can change. He laments a culture in "progressive spaces on the left" in which people are more invested in saying the right things or being credited with the right beliefs than in real transformation. Reseda rejects the ways the left wields shame while calling it activism, canceling people on the internet or casting people out instead of centering the notion that people can change. "That's why I actually, like, really don't fuck with internet woke culture at all," he says.

At this point as I listened to Hemphill and Reseda's conversation, three things happened.

First, I recalled the essay by Alicia Garza I shared in the introduction, where Garza explained her choice to participate in the Women's March in 2017. In that essay, Garza also argued that justice movements need to decide whether we think people are capable of transformation or not. We must believe they are (or what are we even doing?). We must also walk with folks newer in their learning journey, just as someone, at some point, walked with us.

Second, I inhaled with recognition and exhaled in relief. Here were two people bravely exploring, *out loud*, a phenomenon I've been thinking about with concern.

Third, I got nervous. The poet and memoirist Mary Karr once said that one of the most important questions she'd ever been asked was "What would you write if you weren't afraid?" I've been haunted ever since I read that question. And one of *my* answers to that question—well, we're about to come on up and into it.

It's this: We've got fundamentalism growing in white anti-racist culture. And purity tests and shame in abundance. In our longing for certitude, we've become invested in the five-point lists we carry around in our pockets to determine who the enemy is and ensure we stay safely away from them.

Stark lines.

If we're going to be serious about the generational work of transforming white communities, we've got to walk away from the temptations and tendencies to wield shame as a weapon. *Collectively* those of us who are white need to dramatically change the tone and environment in which we lean into the work of changing our relationships to race and racism. We need to build thoughtful relationships with other white people who are at different points on the continuum of antiracism: already working to change; wanting to change; or, if they haven't begun, might be persuaded to begin.

It's scary for me to write about this for the same reason it's hard to give up purity tests and shame. When we're invested in being strong in our commitment to antiracism, it's natural to worry that engaging other white folks with empathy, curiosity, or a willingness to be in relationship may jeopardize our credibility. We can find ourselves, sometimes subconsciously, almost compelled to stand at a distance from them. We might get loud about how they've failed our purity test. Toss shame at them.

Grief is present when we acknowledge white supremacy's impact on our lives. If antiracism is the work of building a landing place for it—to land as love, justice, connection—well, purity tests don't help others learn how to build. Purity tests expel them from the project before they begin.

Fundamentalism is as familiar to me as home. And it's a stunting worldview and way of treating other human beings.

Despite feeling clear about the truth of this, I'm still afraid to write it. The risks of being misunderstood are real.

But afraid or not, this is what I'd write about if I weren't. So, afraid or not, here we go.

Internet woke culture. Reseda's phrase brilliantly describes some of the worst white behavior when it comes to antiracism.

A friend of mine, Jen Louden, is a feminist-committed writer and writing coach. Over the course of her career, she's convened retreats and curated communal spaces of various kinds, all in support of the well-being and self-realization of women. During launch efforts for her book *Why Bother? Discover the Desire for What's Next,* she reached out to someone who was in her professional network, but not someone she knew personally (we'll call him Steve).

Jen asked Steve if his online community might benefit by engaging in the conversations *Why Bother?* made possible. If so, she'd be glad to send him a free copy of her book.

Steve said yes. When he wrote again later, he told Jen, "The book is great." He congratulated her. Then he quickly changed course and moved into a verbose, patronizing lecture—complete with a link to an article about the high rates of coronavirus among Latinx agricultural workers. (Just to be clear, Steve does not work in the agricultural sector.) He said he couldn't give any public attention to Jen's book. Neither her website nor her Facebook feed displayed enough racial diversity in them. "It pains me to say this," he wrote. "My sense is recently you've been trying to bring more attention to these issues."

Jen was stunned. Steve didn't say anything critical about her actual work. Not surprising, in fact. Her book is attentive to intersectional discussions of the different ways sexism and being socialized as women play out in diverse women's lives. It also engages in clear, authentic-to-her-experience naming of Jen's awareness of her own privileges as a racially white woman.

Meanwhile, Jen has published blog series highlighting Black and BIPOC voices. She'd also centered diverse "Why bother?" stories as part of her book launch. Steve ignored all of this.

And Jen has Black clients and students. But she's spent time wrestling with the ethics of images on her website. It seemed too easy to inadvertently end up using women of color as a marketing tool or "to make me look good." So, unless clients freely offered their images after one invitation, Jen had decided she would not pressure them to share these. She'd also made a conscious decision years prior to take her justice work off Facebook because she realized it felt hollow or performative to her. Her own posts about racism had started to feel empty or attention-seeking. She had mindfully decided to focus on working in ways that were authentic and embodied.

Jen chose to tell Steve none of this. She was angry.

Jen replied by saying it was painful Steve would jump to judgment without asking her any actual questions. She would not dignify his response, she wrote, by justifying "my work in racial and social justice work to you because it doesn't show up in my FB feed where you can easily see and judge it sufficient." She closed her email this way: "Please continue your great work in the world and [may you] realize that things aren't as easy to judge on the surface by your standards."

What came next was worse.

Steve posted screenshots of this email exchange in a professional online forum with hundreds of members. He turned Jen into an object lesson, with framing comments like: "To all my members out their [*sic*] posting anti-racist things on their FB feed . . . this is classic. This is a classic example of how white leaders respond."

He invoked the language of "white fragility" to further excoriate this person he barely knew—as either a leader or a human.

And he did all of this without Jen's consent or knowledge— let alone without an opportunity to be in dialogue or to respond.

Jen learned by accident what had been put up. When she did, she went to two friends (also white) with whom she'd been part of a personal and professional support group for fifteen years, as they were friends with Steve and she knew one was part of the group. She asked if they knew anything about this. One of them immediately shared screenshots in which this same friend was tagged.

Now Jen was aghast.

Months had passed and no one—including these friends— had told her this happened? When she asked for an explanation, among the responses was a chastising query as to why Jen had responded so angrily to Steve in the first place.

Jen couldn't understand how her friends could think Steve's response to her had been valid, let alone helpful. Worse, how could they have overlooked Steve's profoundly unethical behavior in sharing a personal email exchange without her permission, and his posturing as if doing so was activism and not just random shaming?

His breach of personal and professional trust is difficult to overstate. Equally difficult to overstate would be the personal harm done to Jen.

Internet woke culture. White antiracism. We're in a moment of needing to really ask and answer: What kind of culture do we want to grow?

Neither Reseda nor Hemphill wants to grow cultures in which harmful behavior is given a pass. Quite the opposite. They want to invite us to live more fully into relationships and create communities of healing. This includes investing with intention in the ways we treat one another.

I'm obviously suspicious of the public mocking of "wokeness" by the political right. It's part of the same agenda suppressing the teaching of U.S. racial history and creating conditions for white nationalism to grow in our social and political life. But some dynamics playing out in spaces where the responsibilities of white people are the focus are taking us in the wrong direction. To be specific: Calling people out versus calling them in. Vitriolic public arguments about cancel culture. Dismissing people as "problematic" and thus unworthy of engagement.

Accountability is a prominent theme in the collective project of white antiracism. We emphasize that white people need to hold other white people accountable. We need to hold ourselves accountable for how we show up to racial justice and be accountable to people of color. All rightly so.

Back when I was at Union, the importance of having a community of accountability was emphasized in all our learning. Cone used to press us: Who were we in relationship with as we thought, wrote, and made justice claims about liberation? What community of accountability kept us rooted, relevant, and real? To put it another way, to whom were we accountable? Do the people I claim to care about and be standing with know it? Am I in real relationships with them?

I was also describing a form of accountability earlier when I talked about having people on speed dial—knowing who's going to pick up when I call for support because I need to act with courage, take responsibility for a mistake, or redress a harm I've caused. Having people who will encourage and strategize with me, but also be honest, is a necessary practice of accountability.

Another form of accountability comes through creating structures to cultivate it. Our local SURJ chapter is laser-focused on getting more white people off the sidelines for justice in Des Moines and building white skills for antiracism. This is one way we're trying to respond to the call of people of color for us to do work in our own communities. But we *always* do that in concert with carefully tended organizational relationships with Black- and Brown-led organizations—our accountability partners (see chapter 10).

Accountability is essential in all justice work. But as we can see in the Whoopi Goldberg example, what accountability means isn't straightforward. And when fundamentalist postures, purity tests, and shame start to become conflated with accountability, we end up stunted.

Some years back a soccer coach I know had her team of high schoolers over to her home for dinner at the end of the season. As the team entered the apartment, they said, "Wow, Coach Kennedy, when you told us your address in class, we were worried you lived in the ghetto!"

Coach Kennedy lived near a neighborhood that was very racially diverse and had many working-class and low-income people in it. She was disturbed by the comments. But she also wanted to handle them in a way that might enable learning. She knew if she invoked shame, the players would likely shut down.

She waited until they'd had a nice meal together, trying the whole time to imagine how she might engage the comments constructively. Then in the post-dinner conversation, she said, "Hey, I want to ask a question. When you got here, you said something about having been afraid I lived in the ghetto. What did you mean?"

The young people looked at each other. One of them said, "Well, you know . . . a ghetto is where there are high crime rates."

"Oh!" Kennedy responded. "Do I live near a dangerous neighborhood? What are the crime rates around here?"

The players looked at one another and then shrugged. No, they admitted. They had no idea what the crime rates were in the nearby neighborhood.

"Okay, well then, what's a ghetto?"

"You know," another player said, "a ghetto is like Harlem."

"You've been to Harlem?" the coach asked with enthusiasm. "I spent a lot of time in Harlem some years ago. It's such a dynamic, vibrant place. Such an amazing history of justice organizing, music, literature—you know the Harlem Renaissance, right? And Harlem is still this hub of Black creativity and Black community in New York City! That's what you meant?"

"Well, no," the players acknowledged. None of them had been to Harlem.

"Okay, so what's a ghetto?"

The players were quiet.

"Is a ghetto a place where a lot of Black and Latinx people live? Or where there are poor people? Is that what you meant?"

The teammates started shaking their head no vigorously. "No, we didn't say that! That's not what we meant!"

After a minute, one of the players said, "Okay, Coach, are you telling us we shouldn't use the word *ghetto*?"

"Look, I haven't *told* you anything," said the coach. "You used the term, I'm asking you to be clear what you meant."

The players nodded. "We get it."

Coach Kennedy engaged in an accountable conversation. This conversation also presumed transformed understanding and different behavior in the future was possible.

The culture that's grown around antiracism can make it difficult to even imagine this kind of approach anymore. In fact, I'm fresh off a very different kind of experience in which healing and hopes for transformative justice were nearly throttled by attempts to weaponize shame that was roaring through a communal context.

Let me set the stage.

I recently found myself in the difficult situation of being associated with an event that caused a great deal of racial harm. The equity and inclusion office at my university—of which I was a senior leader—cosponsored an event to engage entering first-year college students in some basic dialogues about diversity, equity, and inclusion (DEI). The purpose was to tee new students up toward alignment with our DEI commitments the moment they came to campus.

These kinds of events are difficult to do well. This is especially true with a group of seven hundred people whose average age is about nineteen, students from wildly different families and communities and from all over the country.

How do you do something educationally meaningful when

folks are at such different starting points? How do you not go so deep you lose students for whom these conversations are new? How do you not stay so shallow the event feels hollow to students who *live* the challenges a lack of diversity, equity, and inclusion pose every day? How do you encourage white (and male, hetero, cisgender, able-bodied) students to participate—because learning can't happen if folks can't bring their selves into the room—but avoid exposing students of color (and white women, queer, trans, and disabled students) to the hurt of comments that are ill informed or worse?

Tough stuff. And to be clear, these challenging questions are present for any of us trying to shift the culture in our various organizations.

At my school, we'd hired an outside group to facilitate. They were to offer a workshop that navigated these tensions and encouraged students to develop appreciative curiosity about what it means to create a campus climate in which everyone experiences belonging. But the event went shockingly, painfully off the rails.

A poorly moderated open microphone session exposed students of color to racial ignorance and bias (harm number one) of white peers. For example, a white student insisted (aggressively) that "reverse racism is just as bad for white people!" Others said things like "The worst thing to be is a Black female in this country" or "I feel so bad for *those* people." While these latter kinds of comments signaled some recognition of racial and gender oppression, for Black and Brown students in a room of mostly white students, it was a painful, reductive caricature of their lives, not to mention a terrible way to be "welcomed" to the campus community.

The statements were not unpacked or redirected (harm number two). Left standing, they were also potentially received by the white students as "things that are okay to say" (harm number three). Many students, especially students of color, experienced significant emotional distress.

In short, an experience intended to increase our collective capacity to create a community of belonging threw the sense of belonging of students of color into peril before the first week of classes even got underway. So awful.

I found myself in the professional position of needing to apologize on behalf of the institution and my office. I also apologized personally, as myself.

The fallout was a painful reminder to me of how difficult the public work of antiracism is. It was a humbling reminder that regardless of the length of one's journey, we remain vulnerable to missteps. It was also a real-time lesson that no matter how good the intention, the actual experience itself is what leaves the impact.

Difficult days followed for the students who were negatively affected. Difficult days for my coworkers and colleagues who cared about advancing racial justice at our school. Difficult days for me, as I grieved the pain and harm students experienced, but also—to be frank—sat with a heck of a lot of student anger and a sense of betrayal directed pointedly at me.

Fast-forward. I was part of a team that designed a response. One part of the response included my leading a kind of counter-workshop. There we would create a space for students to process the experience and unpack some of the harmful comments made during the original event. We wanted to create an opportunity for reconnection and develop a sounder communal understanding of how those comments hurt.

The workshop went well. We laid out guidelines for how we would engage. I made sure the dialogue moved slowly, especially since there was already pain in the room. At different points, people pointed back to frightening and frustrating dynamics that had emerged in the original workshop. It had gotten heated, raucous, and very chaotic as the moderator failed repeatedly to step in in a constructive manner.

A specific thing that happened late in that ninety-minute discussion became important later. A young white man raised his hand after listening for a long time. He shared timidly and said something along these lines: "I don't really understand all of this. I see why some people were upset at what happened. But I was upset, too. When things got out of control, I kept hearing all these people saying how much they hate white men." He went on to say that later that night, he and some other white students had overheard students of color saying how much white men suck and how angry they were at white people. It felt so bad, he told us. He said he'd ended up wondering if he should be afraid for his safety.

Given the nature of the conversation to that point, I knew it had taken courage for him to raise his hand. So I was glad he'd spoken up and thanked him for his vulnerability. I validated his confusion. I didn't validate the assumptions hovering in his description: that he was equally victimized or that no prior history helped explain why people of color (or white women) would mistrust white men. But I know what happens in most white homes and had every reason to assume he hadn't yet been taught things he deserved to have been taught. I absolutely believed he really was confused. So, I started there.

I went on to suggest that white supremacy and other systems of oppression affect all our lives and can end up making us enemies. I explained that the harm those systems cause some of us can lead us to a lack of trust or dislike (and sometimes even hate!) of those we see benefiting from those same systems, but not acting against them or even noticing that we're suffering. I explained that the opposite can also be true: Those of us insulated from harm can learn to challenge those systems. When we do, we make it a little more possible for trust and relationship to emerge.

I also said something about how patriarchy and racism hurt white men, too. I remember sharing an example of how hard it is for men who experience sexual assault to come forward. This is one example that shows we all have a stake in challenging isms and learning to do it together.

I encouraged him to stay curious. I showed him empathy.

When the workshop was over, I sought him out—along with two other young white men with him—to speak further. I invited them to spaces on campus where men are exploring the effects of masculinity on their lives and white people are seeking to grow in antiracism.

The exchange was gentle—on both our parts. It was framed educationally. He didn't leave convinced by me of any particular perspective or with any lack of clarity about what I believed about racism. We did leave with the possibility of further conversation.

And one more thing. What this young man had said was reasonable. In the workshop that had gone sideways, the room had become full of explosive energy. A lot of very angry young people had said some pretty furious things. I knew from talking with Black, Latinx, and other students of color later that they felt afraid because of what they'd heard their white peers say. In the process of rallying a sense of communal strength in response to that fear, some words had been uttered in some spaces that implied a readiness to retaliate if necessary. (Such words had been spoken in pain and they weren't directed at any specific white student.)

It had been an incredibly perilous moment in the life of a campus community that was not even actually (yet) a community. None of what happened was the fault of any of the actual nineteen-year-olds who were part of it.

A couple of days later, I got word from a colleague that a small cohort of student leaders who'd been at my counter-workshop had come to her and a student leadership board to complain. These students reported that I'd facilitated a conversation that caused even more harm. They were unhappy with my leadership.

I was shocked and confused. What had I missed? Had people been upset? I started to second-guess my assessment of my workshop.

It had felt honest and authentic. Both the comments made and the fact folks lingered for more conversation after it was over left me assessing it as a small but meaningful step toward communal healing. The dialogue had been connective. The energy felt good.

In short order, I came to understand my exchange with the young white man had been deemed problematic. As I listened to reports of their complaints, I learned this meant I shouldn't have engaged him. I should have "shut him down."

I also recalled there were at least three Black staff members in the space that day, two of whom are women and one who is nonbinary. These individuals hadn't been irate. They'd participated fully for the entire dialogue and been among those who'd lingered afterward.

As I was replaying and sorting all of this in my mind, I learned something else. With one exception, the students irate with me were white. (The one who wasn't white wasn't Black and had actually left before the young white man had spoken. His anger came from secondhand reports white peers had given him.)

A white rage machine was churning. "Throw him away," it was saying. That guy didn't pass the test. He needed to be cast out because he was impure.

The rage machine was also saying that my willingness to engage such a person, let alone to have the audacity to do so with empathy and in a spirit of connection, had rendered me impure as well. I might need to be cast out, too.

I believe these students were genuinely concerned about accountability. And I need to resist the temptation to throw shame back at them.

But there are several immediate implications revealed in the call to "shut him down."

First, these students were barely older than this young man. They could have easily been him just a year or two before. Their desire to shut him down was ironic in this regard. But when white people begin to mobilize in ways that draw on fundamentalist tendencies, it's not unusual for us to do it against or in response to folks who *we ourselves were at some point*—maybe even not that long ago.

I'll be blunt: We need to find the courage to name such hypocrisy in and among ourselves. We must boldly refuse to participate in it.

Second, when the temptation to behave in this way emerges, we have to ask ourselves: Where do we think this young man is going to learn if those of us poised to have meaningful, non-shaming engagements reject him?

On the one hand, this is a basic pragmatic question. We need to engage other white folks anywhere we can. That's what doing work in our own communities requires.

On the other hand, the white students' self-righteous rage was itself a stunning expression of white privilege. The work people of color have insisted we do is *not* to point out and distance ourselves from every white person who doesn't pass our purity test.

That doesn't move the needle on justice. When we walk away, we leave more work for communities of color, who will inevitably at some point have to deal with white folks we cast out.

Third—on the matter of tone. Setting aside that we have a moral obligation not to dehumanize one another (we're coming back to that), there's another pragmatic issue here. How we talk to each other matters! It's human nature to shut down and quit if we're constantly told we're doing things wrong. On the flip side, when we're taken seriously, we're far more likely to keep seeking to grow. When our growth is acknowledged, we're more likely to keep going. That's just how we're hardwired as humans.

I'm not suggesting we can just gently educate our way to antiracism or that existing systems will be changed with kind words.

But in many cases patience, empathy, curiosity, and a willingness to connect with folks not yet at the point where others of us may be (but haven't always been) are far more effective in the long haul than shutting people down. Those relationships are also vital to continue to amass collective power for our organizing to challenge and change. We need each other!

Finally: shutting people down is dangerous. Let's think about this young white man as just one of many who didn't have modeled by their elders what they needed. He brings his genuine confusion to a space where we're talking about white supremacy and the need to change and dismantle the systems that harm all of us. There he learns he's unworthy of being in the room because he isn't yet clear what we're talking about, doesn't have access to the right lingo—and so, well, "Bye-bye—get out!"

Where's this guy going to go?

If we're lucky, he'll just check out altogether. *If we're lucky.*

If we're unlucky, he's going to find folks happy to welcome him with open arms and tell him he absolutely belongs—just as he is. He'll find people eager to affirm his whiteness and maleness—just as they are.

You may remember recent reports of incidents in which a complex or campus has been covered in the middle of the night with flyers that read: "It's Okay to Be White." The folks behind such incidents are trolling for young people precisely like this one.

I'm not sure what to say when I'm asked what we do in a time when threats against those of us who dare to take our racial justice, antiracism, and other forms of anti-oppression commitments public are on the rise. There are no obvious immediate solutions other than knowing we need to relentlessly build relationships so we can sustain our courage and have each other's back.

And I really have no idea what I can do about those who've been sucked into conspiracy theories and election denial and seem hell-bent on taking us back into unapologetic white male dominance (and have so many guns).

But I do know this: We can stop handing white nationalists such easy recruits. If we don't fight for young men like the one who came into my workshop, we'll have turned off and away someone who was curious enough to show up and who might decide to engage with the liberating work of disentangling their whiteness and maleness from white supremacy and sexism. We may feel self-satisfied once we "shut him down." But he'll still be out there, ripe for the picking by those more than happy to engage his confusion and curiosity and deploy it to strengthen white supremacy and further destroy our democracy.

These preceding observations about the implications of casting people out with such ease may seem obvious. But shame is a heck of a thing. I can easily imagine those white students rebutting—or not even being able to hear—any of the things I just said. Reseda's right: Once shame is in the room, it's like someone's pulled out a gun.

Shame in the room affected how Jen Louden responded once she'd learned of Steve's behavior and the involvement of her friends—people who now get paid to offer DEI work in various organizations. Jen did have one-on-one conversations with some of the people involved. But while one of them expressed some regret, no one apologized or named Steve's behavior as wrong.

She told me she regretted that she didn't convene everyone involved. "It would have been much better for me to have called a meeting of the entire group and explained to them how I felt Steve had done something truly egregious and performative, but I was so triggered with shame that somehow I was in the wrong, even though most of my brain knew I wasn't that . . . I never called a group meeting. I think that's an interesting part of the shame story. I couldn't stand up for myself. I couldn't articulate what was wrong. I obsessed about it for years and it caused me no end of confusion and pain."

We need to surface deeper undercurrents in our longing to create justice that have to do with moral matters such as how seriously we take innate human worth or how, in reality, we're all interconnected. These undercurrents point toward frameworks we might build if we want to grow cultures around antiracism and other forms of liberation work that are capable of enabling the change we must have. We need frameworks that help us refuse to dehumanize one another—including other white people. When we dehumanize, we are in fact mirroring the same logic— "othering" other human beings—on which systems of racism and white supremacy are themselves built.

When I think about the rage with which those white students

wanted me to excise this young person (and maybe me), I feel sure they felt a shame threat. As if their proximity to him would expose their sense of worthlessness, too.

Shame is an ongoing challenge for white people. Shame will remain an ongoing challenge until the day we eradicate white supremacy, until we heal.

There's a layer added to that inner turmoil, too. As we grow aware of the impact of racism in our lives, we realize we've been so untrustworthy that our relationships with Black and Brown people are typically tenuous—if we have any at all. It's easy to imagine we keep our reputation and such relationships only by othering other white folks who don't pass the purity tests. Performing public rage at other whites can become its own purity test.

Going hard on that young male student was a way for those other white students to try to perform credibility for their Black and Brown peers. Growing white antiracism on this kind of foundation will fail us. It's already failing us.

There is a time and a place to reject and draw stark lines of *NO!* around certain kinds of behavior. A few years after the Witness Our Welcome debacle I described in chapter 4, I was present at a smaller, local, queer church gathering. This time a keynote speaker, who was a gay white Episcopal priest, was talking about the challenges of navigating different views on LGBTQ+ inclusion between churches in North America and in Africa. Important context: In the Episcopal Church, bishops are called *primates*. With no small amount of glee at his own cleverness, this priest began to raise his voice in anger at anti-LGBTQ+ views among African churches. He barked, "So these primates from Africa come over here and want to 'monkey around ...'" and proceeded to repeat versions of this phrase several times. This is the kind of case in which it was completely appropriate that someone in the gathering stood up mid-presentation and stopped him by yelling, "Shame on you!" And fully interrupted the proceedings. (Out of which chaos—far more dramatic than what ensued at WOW because the speaker both had the mic and was recalcitrant—ensued.)

But if shame becomes a primary tool in all our antiracist engagements, it's like wielding a hammer. Soon everything—every comment, fumble, moment that exposes someone as having more to learn—starts to look like a nail. ("You thought it was okay to say *ghetto*!? Get out! No transformation for you!!")

I understand why both Richie Reseda and Alicia Garza worry we've lost a belief in the capacity of people to transform. I felt despair on my campus about what these students seemed to have learned in the contemporary conversation about race and white people. Their desire to throw that young man out had nothing to do with interrupting actual harm. He'd made no accusations, didn't use racist analysis. He simply shared confusion and fear. But the toxin of shame made it impossible for his peers to see him as a fellow human or imagine he might be capable of growth.

We've got to embark on a fast from shame.

We need, instead, to build notions of accountability on the assumption that we belong. No one is expendable. Because we are all necessary.

We're "born to belonging," wrote Mab Segrest in 2002. Segrest, a white southerner and antiracism activist, was drawing on a South African principle often paraphrased in English, from Zulu, as "I am because you are." Our humanity is tied up in one another. We are literally interconnected.

People are yearning to belong, Alicia Garza explained to

Prentis Hemphill in 2022 after Hemphill asked Garza to share some of her wisdom and realizations from being in leadership.[3] People need "to be seen, heard, and valued," Garza explained. She went on to say "we need tools in this movement for how it is that we belong to each other and how we belong in this movement that aren't deeply divisive." We really won't get where we need to go if we can't find a way to create belonging with one another.

A framework of belonging is a way to radically reunderstand accountability.

Not long ago I was part of a conversation with a group of white antiracist activists from different parts of the country, all working in different settings. Among the participants was Kerri Kelly, executive director of CTZNWELL, an organization working to move from our society's obsession with "personal wellness" to "a culture of wellness" that democratizes well-being.[4] CTZN-WELL acknowledges that ending white supremacy is part of the work of creating a well culture. It sees the interconnections between self and systems that Hemphill and Reseda were talking about.

The participants were exploring opportunities and challenges in mobilizing white people for racial justice. And at one point, Kelly said that part of what's going on in the current fiery clashes over cancel culture is actually a conversation about accountability that we don't quite know how to have.

That conversation is actually about belonging: "I am holding you accountable," explains Kelly, "because *I need you.* I'm holding you accountable *because you matter.* I am holding you accountable *because you are necessary.*"

Accountability as belonging can look like coming together across racial lines to remember and honor our shared racial history.

Resmaa Menakem's understanding of white supremacy as

racial trauma for oppressed and oppressor alike leads him to emphasize bodies and culture because of the ways trauma lives in the body. White-body supremacy, as Menakem calls it, "let loose" in 1691, "begins in your body, ripples out to other bodies, and then to our collective body."[5] Menakem's work proceeds to envision and invite embodied antiracist education rooted in practices that heal our bodies and our collective body. We need to, and through such practices we can, build new, healthier—antiracist—*cultures* (not just concepts, see chapter 5).

There are embodied practices in the work Bryan Stevenson (author of *Just Mercy*, which recounts his entrée into legal work overturning unjust death-row convictions) has invited Americans to do. He's also created ways for us to do it.

We are all *necessary* for the healing work our communities need to undergo in order to become civic bodies of justice and flourishing. So Stevenson's Equal Justice Initiative has developed the Community Remembrance Project. The project aims to establish memorials in all 805 counties where we know a lynching took place between 1877 and 1950.[6] Coalitions of people at the local level can partner with the Community Remembrance Project to move through a process of learning about what happened and understanding how the racial terror of lynching still shapes so much of our U.S. racial contexts today.

Facing and telling the truth about our shared history together, as difficult as that process is, can change the conditions and relationships in our communities and make a more just future possible. When local communities move through the various processes the Community Remembrance Project supports, they culminate by collecting soil from a lynching site at the National Memorial for Peace and Justice in Montgomery, Alabama—which helps move our national remembrance forward. And together they erect a historical marker at the lynching site.

Similar projects are taking place all over the United States. *Acts of Reparation* is a film project created by Selina Lewis Davidson and Macky Alston.[7] Davidson, who is Black, and Alston, who is white, have been friends for twenty-five years. They are both invested in understanding their own familial histories in relationship to enslavement and Native American genocide. In *Acts of Reparation* they bring their exploration of their own legacies into dialogue with six different projects in which groups of Americans are being accountable, today, to history and to one another.

One of the projects focuses on Alston. A descendant of enslavers, Alston meets historian Mamie Hillman when he sells his portion of an inherited plantation and gives the money to a Black-, queer-led justice group as an act of reparation. Through this relationship Ms. Hillman and Alston find a "lost cemetery" where Black ancestors in the community are buried. Together they help organize a communal initiative to repair and restore the cemetery. Malachi Larrabee-Garza, in Oakland, engages in work to connect philanthropists descended from enslavers with Black Lives Matter activists. These reparative justice projects create deep connective ties among people and communities who come together as they grow accountability.

As with the Community Remembrance Project, resources for those of us who want to grow such work in our own community have been created surrounding the *Acts of Reparation* project. One of these is an initiative to bring white people wanting to explore and deepen our relationship to reparative justice into six-week circles of practice.

"You are necessary" is the opposite of being expendable. "You matter" is the opposite of being worthless. We belong to one another and can do the work of creating such belonging, in relationship, through accountable practices.

How might white antiracist cultures shift if we explicitly begin with such presumptions?

The models being generated by healers like Menakem, Hemphill, Reseda, and others can help us find the courage to tear up the five-point lists we use as weapons. These practitioners invite us to draw on the wisdom of our bodies to heal ourselves as we learn to recognize and then refuse the ways we've internalized these systems. Communal dialogues and rituals like those being supported by the Community Remembrance Project and the circles and projects invited by *Acts of Reparation* are making models available to everyday Americans in our local communities to understand how we can move forward in a different way.

The healing these different initiatives envision is collective. They presume interconnectedness. They assume we belong. They know we need to find our way back to ourselves and to one another.

Inherited legacies of white supremacy deceive us into believing we don't belong to one another. They would keep us acting out of the trauma and hurt we carry in our bodies toward other human beings; even in our process of trying to deepen our capacity for antiracism.

Belonging as an unshakable conviction is a necessary antidote.

White people working in our own communities can insist that learning and growth are necessary, as is redress of harm when it is committed. But we can go hard on principle, be clear about practices, while staying gentle on people. And we owe it to one another not to dehumanize any one of us.

I'm not putting out a universal call here. The multiracial work of justice requires different things from different people in different communities at different times. Doing work in *my* racial community remains my focus. But the models I've described above also help us become better able to turn away from shame and resist the allure of purity tests. None of us chose the conditions of our birth. Nor did any of us create these systems currently damaging our humanity and alienating us from one another.

Accountability as belonging asks us to create strategies to help us say no to the temptation to take our pain out on each other. Instead, I am granted permission to direct my anger at the systems and legacies harming all of us, rather than at you the person and people I need. You who matter. You who are necessary in this difficult collective project. More space is created to grieve the ways these legacies have cost us all so much.

A framework of belonging makes me as invested in your growth as I am in my own. It releases me from the false expectation that perfection is a possibility or the goal. Instead, the goal is continuing to show up even when doing so means at some point I'll have to take responsibility for harm I cause.

Belonging makes it possible for me to choose to walk alongside you as you try to make sense of what these legacies have done to you. It asks you to walk alongside me as I do the same. Accountability as belonging presumes you are worthy. You are invited, offered support, and lovingly challenged to come in, to come back.

Accountability as belonging is being able to say to a confused and frightened nineteen-year-old, "Come, let's sit down and look at this together. I'm invested in you finding a way to the table. We need you and you, too, deserve to heal."

This is also a good moment to note: Just as we learn discernment most deeply in relationships and community, accountability as belonging is best practiced and most meaningful in local contexts. We need to build physical relationships with one another. We need to create spaces where we build a container that makes possible what a brilliant friend of mine calls secure attachment (thank you, Kelsi Cooper; see chapter 9). Secure attachments are built through intentional practices we do and repeat with one another to stay in relationship. They require us to pay attention to and figure out how we create agreements to stay in process with one another. This is not unlike how a spiritual community might participate in repeated rituals or a class of students might agree to guidelines for difficult dialogues over a twelve-week semester (see chapter 9).

I was held accountable in a mighty way after students at my university were harmed by an experience for which I held real responsibility. It mattered that we were in proximate relationships so we could engage in granular, repair-focused dialogue about specific forms of redress that were necessary and that these were tethered to the original incident.

In addition to a more organized, public response, countless invitations to share a cup of coffee with Black and Brown students, to hear and hold the hurt and anger, were meaningful ways to honor the truth that we are all interconnected. The ability to attend directly to those relationships (even when the invitation was declined) mattered to what came next.

Follow-up with the young man in my workshop and ongoing dialogue about his confusion remained possible because we were in relationship. This mattered to what came next, too.

There is so little about which we can be certain as we engage in white antiracism. But the premise of taking such a journey at all begins with a belief that people can change. I can. You can. It presumes we need one another to survive. As we journey together, we need to know—and when we forget, we can practice reminding one another—that an invitation to be accountable is one of the greatest affirmations of worth and belonging we can possibly offer or receive.

TAKE A NEXT STEP

1. Reflect on your relationships with shame—specifically, racial shame. Where did it come from? Continue to explicitly think about the difference between shame and guilt. Identify an antiracist practice you can commit to that seems to take responsibility for responding to racial harm.

2. Engage with an activist or thinker whose work pays attention to our bodies and our connections to one another. Resmaa Menakem offers practices that can enable "resilience, discernment, and the ability to tolerate discomfort." Sonya Renee Taylor's The Body Is Not an Apology project offers a framework of radical self-love and tools to dismantle the shame we carry in and about our bodies as a result of oppression. CTZNWELL connects wellness with ending white supremacy, economic injustice, and lack of access to health care and connects us to others to shift the culture. The Equal Justice Initiative's Community Remembrance Project collaborates with local coalitions to memorialize racial violence and deepen our communal commitment to justice. (There are more resources that take these kinds of healing approaches listed in the Further Resources section at the back of this book.)

3. Have an explicit conversation about *transformation* in the antiracism group you are part of. (If you aren't part of one yet, join one.) What do we believe about our own and other people's abilities to change? Identify specific norms and practices the group will develop to support transformation within ourselves and in one another.

8

So, What *Do* We Do with Our Families?

My older child started talking really early. Her verbal acumen made her a force to be reckoned with. She couldn't have yet been three the day she came down the steps of our house, slowly spelling at the top of her lungs, "P-O-R-N! [pause] P-O-R-N!"

I'll leave it to you to speculate about what could have happened there.

During the same years she was finding so many words, H. also spent a fair amount of time at her grandparents' house. Grandma and Grandpa loved her very much, and the occasional breaks from the grind of parenting a toddler with an infant in tow were a godsend to my then-partner and I. We were very, very tired.

During the same years she was finding so many words, H. also had a beloved baby doll. Her doll was Black.

One day H. came home after a weekend with the grandparents. In a random moment of play she picked up her doll, held it in the air, and said to me and Chris, "*Black* baby."

Chris and I looked at each other. "What?"

To be clear, we weren't concerned H. might be noticing and naming the doll's race. We've attempted to raise our two white children in a race-conscious, justice-affirming way since birth. But H.'s language and tone didn't signal that type of healthy affirmation of all kinds of visible differences.

Plus, while we had said things like "Look at this baby's beautiful brown skin," or—of another doll—"This baby has beautiful peach skin," we'd never referred to the doll in that way, just as we hadn't referred to any of her dolls with light skin as "white baby." We suspected H. was mimicking a reference to her doll made by family she'd just been with and that the reference hadn't been in authentic celebration.

So, now we had to decide what to do.

Our white families got exposed in 2016, and the exposure has continued ever since. Myriads of white Americans who were fully horrified by Donald Trump and his racist hate had family members who voted him into office.

Whereas before political differences had been somewhere on a spectrum of "reasonable people can disagree," now a "willingness to align with hate" was sitting next to us at the extended family meal table. Add to this the political pressure cooker we're all living in, combined with a growing culture of disdain for attempts to engage meaningfully about our current state of civic affairs (I'm trying so hard not to use the word *polarized* here), and . . . well . . . *presto*. The temptation to not go home at all or to go but keep it short and our mouths shut shot off the charts.

I remember talking with Chris about whether we'd join the usual Christmas celebration a month after the election. This would have been to the "*Black* baby" branch of our eclectically grafted family tree. Our absence would have created shock waves.

We'd known full well racism was already in the room. We'd engaged with it, along with homophobia, in various ways for years by that point. But the intensity of pain and the feelings of betrayal accompanying the realization that the people who raised you and loved up on your kids would vote for someone so maliciously out to get you and those same kids were almost unbearable.

I also didn't want to sit anywhere near one particular brother-in-law. Let alone try to be yuletide gay.

I've heard white people from nearly every age group, class bracket, and educational background and so many parts of the country talk about how tough, or how much tougher, family gatherings became after 2016. This means, of course, the conditions enabling that white vote were already in the room.

The election revealed a long-existing failure to invest deeply in racially just change in our most intimate, or at least most long-term, relationships.

White racial bonding has long been alive and well in white families.[1] For just as long, the many of us who've wanted to check or challenge it have found ourselves caught in the sticky web of white silence.

It's also reasonable, then, to see white families as powerful places for civic impact. Transformed white family networks have the potential to enable collective and generational changes we must have.

Families aren't and can't be the only places. But they are powerful places.

In my mid-forties I was surprised to find myself writing a book about parenting. Part of me was even a little embarrassed.

200 □ Antiracism as Daily Practice

There was a time I'd have considered that to be just touchy-feely stuff. Not real racial justice work. Only strategic activism counted for me—hard-edged work on reparations and other matters.

But Ferguson burned when my children were young. I realized intentionally mentoring white kids and youth into antiracism was vital to raising a generation more likely to be the kind of friends, coworkers, classmates, and civic neighbors their friends, coworkers, classmates, and civic neighbors of color deserve. I started to believe that taking white silence and passivity head on in our families was a necessary form of social change.

That little public library in rural Iowa I described in chapter 6 was onto something.

We have this mantra in the United States. When racism shows up in kids' lives, it's because someone's taught it. I've even seen "Racism Is Learned" underneath a child's face plastered on a billboard. The implied takeaway is "so don't teach kids to be racist." But the truth is so much more complicated. Yes, none of us are born racist. But it's antiracism, not racism, that has to be explicitly taught. When we do nothing, racism predictably shows up. That's because we start breathing its smog (psychologist Beverly Daniel Tatum's metaphor[2]) from the moment of our first cry.

As I reckoned with this as a parent, I also began to realize the whole white kids thing wasn't an individualistic matter. It's a collective one. It isn't just about how I parent my own kids. It pertains to how I (and all of us) show up in my (our) extended family networks.

It's my job to teach my daughter to love and affirm difference by cuddling a Black baby doll with her and talking about its beautiful brown skin. It's my job to insist she unlearn the othering version of "*Black* baby" she picked up from family elders.

But my job doesn't stop there. It's also my job to engage those family members and the family culture where she picked that up. They're part of my collective (and hers, too).

Creating a world in which we are all seen as worthy of deserving conditions in which we can flourish thus has everything to do with what we do in our families. Breaking silence in white families, then, over and over again as a long-haul practice, absolutely has the potential to change civic life.

Meanwhile white antiracism is relational. It takes time. It's almost always slow. And as we've already talked about, a basic premise of accountability as belonging is cultivating a willingness to build relationships with other white people.

We're usually in our family relationships, in some way, shape, form, or mess, over the long haul. So families are a great place to do that relational work.

It can also be a tough place, too, of course. Ruining a good party is hard in any space.[3] But family might be the hardest because there are all these preexisting younger versions of ourselves in those spaces. These younger selves have all kinds of complicated relationships in the culture.

Many of us struggle with how to show up authentically in our families of origin. Or even know what it means to do that.

When I became a vegetarian in college, I recall the moment my aunt heard this news. I was so proud. She promptly scolded me. "Jenny, you have relatives who are ranchers!" she said bitterly. "How can you not eat meat?"

I suddenly felt so disloyal. To her and somehow to the entire Harvey clan.

A preexisting Jen was already there! She complicated emerging Jen's ability to show up.

Then there was the ribbing at every extended family gathering. I ranged from being a problem ("Well, what *can* she eat?"

asks the person cooking) to an object of fascination. The repeated retelling of the time my dad found a box of Big Mac Attack T-shirts in an alley and I decided to wear one every day for the rest of the school year. What fun! This family memory took on a whole new comedic tinge now that I'd changed my dietary convictions.

Side note: This is actually a great and true story. Let me tell you, I spent a lot of second-grade political capital trying to convince my incredulous classmates—who for some reason found it impossible to believe I owned twenty Big Mac Attack T-shirts—that I wasn't wearing the same (unwashed, they presumed) T-shirt every day.

And that's it right there. A simple dietary choice conjured earlier Jens, along with all sorts of family dynamics they were already part of; so much so that at times it would have been easier to just smile and eat the damn hamburger. I was tempted more than once.

But while food is bound up in identity and history, it's got nothing on race. Take the politics involved, and the misinformation or lack of information about racism so many white folks suffer from. Add layers of feelings: the all-kinds-of-feelings our families elicit and the shame that always hovers about, guilt, fear, or every other feeling race can elicit.

When Chris went to talk about the doll with the grandparents, she wasn't just facing that tough conversation. She was potentially raising every other conflict she'd had with her parents about any number of points of difference with them from prior stages of her life. She was contending with the existing power dynamics so often present in intergenerational family relationships. In her case, she was making herself vulnerable to revisiting prior experiences of being treated in ways that were minimizing and dismissive.

Here's my Pollyannaish reframe. If antiracism is a practice and building moral muscles for behavioral changes is the journey, then showing up differently in our families offers a lot of bang for our buck. Simply put, if we can learn to do it there, we can do it anywhere.

So, what *do* we do with them?

Every family is different, so there's no template you can just pick up and transfer to any other set of relationships.

But whatever it looks like, we need a heck of a lot more open conversations about what goes on in our families. Those of us trying to figure out how to do our part need the nourishment and growth that can come from sharing and exploring with one another what it can look like, what it feels like. We need to break our silence with one another about the million different ways we're trying to break white silence in our families.

My response to "What *do* we do?" looks something like this: We need to *stay in it*; then *stay in it again*; and then we need to stay in it some more until it's clearly *time to leave*.

Here are some of my own very imperfect, very incomplete (and, frankly, very vulnerable) experiences of trying, with all of my flawed might, simply to stay.

White silence tempts us to put our heads down and hope red flags will go away. (They won't.) We knew we couldn't let the "*Black* baby" comment slide. I remember saying to Chris, "Ummm, so you or me? Rock, paper, scissors?"

We also knew it didn't matter whether we could succeed in explaining to the grandparents what wasn't okay about what they'd said about the doll. We needed to address it regardless.

But we did strategize. For example, I kept thinking how bad it would have felt if Black family members had been present when H. had said that. Could we humanize the harm of othering a doll with the tone just channeled through H.'s sweet little toddler mouth? Could we ask them to imagine how our nephews or sister-in-law would have experienced that moment?

We also practiced. "It's not bad to notice this doll is Black and beautiful. We want H. to learn that. But it's not okay to use the word *black* to imply something about this doll isn't just as normal and good as her other dolls. It seems like maybe that's what you did."

Mostly we just agreed ahead of time that whatever happened, a boundary needed to be set.

Chris called nervously. "We need to talk." Then off she went.

It was not an easy conversation. Actually, that's an understatement. The conversation was a disaster.

The grandparents were not gentle with her or curious about her concern. They denied there was anything wrong with what they'd said. Every attempt to explore that claim with them only made it clearer something was *definitely* wrong with what they'd said.

They weren't receptive to that feedback, either. Also (see above) hard family dynamics showed up in a major way. Long-standing tendencies by one parent to show up with condescension and barely sublimated anger when anyone forgot their place and challenged him combined with challenging dynamics between the two parents—one parent more receptive to learning but committed to not breaking ranks with the other.

This is how it felt on our side, anyway. The grandparents might remember differently. And I wasn't there. But I did hold space as Chris described how her attempt to lean in and explain had landed her on the receiving end of acrimony and accusation.

She didn't get through.

Eventually, she'd had to just end the not-conversation. "Well, we're not going to have this," she said. "Whether you get it or not, if you want H. to come over, you can't talk about Black people like that. If you won't agree, you can't be around her unsupervised."

They were pissed.

Over the next few days, a series of furtive phone calls took place, usually initiated by Grandma, who was trying to broker a peace deal. None got far. Then a call initiated by Grandpa went so sideways that Chris ended the whole thing. "Look, I'm not talking about this anymore. You'll either agree or you won't."

After that, we didn't hear from them for three full months.

Three uncomfortable, angsty months. Three months with no child-care breaks. Three months during which a confused toddler missed her grandparents.

Then, about as abruptly, we won.

One day they just called. "Okay. It won't happen again. Can we see H.?"

We never talked about the doll incident again. Probably they never understood it in the way we'd hoped. But they did understand our values mattered to us enough that we would speak them and stand firm. We came back into our relationship in a spirit of kindness. We brought with us fresh homemade dinner rolls and one happy toddler.

Our decision to not relitigate the incident wasn't a return to white silence. It was more a peace agreement secured by successfully creating a new norm in the family. We'd been clear and a boundary had been established.

We also knew our verbal toddler would give it away if the boundary got crossed again.

In the years that followed, we took different approaches. The "absolutely not" rule remained firmly in place when the kids were too young to speak for themselves. It was never revoked exactly, but race talk was a constant stream of conversation in our home. So as our kids got older, they took the conversations to the grandparents.

We fumbled our way into building habits that could apply to lots of situations. I'm thinking especially of families where kids have more than one home and different values exist in each.

For example, we were never apologetic about talking about race. It was part of our family life. Our kids got to take it out the door with them.

We kept validating the assumption that these are conversations we have with people. Especially people with whom we talk about all the other things in our lives. Race and a longing for justice are not taboo subjects to avoid. We never wanted our children to think they were supposed to shrink their values just because they bumped against someone else's—including those of adults.

We also encouraged them to pursue their earnest questions, even if they felt awkward. This got really exciting when the 2016 election ramped up. "Why do Grandma and Grandpa support Trump? How can they like someone who is mean to women and Black people?" I remember so many questions about immigrants.

We validated the questions. We never let the grandparents off the hook. But we also never dehumanized or disparaged them.

We'd say things like "It's hard for us to understand that, too, when we know they like to do good in the world. It makes us really sad they don't see how hateful that is."

We'd say, "I don't know. But it's a great question. I think it would be fine for you to ask them."

(And our kids did. Many times. On repeat.)

One day they came home and told us the grandparents had

said Trump would "keep us safe." Our kids called bullshit. They matter-of-factly told us they'd explained: "People crossing the border don't make us unsafe. They're trying to feed their babies."

We got to connect some dots from that particular report. We talked about how racist stories describing dark-skinned people as dangerous are used to justify terrorizing people who are fleeing violence or are hungry. We explained this was connected to the full story we rarely learn, which is that the United States actually took Mexico's land and moved the border—and that this happened not so long ago.

I had no doubt this conversation might end up back at the grandparents' house, too. That was fine with me.

This wasn't calculated or disingenuous. We weren't deploying our kids to do antiracism work under cover. Our kids' relationship with their grandparents was real. It was authentic. And as long as the environment wasn't unsafe emotionally or otherwise (that's a different matter), we supported them in bringing the moral values they were developing into challenging conversations in that space, even when we weren't there.

Also, we didn't expect our kids to do anything we weren't also willing and able to do, too. Our relationship with the grandparents wasn't as direct or close as our children's. But when we spent time with them, we wore our own antiracist commitments on our sleeves.

And these are some of the kinds of practices I think of as *staying in it.*

We stay in it when we refuse to cordon off our commitments from spaces even when they make our families ill at ease. We stay in it when we reject pervasive messages that we're supposed to avoid hot topics with our families of origin. We stay in it when we don't shrink or shirk just because there may be land mines lying about.

Staying in it doesn't mean provoking disagreement or yelling matches when someone doesn't see something the same way we do. There's a time to push back hard, and there's a time to set firm boundaries. There may even be a time to argue. But I don't think staying true to antiracist commitments means having to "win an argument about an issue" every time we go home. Arguing and yelling about racism really aren't sustainable. They're not a way to stay.

Now, to be sure, avoiding arguing and provocation doesn't mean every interaction will go well. Sometimes merely refusing to cordon off our commitments is experienced as provocation.

I remember the time a totally banal question got me all tied up in knots. "Jen, what are you teaching this semester?" Someone was making small talk. Well, I was teaching reparations for enslavement. So I said that.

The emotional intensity escalated immediately. I found myself flustered when someone asked sarcastically, "Okay, well, I'm Irish, where's my reparations?"

My response was feeble. "I don't know. I guess I'm focusing on me and my community's responsibility for making things right."

That exchange felt decidedly not great. I felt like I'd failed by not coming up with a better response. I also left feeling like I'd let myself get bullied a little bit.

When I look back at this incident from the perspective of staying in it, I see that maybe this failure was its own kind of success. I'd known it would be a whole lot easier to evade when asked about my teaching. I could have said, "I'm teaching history," and that would have technically been true. But it wouldn't have been authentic. I'd have been choosing ease over my values.

Staying in it is a decision to take up space. It's the attempt to show ourselves in the fullness of our beliefs and commitments, regardless of whether others get it. It's a repeated choice to not hide. I wasn't trying to score a point when I said *reparations.* I was just trying to be my actual self.

I think that's the messy, nuanced journey at the heart of what staying asks of us. A willingness to make dis-ease part of the family culture. Developing the resilience to keep showing ourselves even when that means the relationships get uncomfortable.

In fact, discomfort can be quite productive. Whenever my favorite yoga teacher has us hold a terrible pose like Side Plank or Chair for longer than my desire for ease wants, my body begins to shake. Without fail, I soon hear my teacher's voice reminding the class that seeds vibrate at a microscopic level before they germinate. That's the precursor for the dormant life inside being able to break through.

I am unable to confirm the science behind this explanation. But the metaphor makes sense to me anyway. So often in life, it's only when things get shaken up that new things can grow.

Invitation and dialogue are not words we associate with racism and antiracism very much these days. But the loss of those words is costing us all so much.

So it's worth giving some thought to *how* we engage our families. Long-haul relationships are especially good places to avoid throwing shame and shutting people down. They are especially good places to figure out how to practice curiosity and root that curiosity in an attempt to sustain connection.

In 2020, *The Atlantic* published a story on the remarkable success People's Action had in changing would-be Trump voters' minds and securing a vote for Biden.[4] Similar reporting has been done on getting through vaccine hesitancy in an environment rife with misinformation and fear around COVID.

In every case, it's clear "facts and talking points do not change minds."[5] And starting by arguing one's own opinion ends most dialogues before they even begin. The National Coalition Building Institute (NCBI), which has a decades-long track record of bringing people together around issues of oppression (especially racism and discrimination), concurs. It adds that shame and guilt can even lock discriminatory attitudes in place.

The voting study found that building some sense of intimacy and connection goes a long way to create conditions for the kind of dialogue that might allow room for a mind to change. Acknowledging shared values is also a powerful way to frame a dialogue when seismic differences are deeply entrenched.

I'm a part-time local in a mountain town in which local residents who are conservative (on everything from guns to queer people) are neighbors with locals who are earthy-crunchy types. In summer of 2022, an LGBTQ+-affirming float took part in a Fourth of July parade for the second time ever. Somehow, during that same parade—or so the Facebook claim went—a six-year-old ended up in possession of a condom.

Rage, inflected with barely veiled threats of violence, erupted on social media directed at the queer locals (mostly young people). Now, there had been baskets of condoms on the float. But the participants insisted they'd never thrown them into the crowd. They'd handed them out only on request and most certainly had not given any to children.

For forty-eight hours these two communities within one community separately roiled. Then a parent of one of the queer youth observed, "It seems to me the first thing we've got to do is sit down and find some agreement. Like 'we all agree that none of us wants a six-year-old sexualized in any way, shape, or form.'"

That's a shared value.

This parent and another leader proceeded to invite precisely such a dialogue. Lo and behold, their approach resulted in rapid de-escalation and an unanticipated apology for homophobia and transphobia expressed in the heat of the moment. The conversation also gave way to some surprising possibilities for a mini-coalition around some specific issues down the road (maybe). De-escalation alone helped cut through the misinformation and get to the bottom of what happened, which indeed exonerated the queer people.

All of this is easier said than done, for sure. It's especially hard when we find someone's views abhorrent (and really want to win!). Not a one of these is about finding a mushy middle ground where we compromise our convictions for civility as the end goal. Nor is any of this exploration throwing cold water on the value of speaking fully and directly about one's own values.

NCBI has developed a relationship-based model grounded in the understanding that attitudes are most likely to shift when we hear (and share) stories. They teach a dialogue method that aims to sustain connection by noticing our tone and minimizing defensiveness. They teach people to try to consciously bracket or set down (only temporarily!) one's own "ouch" that arises in a moment when a prejudicial comment of some sort has been articulated. The rationale is that two ouches bumping against each other can't create space for the kind of engagement in which a shift can emerge. Their method suggests one ask questions and listen for the pain underneath the ism that has shown up.

NCBI's assessment of the presence of pain is not an outlier. Pain and fear often lie underneath bigotry and bias. The adage may sound trite, but it's true. Hurt people hurt people.

The hurt may come from the harm white supremacy causes white people, which we then turn on people of color—acting out oppression while continuing to participate in a violent system that malforms us as we do. It may be hurt caused by other forms of oppression and suffering that we then pick up and use like a weapon, as we scapegoat and target communities of color and/or religious minorities. Often it's a tangled mess of both of these. We're all living in a world in which many systems of violence and injustice are knocking us around in all kinds of ways every day.

But what changes if I can hear a wound in the snarl "I'm Irish, where's my reparations?" What changes in me if I assume some experience of pain or fear is implicated in the choice to refer to a doll as "*Black* baby"?

What shifts is not my insistence about not letting such comments slide.

But I might release the assumption that clear-cut victory, secured by convincing every member of my family to see things my way beyond a shadow of a doubt (and in one conversation!), is the only goal. What shifts is the possibility of empathy, which might help me find some internal spaciousness for curiosity. Maybe it begins to feel feasible to move into an emotional tone and tenor that renders some meaningful connection more viable. And with connection I keep alive the possibility that when the conversation doesn't go down the path I hope it would this time, I can (we can) loop back again later because I haven't scorched the earth.

"Tell me more about why you're so afraid of people crossing the border. You're a compassionate person and I know you'd do anything for your own kids or grandkids. Have you had an experience that makes you feel so strongly about protecting our borders? (When did our family cross the border?)"

"I'm committed to H.'s learning the whole story of U.S. history. I know you value education. You're always so proud of how hard she works at school. Why does her learning about this part frustrate you so? (What were you taught about U.S. history?)"

"I've been learning about the destruction of Black communities when the interstate was built in Des Moines. It dawned on me your parents were here when that happened. Did they ever talk about this? (I have a friend whose family lost her business. It's been painful to learn how these emotional and economic losses still affect all of them. I feel sad about it and wonder how it affected our family.)"

Staying takes many different forms, even in the same family. We stayed through so many different kinds of moments over the years. The moment someone blurted out a racially biased association in a game of Catch Phrase at Christmas, and our immediate response was "Hey, no. Nope." A conversation about neighborhood frustrations in which a derogatory racial-religious term was used and a puzzled look was given in response, accompanied by "I'm not sure what you mean by that term"—if just to interrupt.

Sometimes it was an ask: "Can you watch the kids? We're going to a protest." An honest response to the question "How are things at work?" "Well, I'm excited because students of color are . . ." and then describing a justice project the asker might feel stretched by (but on a good day, which might engender follow-up questions anyway). An invitation to join when there was a shared value we could acknowledge. "Hey, we're working with friends who are sponsoring two asylum seekers and they need to furnish an apartment. Do you have any furniture you want to share?" (In a Catholic family it's pretty hard to fight about that kind of giving, regardless of the politics.)

Over time we felt subtle shifts in family dynamics. Whatever may have been said when we weren't present, remarks that otherwise might have been made in shared family space decreased. It was almost like everyone realized we couldn't be counted on to look the other way if something came up. So everyone started paying more attention to avoid that scenario.

It was kind of like being a sore thumb. A pea under the mattress. A bit of an irritant simply by being in the room in our fullness. We were a constant source of some level of dis-ease.

The shifts enabled other possibilities. One person, more open than others, refers in an individual conversation to an interaction from shared space. A new conversation—and a new connection—develops in that relationship. ("I couldn't believe Tabitha made that comment during Catch Phrase! Why would she think that's okay?")

Over time, racial dialogue in the web of our relational lives grew, even though political and moral differences—huge ones—persisted. It was always very layered. But white silence lost its suffocating grip.

Then one night something big happened.

We'd gone out for pizza. Three generations were at the table. A sister started talking about a child in her elementary class. She'd learned his parents were undocumented and he was not. He was missing a lot of school.

I got nervous. It was post-2016. ICE was doing a lot of raids. Families were terrified. Many were hiding. Where was this going?

She began to say it never occurred to her a child in her class could be so afraid. She also said she'd heard that a lot of immigrants really love their home countries and would rather be there. They come only because they find no other choice.

Then she turned to me. "Jen, is that true? People would rather stay home?" Curious. Earnest. Gentle.

I couldn't believe this moment had come. I'd worried the opening salvo was headed toward complaint about the child or would pivot to frustration with a government that left underpaid and overworked teachers (she was underpaid and overworked) to deal with the disruptions of frequent absences, language barriers, or some other impact of immigration on underfunded schools.

(Let's notice: That second possibility would have been a perfect example of real suffering. Teachers have been maligned and denied the support they need and deserve in our civic environment. That suffering can easily be turned on another group as a scapegoat.)

But nope. She leaned into empathy. She acknowledged there was something she hadn't thought about before that was worth understanding now.

It was also a big deal she hadn't pulled me aside privately. She asked right in front of everyone. This included family who held undocumented immigrants in disdain and elders who got mad if you raised anything political because it caused stress. *No one* besides Chris and me had ever done *that*.

I was on cloud nine.

So guess what I did.

Well, imagine there's a shy turtle that's tentatively poked its head out of its shell in a brand-new environment it finds a bit scary. Imagine you want that little creature to poke its head out further, look around a bit, maybe even engage the space further.

You'd probably be wise, in such a case, to sit very still. Be gentle. Speak softly.

I did exactly none of that.

I basically rushed up to the turtle in eager joy, got right in its face, and shouted, "Welcome!" as loud as I could.

"Yes, of course people would rather be home! They love their countries as much as we do! Think how desperate you'd have to be to take such a dangerous trip! Or leave your children behind or send them ahead! Then you get here, and people say such hateful things about you! Now ICE is scaring the hell out of these vulnerable families!"

At. The. Top. Of. My. Emotional. Lungs.

I'm sure my passion felt like barrage. My rush to connect a pontification.

Instead of responding with the empathetic, curious energy that had just been extended to me—which might have given way to a back-and-forth—I made statements. Gave my views. Which, by the way, everyone at the table already knew.

That there was nothing untrue about what I said is irrelevant. I didn't need to pile on. What I needed to do was receive the opportunity and build on and deepen a relationship where a newly emerging shared value had just dared poke its little head out.

Wow, was that conversation abruptly over.

When I got quiet, everyone at the table kind of looked at each other like *Well, that was fun.* They looked back down at their pizza.

Dammit.

I so wish I'd have said something like, "Yeah, people are really afraid right now and surely longing for the comfort of home," and gone on with any number of follow-ups.

Like:

"Tell us more about your student. You must be worried about him. Have you ever met his family?"

Or "I wonder what it would be like for H. or E. to be here legally, knowing they might come home any random day after school and find me gone. It must be hard to realize your student's going through that."

Or even, "This makes me sad since Iowa used to be proud about how it welcomed refugees. Undocumented people are basically refugees who couldn't get papers. Do you get support as you support these students? Because this seems like a hard job." (Okay, see? Even that response is a little preachy compared to the first two, but it's still way better than what I did.)

My point in sharing this story is not to belabor that I flubbed it.

My point is to notice that in a family culture where dis-ease had been a constant for almost fifteen years, someone touched and then risked sharing a point of grief.

That moment has stayed with me as a reminder of what sometimes begins to grow if we can find a way to stay.

One expectation articulated in the collective project of white antiracism is this: White people trying to do better have access to the white people who also need to do much better, so it is our *responsibility* to stay engaged. Even when it's tough.

After the youth of Ferguson rose up to say "enough!" and Black Lives Matter became more widely known, the Public Religion Research Institute found that 91 percent of white Americans did not have a meaningful, sustained relationship with anyone who was not white.[6] This figure was cited to explain the huge disparities between how white and Black Americans understood the killings of Black people by police.

Ninety-one percent. That figure is stunning. It makes clear why staying in relationship matters. Especially when we understand that culture change requires a massive shift in which so many of us integrate antiracism and other dimensions of justice and belonging into our lives, like Rebecca Solnit talks about.

I was reminded about the rooms white people have access to when my friend Bruce described a night out at a club a few months ago. Out to enjoy the music, he was introduced to a friend of a friend. He learned this white woman worked in the upper levels of an organization that had recently moved to place armed security officers inside local grocery stores. "To prevent theft," the rationale went. After engaging in conversation over the course of the evening, Bruce said, "Hey, while we're talking, can I ask you a question?" "Sure," she said. "I'm wondering if you all have thought about the likelihood one of those officers shoots a Black person, or how it feels to Black shoppers to have those officers strolling around? I'm also really curious about what kind of de-escalation training they have—because if they don't, it makes me think you are expecting them to use their gun in response to theft." He went on to share with her how nervous it made him to bring his young kids and their friends (which included a number of Black kids) into the store after a sporting event or other social outing.

By the end of the night he had a commitment that she would raise the issue with her team. "I'm at the table where those decisions get made," she said. She invited him to reach out to follow up. There are no guarantees a change will come from Bruce's speaking up at a club—though it might help push things along if community organizing is also taking place. But it's a reminder that we have things we can say and do in white circles.

Still, there's a paradoxical tension in this expectation to stay in relationship. It's a suspicious observation about the pernicious consequences when white people do stay.

I've heard it asked this way: "What on earth is going on with white people who stay? How can you sit and pass the mashed potatoes to folks who couldn't care less or might even be a-okay with the racist violence and harm raining down on communities of color?" If we're able to stay, the critical query goes, we must not be pushing hard enough.

This query is on point. Think about my great-uncle's choice

to stay and even raise the next generations in a church that said segregation was desirable. It's on point in cases when I've left racism unaddressed as I exited a space or conversation but maintained connection (by staying silent) with the people among whom it manifested.

Curiosity and an attempt to connect can't be confused with silent acquiescence. Family cultures won't shift if we go home but keep quiet. We have to destabilize white silence. That's how we weaken the white racial bonding that occurs in our relationships when we comply with existing familial racial practices.

But there's nuance here, too. Getting kicked out isn't the goal for its own sake.

Like so many of the other paradoxes white antiracism requires us to navigate, this too asks us to live into antiracism in complex landscapes.

In the midst of this complexity, then, another matter of broken relationships asks for consideration, too.

Stay in it; then *stay in it again*; and then stay in it some more *until it's clearly time to leave.*

What about this leaving part?

I never did find a way to sit near one brother-in-law—not for the long haul. I did try. And for quite a while. After all, we were in the same family for nearly twenty years. Our kids were close when they were young. We connected over NFL football for a time. I even sent him a card in the actual mail once, because I knew he'd had to stretch to attend our same-sex wedding. I wanted him to know the stretch mattered.

And there was a time some shifts emerged.

A week after the 2016 election, I'd heard an organizer of color (I can't remember who and can't find the flyer) say on a national

SURJ call, "Hey, white folks, this is not a moment to go around disparaging your people. In the coming months there's going to be some voter's remorse in your communities. It's your job to be there when that happens."

He was right.

Midway through the forty-fifth presidency at a family graduation gathering, my brother-in-law surprised me with a genuinely lighthearted joke about how maybe he should read *Raising White Kids*. So we could debate, he teased. Then he made a comment about how it seemed like no one can even talk to anyone they disagree with anymore—so maybe he and I should try (just think—he thought no one could talk anymore way back in 2018ish!). I teased back: "Well, if you ever decide you'll read it, I'll give you a free copy and you can tell me all the things I got wrong. I'd love to have that conversation."

This unexpected exchange gave way to a series of texts. We started to carefully, gently, a little playfully, talk *some* politics. He thanked me for being a good aunt to his daughters as we engaged. Then he made an unsolicited, self-deprecating joke. He said, "Maybe we should write a book together. I'd call it *How Hatred of Hillary Clinton Made Me Vote for a Moron*."

Oh my god. Here was the voter's remorse that organizer had talked about! This time I didn't yell "Welcome!" in the turtle's face.

I took a deep breath. I leaned in. "Well, good news," I said back. "You're going to get a redo in 2020. And we need you."

He responded. "I've got you."

But by the time 2020 rolled around, the rage and the misinformation peddled in our social media rabbit holes had done its work. I was frantic to help flip Iowa blue and felt obligated to talk to anyone I had a relationship with who had voted for Trump the first time around. I reached out to my brother-in-law, taking a playful tone to offer a serious reminder of our conversations a year or so prior. I pointed back to his "I've got you."

But what came back my way was rage. Full throttle.

Within a short period of time, it became clear that curiosity or any attempt to stay connected was off the table and inappropriate—not just for me, but for my precious little queer family.

The radicalization of members of white communities is real. There are no easy answers for how to stop it.

I felt that nightmare Solnit also talks about nipping at my heels and ended the relationship.[7]

It was time to go.

But families are complicated and interconnected. A decision to set a hard boundary around one relationship necessarily tests others. What and how to talk about what happened with the next generation can be anything but clear. Do you spend time with members who haven't set a similar boundary? How, when, and under what conditions?

Our leaving had layered and painful consequences we'll all be living with for a very long time because of all of these complexities. But while I wouldn't have chosen that outcome, I don't for a moment regret my decision to speak truthfully and be fully seen.

Also, even if everyone is white, saying no to racism causes family strain. The need to leave may also not result from just one thing. Sexism makes it hard for men to break ranks with misogyny (and other men). Queer-hatred makes family think they're doing you a favor when they embrace you—a perilous way to live, because those chips can be called in at any time. In our case, sexual orientation and gender identity became channels through which family members attempted to get us back in line, a stepping out of line we had taken most consistently in our commitments to antiracism.

Dis-ease can allow new things to grow. But it's also true that when any of us in a family system persist, the dis-ease can engender such powerful shakes that the whole system comes crashing down. Sometimes it pulls several layers of oppression down on us as it does.

That's what it looked like when my necessary leaving arrived. Yours may never come. (Or maybe it has already. And if it has, I hope you know you're not alone.) The effort to stay in it is not about displaying a kind of vulnerability that puts you in jeopardy of emotional or other kinds of harm.

These are hard truths to acknowledge. But I'm also coming to realize loss doesn't mean it's the end of the story. It doesn't even mean it's a bad ending.

My children have lost a great deal because of the way racism and other forms of oppression have affected their experiences of biological family. But my children continue to be okay. From the baby doll experience to today, I see the sheer beauty that interrupting the damaging effects of oppression is bringing into their lives. I feel that same beauty growing in mine as I keep learning to be an interrupter. That's the other side of such familial loss. Insisting that, consequences be damned, we'll keep working to build a place for love is already bringing new ways of being into existence.

And also . . . given the pain in the last story, I'd be remiss if I didn't say it wasn't the only truth in a period of time that was incredibly difficult on this branch of our family tree. A handwritten letter to an elder—one that invoked shared values, expressed empathy, demonstrated an appreciation for theirs, and made clear the devastation the forty-fifth presidency had done to beloveds in their family—had a different, shocking outcome. That result was a very short email I received back—one we also never revisited. It simply said: *I love you. I'm sad you're hurting and scared. I want you to know you don't have to worry about my vote.*

Stay in it; then *stay in it again*; and then in it *again* until it's clearly time to leave.

Then, if we have to leave, we leave with authenticity and clarity. We can depart with the kind of authenticity and clarity that may mean the leaving isn't permanent—who knows? Or if it is permanent, we can *know with certainty* a footprint remains behind. Perhaps even a trail of breadcrumbs.

We will never know in the moment whether one day we may look up and find that someone has decided to follow. But even without certainty that that day will ever come, we begin to know and even feel ourselves "becoming the good ancestors"[8] white children most certainly need and everyone's children deserve.

Portals of possibility are everywhere, just waiting for us to open them.

TAKE A NEXT STEP

1. Take a careful inventory of your familial relationships. What racial values do you live in those relationships? Where is dis-ease necessary? How do you want to put your values on your sleeve? Imagine who you want to be in that set of relationships and identify one next step you need to take to do that.

2. Start a conversation with a family member open to your growing behavioral investment in antiracism. Ask about their investment and describe the shifts in your family's racial culture you want. What is one way you can support each other in trying to move it in that direction? Practice the racial conversations you already know come up in your family, and create a conversation that might lead to a different one.

3. Take your experience with your family or an attempt you made in that space into dialogue with people outside of

your family whom you are engaged in antiracism with. Share this experience to get support and grow accountability. Rely on them to help you create a plan for one proactive engagement or intervention, appropriate to your family context, and try it out. Get support to stay in it.

9

Mapping Our Spheres of Influence

Kelsi Cooper (they/them) is a parent. They are a pastor in the Southwest. They are also a longtime antiracism and anti-oppression educator, facilitator, and consultant.

On top of the challenges Cooper and their family went through as the pandemic hit, Cooper became deeply involved in the protests in their local community in 2020. They already had relationships with organizers. And because they are white, they were called on to play a particular role.

In many communities, white people already engaged in justice work similarly stepped up in the aftermath of George Floyd's murder. In my own, the goal was to support Black leaders in remaining front and center and setting the agenda, but also to share the labor and do as much heavy lifting as we could. White people did things like pass out water at rallies, take care of logistical tasks like getting megaphones where they needed to be, and raise money to buy the orange vests needed by folks charged with keeping protestors safe at rallies—for example, legal observers or medical care teams.

Cooper drove a car. Planning for protests included having a car at the ready if leaders found themselves at risk of arrest, assault, or some targeted danger. Cooper played a key role in trying to create more safety for Black folks on the front lines.

At the same time, given their years of work, Cooper scaled up their facilitation and consulting. The upswell of consciousness rocking the nation led so many entities to seek out experienced workshop leaders and anti-oppression trainers. Cooper found the work they were already doing with a team of Black colleagues in intense demand.

So much was happening. It was all a lot.

Today, Cooper is not working in the same way. They aren't working on the same scale as they were at the height of 2020's frenzy. They've gone from formal antiracism training work, and lots of it, in as many different places as asked for it, to moving slowly and with incredible depth and presence. They are laser-focused on their work with a group of people doing mutual aid, all of which goes directly to support Black people locally and the community school they co-created with one of the organizers also part of that group.

"What are the practices I would have pride about passing on?" Cooper is asking these days. "If my kids were doing X, Y, and Z inside of their relationships across race? . . . Or what are the behaviors inside of white bodies that I could be like, 'That got transformed in this generation. . . . I'm proud of that, it's continuing'?" Cooper is invested in practices in their life and with a few other families, seeking to embody intentional responses to that question. At the heart of it, for Cooper, is high-quality close relationships in their sphere of influence.

*   *   *

We all have a sphere of influence. In fact, we have many of them. These are the day-in and day-out life places where the millions of us learning to act in different ways can move the needle for transformation. Regardless of family status, level of education, work situation, age, or anything else, we all have the capacity to have an impact.

Communities of color, especially Black communities, have long legacies of assuming the necessity of connecting with others, plugging in to create some kind of change or contribute to the well-being of their community. When I began working primarily with students of color at my university, I discovered that within a few months into their first semester—even if they'd moved from out of state—Black students were in meaningful connection with local Black community groups (a church, a YMCA, an after-school program dedicated to the well-being of youth, and so forth).

As a university, we were eagerly growing service-learning opportunities and finding ways to ensure students got academic credit for community engagement. But from the moment they stepped on campus, most Black students began doing that on their own and outside the formal system.

Being oriented to participate in generative mutual support is a response to generations of needing to do so. Pervasive racism has meant communities of color have always known they couldn't count on formal structures (universities, for example!) to meet their needs. They've always created alternative means to survive and thrive. A sense of collective collaboration as life necessity grows from historical and contemporary experiences of marginalization.

Such dispositions are far less common among white Americans. Our lack of a history of needing to organize for survival, especially among the more economically secure, has left us with more individualistic orientations. We tend to be less clear about how change happens. We are less likely to presume we can play a role in bringing meaningful change in our communities. When we do presume we can play such a role, our orientations are often toward charity and volunteerism instead of mutual aid and strategic justice.

I'm speaking in generalizations and tendencies, of course. It takes only a five-minute conversation with someone like Cooper to understand that we can develop an orientation to collective care. We can learn how to make change.

So as we nurture our yearning to be part of meaningful, just change and tarry (thank you again, George Yancy) with the question of transforming white communities, it's worth developing intentional awareness about our spheres of influence.

My spheres of influence are the parts of my life where my presence makes a difference. Where it affects what the space or place is like. My workplace is a sphere of influence. So is my family—both my family of origin and my chosen family. My neighborhood may be a sphere of influence. My child's school surely is. So are the local recreational sports leagues or music programs or whatever else I or my kids might be involved in. The list goes on and on.

Once we've identified these spheres, we can map a plan for being change agents in our day-to-day lives.

I'd lived in the suburbs of Des Moines for more than eight years when a flyer showed up on my front door. It announced that some of my neighbors were creating a neighborhood association. They'd already given the association a fancy name that hearkened back to the days the neighborhood had first been zoned for development.

I didn't feel great when I read the flyer, and frankly, the name they were giving the association annoyed me. I know enough about the histories of the suburbs to know that, whether intentional or not, white racial bonding (as well as middle- to upperclass Christian bonding) often gels in these kinds of associations.

I immediately decided I wanted nothing to do with this project. I didn't turn in the form. I didn't send in any dues. I brazenly ignored the occasional invitations to block parties.

If you're seeing red flags in my behavior, I say sincerely that I'm glad you do. Without consciously processing the fact I was doing so, I basically decided I'd sit on the sidelines while something I knew could be a breeding ground for racism grew right under my nose.

About two years into its existence, the association conducted a survey. It included questions about what people liked and didn't like about our neighborhood. Once again I didn't participate, because this exercise made the hair on my arms stand up.

When the survey results were stuffed into our mailboxes—whether we wanted them or not—they were shared in a tone that oozed (white) Iowa nice.

For those of you who don't live in the Midwest, Iowa nice is a singsongy pleasant tone that is passive-aggressive as all get-out. My sister who's an occasional stand-up comic described it once in a skit. Someone comes up to her and says, "Wow, that's a nice haircut. . . . Did you cut it yourself?" Or another actual thing said to her at work once: "You did a great job in your presentation today. . . . I wasn't expecting such good work from you!"

Here are some of the Iowa nice survey results that landed in my mailbox:

"We like the manicured flower beds in the front of our houses."

"We don't like extra vehicles parked in some front yards."

"We like it when everyone decorates their houses for the holidays."

"We don't like it when some of us forget to put our trash cans away quickly after pickup day."

The list went on.

The *we* part bothered me the most. *We* who?

I thought of my neighbors a few houses down. This was a multigenerational Black family headed by a matriarch who cared for six or seven of her siblings' children. I'd gotten to know her family over the years. I knew a desire to access public schools in a district that had more resources than Des Moines was one of several reasons they'd chosen to live there. There were always lots of people coming and going. Lots of cars.

To me the report felt hostile to families like theirs. I wondered how it felt to my neighbor.

I grumbled aloud about it to another neighbor. This was a white family in which the dad was a veteran who'd done several tours in Iraq. They had four children under the age of six. Both parents worked really hard. They had an RV sitting in their yard. It was the only way they could take road trips to see family that the mom, in particular, missed terribly. I told them I thought the survey was obnoxious. They told me someone had recently called in an anonymous complaint about their RV. They'd been given a citation, along with a short window in which to figure out what they were going to do to store it in a manner that aligned with "code."

That made me mad.

I stayed uninvolved.

A couple more years passed. A new Black family moved in

down the street. One Saturday, when they'd been there about nine months, I was driving past their house and saw a police car out front with its lights on. The woman, who seemed to be the head of the household, a few young children, and one other adult were sitting in the driveway. It was a beautiful warm afternoon. They seemed to be having a celebration.

I could tell from the adults' faces as they talked to the officer that they hadn't called him. They looked surprised. They were shaking their heads no. Aside from the presence of a police officer, the whole scene seemed serene.

"I wonder what that officer is doing there and if those folks are okay?" I mused aloud. My nine-year-old was in the car. "Should we stop?" they asked. "I don't know," I said. "I kind of want to. But I'm also worried it might embarrass them or make whatever's going on worse. I'm not sure what to do."

I slowed down, then decided to keep driving. I stressed about that choice for the rest of the day. The next day, after talking it through with two different people I trust, I decided I had to follow up.

Marching up and ringing the doorbell didn't seem quite right. I kept trying to puzzle out an unobtrusive way to introduce myself, say hello, and see if I could find a way to acknowledge what I'd seen. I also knew my attempt to engage could be unwelcome, offensive, or any number of things.

I decided if I saw the adults outside, I'd stop and go for it. But I gave myself a deadline. If I hadn't seen anyone outside by a certain day, I'd take a deep breath and ring the doorbell anyway.

That day came. I'd seen no one outside. So I made cookies.

Butterflies in my stomach, I walked down the street, questioning the wisdom of what I was doing.

As I approached the house, I saw a teenager riding his scooter up and down the block. I was fairly certain I'd seen him before and that he lived there. Instead of going to the door I walked over to him.

I introduced myself. I said I wanted to welcome them to the neighborhood and gave him the cookies, and we chatted for a moment. Then I said, "Hey, I don't want to be nosy or get in your business in a way that doesn't feel okay, but I noticed a police officer was here last weekend, and as your neighbor, I just wanted to check in and see if you all were okay."

The young man paused, then said, "I'm going to go get my aunt."

He went inside. I heard him call his aunt's name and tell her there was a neighbor outside who wanted to talk. I heard her respond. She sounded annoyed. I heard her say something I couldn't understand. Then I heard him say back, "No, this one seems nice." I questioned my life choices again.

My neighbor came outside. "Can I help you?"

Now all I could do was explain myself. "I'm so sorry to disturb you. I didn't mean to make you come outside. But I'm one of your neighbors." I pointed toward my house. "I told Jacob I'm not trying to pry, but I saw the police here the other day and I wanted to . . . I don't know . . . just see if you were okay. It seemed like you were surprised he was here. I wanted to tell you I noticed that."

The woman listened. Then she said, "Who are you again?"

I stumbled through another round, saying the same thing with different words. Still she stayed quiet. So I finally said something totally awkward. "Maybe you're like, 'Why is this white woman showing up at my house?' But I know what can happen with police and I want to be a good neighbor. I almost stopped when I saw that police officer here the other day, but I also didn't know if that would have felt bad to you."

She started to nod her head and stepped a little closer. "Okay, I'm going to be honest," she said. "The cop was totally fine. He was actually embarrassed to be here. It's your white neighbors who are the problem. We were just out here celebrating my daughter's birthday. Minding our business. Two white women walked by and stared at us as they passed. I told my boyfriend, 'Just watch.' Sure enough, not ten minutes later, the police car pulled up. He'd gotten a call that we were playing our music too loud. Of course we had music on—but not loud. He had to check it out, but knew it was nonsense from the moment he pulled up."

Now I felt embarrassed, angry, sad. I didn't know what else to say so started with, "I'm sorry that happened to you."

She went on to tell me they'd moved into this house, excited to have more space. They were hoping for more quiet than the options they could afford in Des Moines made possible. In the less than nine months since they had arrived, the police had been called to their house five times.

Every time by an anonymous concerned neighbor.

Every time for nothing more than existing.

She repeated herself to me. "I don't know what kind of neighborhood you all have here, but that's what it's been like. Don't you have a neighborhood association or something? It seems like if you want to be a good neighbor, you should go talk to them."

I was stricken and chastened. Rightly so. In my self-righteous annoyance, I'd abdicated my responsibility and agency for influencing the racial climate on my very own block.

I also had to reckon with another reality. Because I'd not gotten involved before now, I had no obvious or direct path to show solidarity with this new member of our neighborhood. I'd built no relationships in my own neighborhood community that would have made it possible for me to leverage my influence with her or on her behalf in response to racial harassment.

I had ignored this sphere of influence almost completely.

None of us can take on everything in the world. None of us can participate in a full-throttle way in every sphere our daily lives bump into, move through, or are impacted by. I can't be all in at the PTA and knock on doors for political candidates, push the local soccer league to be more inclusive and organize with SURJ, and also be all in at my neighborhood association (plus somehow parent, work, eat, sleep). All of us—regardless of our racial identities—make choices.

But that actually brings us to the point of mapping our spheres of influence. The point is intention and awareness.

My neighborhood was one of the most immediate and direct spaces I could have engaged with, especially given how powerful neighborhood associations can be. Plus I'd had a chance to be in on the ground floor. If there's anyone in my life I want to be present with and for, it's people in my local community. My neighbors! The kids who live on the block and play with my kids.

Cooper's focus shifted at the end of 2020 because the pace of their life had become unsustainable. They had gotten caught in some of the dynamics of white antiracist culture I described earlier—for example, when I wouldn't grieve because I was worried it made me fragile, or when the white woman was exhausted but didn't think she was allowed to set limits. Given their expertise as a trainer and the demands of the moment in which it seemed like so many people were ready, Cooper said, "Let's go." They felt like they should say yes to every ask that came in. They told me that this orientation was complicated—it may have had a little bit of saviorism in it, but it also came from a desire to be a reliable white partner in the work they were doing with Black colleagues.

By the end of 2020, Cooper had yes'ed themselves to the point of developing severe health challenges. I have to assume such a pace also came at a cost to the rest of their family as well, which included a partner and several children.

But something else began to emerge for Cooper as they went through this health crisis and reflected back on the year. They began to reckon with what kind of embodiment (Cooper's word is actually *incarnation*) is necessary to actually transform the conditions of racism. And from Cooper's perspective, the up-swell of demand for antiracism training combined with everything having just gone virtual became something of "a recipe for disaster." While some good work did happen, the systems and practices for what transformational white antiracism requires weren't there.

"When you have trauma happening at that scale," said Cooper, "the trauma from George Floyd, the trauma from the pandemic. We had all this trauma material floating around in our bodies, in our brains, everywhere. And all of a sudden we're all scaling up. We probably should have paused and said, 'Wait, we actually need to slow down.'"

Antiracism trainings began to move at the "speed of trauma and the speed of the internet." Wide breadth. Large scale. Disembodied from one another. Not done in relationship.

Meanwhile, during this same period, Cooper's work with the group of Black activists they *were* in relationship with locally stood as a powerful and compelling contrast. Thanks to a "brilliant Black organizer" named Lake Fitzgerald, the organizing Cooper got pulled into more deeply beginning that summer of 2020 was done so differently. Instead of moving at the speed of trauma and the internet, this group was practicing moving at the speed adrienne maree brown insists is the pace justice work must move, "at the speed of trust."

The values antiracism educators teach are values this group of people are striving to *live* in their local community. "I would say instead of a community of preachers, we're a community of practice," says Cooper. "Antiracism culture has developed this climate in which everyone is looking for a 'hot take.' Our community is striving for 'hot tries.'"

This multiracial group of mostly queer and trans people has developed sustainable mutual aid networks. They've kept an intergenerational Black family who is housing insecure and in which there are several children with disabilities fed for nearly two years. "We are getting diapers to Black moms," Cooper said.

"We aren't talking about Black lives mattering," Cooper said. "We are asking how do we practice Black lives mattering *here?* How do we practice 'land back' *here?* How do we practice 'families belong together' *here?*"

Meanwhile, another quality deeply aligned with careful pace and small scale is attention to a culture of commitment they are consciously growing. They are building a culture in which people opt in to relationship and collective care. They invite one another to move "from a place of desire and capacity."[1] This is in contrast to using group pressure to get folks to do more or guilt tactics if they aren't, which sometimes shape the culture of community organizing.

Fitzgerald and Cooper also ended up taking the lead in developing Communal School (CS). Like so many families, theirs were struggling to navigate virtual school and working from home and were facing hard decisions about what to do when the schools reopened but safety was still uncertain. So, during the second year of the pandemic, a small group of families decided to pool their resources and create a small school.

CS is multiracial. There are four core families. Even when everyone gathers, there are no more than twenty-five people at the most.

"We are village-making." The entire experience is rooted in transformative justice. The participants in CS have created agreements about how they will tend to their relationships with one another. These agreements operate with and among the children, as well as with and among the adults.

Within CS, different people share responsibilities for different parts of the curriculum. Some of the kids in CS are in a hybrid model where they also attend public school part of the day.

As a result, CS has created a structure in which "secure relationship attachments" are possible.

For example, last year as part of their history unit they all went together as families to an Indigenous settlement several hours from where they live. They listened—children and adults together—as the guide told them about the history of their people. There were devastatingly difficult parts of the telling. The guide pulled no punches about the violence, including the massacres of children that were part of the U.S. government's military removal of Native people. Cooper described the children in CS as all having emotional reactions. They experienced horror and fear. The younger ones needed to get close to the adults. Cooper described their young child needing to be held as he listened.

But Cooper went on to say that the depth of engagement all the children manifested was profound and beautiful. They did a craft project with a Native elder during part of their visit. Later the elder told the adults that this group of children was like no other children she'd seen come through. They were so connected. Curious. Joyful.

After that trip some of the white children in the group shared that this history was making them feel ashamed about being white. In response, CS convened what they call a Huddle.

CS has created many such ritualized practices. "We also created Mingus Moments!" said Cooper.[2] Mia Mingus is a transformative justice and disability rights educator and writer. She teaches that mindful tending of the "small things" in our relationships often prevents "big things" from happening; this has been vital to how the relationships in CS are tended. ("I read everything Mingus writes. It informs everything we do in CS," said Cooper. So I've put Mingus in the Further Resources for you, too.)

In a Huddle, CS comes together to mindfully explore something important for the well-being of the people in the group. In this one, they planned and held a radically honest and deep conversation about white shame.

"It was complex, and it was hard, cringey, and intimate," said Cooper. "It ended up bringing everyone in CS closer. And I just kept thinking, *Man, if I'd had this as a kid, I'd be so much different. I wouldn't have caused nearly the harm I caused as I was trying to figure out who I was and what it meant to live in a white body.*"

Yes.

This multiracial community of humans has built a container that can hold such transformative ways of being with one another and in the world.

"What are the practices that I would have pride about passing on?" asks Cooper.

What priorities do I need to set? What relationships do I need to grow if I, too, want to pass on a different way of being in my spheres of influence?

These are the questions I would ask and try to answer if I

were to get a redo on my neighborhood association situation. Whatever the sphere of influences we are in, mapping who we are and what we want to grow is a worthy practice.

For example, in my neighborhood association, I would first have had to carve out time on my calendar. I would have had to give something else up to have been a reliable presence at those meetings.

I probably would have reached out to the person getting things off the ground, too. A face-to-face conversation before the first gathering would have helped that relationship and given me a better feel for what hopes, agendas, and motivations were at work.

I would have also tried to do some research. A local librarian could have helped me learn about the racial history of housing development in my neighborhood. Maybe I would have reached out to our county housing authority's project on redlining in Des Moines so I could bring that historical context to those early meetings. Helping ensure history and my commitment to growing an inclusive culture in our neighborhood that didn't repeat that history would have been an intentional contribution I could bring.

Friends who were already trying to be a presence for antiracist values in their neighborhood associations could have been resources I would have turned to as well. It's rare we have to totally reinvent the wheel or figure something out completely on our own.

The internet may not be so great for building the relationships we need to stay engaged in transformative justice work. But it's ideal for resources. Many organizations have ideas about how neighborhood associations can be places to effect socially just change. Lots of people have thought about racism, economics, and housing.

I would certainly have suggested as an agenda item, at a very early meeting, that we spend some time carefully discussing what we mean by *safety*. This is a word neighborhood associations always bring up. Policing is where white people typically go when we think about safety. I would have wanted to bring in an explicit conversation about the safety and well-being of Black and Brown neighbors from the beginning. "What kind of neighbor-to-neighbor dynamics do we want our association to help grow?" would have been a great question.

Last but not least, before that first meeting I would have probably knocked on the doors of some of my neighbors I had reason to assume might share some of my values. I'd let them know I was planning to be part of the association and share my concerns about it and hopes for it. If they shared those hopes and concerns, I would have asked if they would come to the meetings, too.

We need each other.

Before the conversation with my neighbor ended that day, I told her I would follow up in response to what she'd shared with me. She encouraged me to do so.

I reached out to my local city council representative and told her what had happened. (I did not disclose the identity or location of my neighbor.) I asked her what role she might play in helping our neighborhood address the issue.

She asked me if I would be willing to be part of a conversation that she would arrange between her and the police chief. I said okay.

I called some friends to get help preparing for that meeting. They supported me in figuring out what kinds of questions I should ask the police chief and what strategies to use to try to ensure the conversation was meaningful and not just placation. They encouraged me to be specific, asking how the police department vets 911 calls to determine if they are true emergencies; what policies prevent officers from being used as tools for racial harassment; what consequences there are for the caller who engages in bad faith use of 911—especially repeat offenders; what structures of accountability exist once a department learns of these kinds of problems in their precinct; and how they keep the public informed.

The conversation surprised me. After I shared an overview of the situation (again without saying which neighbor it was) the police chief told me he knew which house I was talking about. He'd pulled the 911 log when our council rep asked for the meeting. He saw exactly what was happening.

He identified some of the ways he'd already given thought to how his officers were being deployed (even before this specific situation) and some of the structures in place for nonemergency calls. He identified some structures they were developing and described a general timeline for when they expected these to be in place.

And then he said to me: "But the really important work here is to get this conversation going in the neighborhood association. Can you get me invited?" (Dammit again.)

He went on to say there'd been upticks in all kinds of calls to the police station. He said he had a vested interest in helping the neighborhood association become a place from which healthier and more neighborly ways of engaging one another could be encouraged, in contrast to the quick move to get police involved in everything. He emphasized this was especially important given the racial disparities he could see in the logbook, which weren't news to him and weren't a problem just in our neighborhood.

He also told me he planned to go by and have a conversation with my neighbor to check in, as well as to see if he could open up more direct communication with her. (When I heard this,

I was extra glad I'd told her I was planning to follow up and gotten her okay. Score one for remembering to be attentive to the fact that when we try to show up in attempted solidarity, our actions can have consequences for people of color.)

The moment I left that meeting I went back to my neighbor's house. She wasn't home, so I left a note that told her how the follow-up had gone. I let her know the police chief was planning to stop by and why. I also left her my cell phone number and said I'd be glad to come over when he did if that felt better to her or if she had any other questions or concerns and wanted to talk more.

I'll close the loop on my story by saying it didn't have a happy, resolved ending. I did have some ongoing communication and exchanges with my neighbor and her nephew. But during the period of time in which I attempted to connect with the neighborhood association, my neighbor and her family moved. Within a month of her family's departure, I realized I was going to be moving as well, and within six months I had. But the lesson about choosing with intention, and really prioritizing the most local places possible for my involvement, has stuck with me.

I hope there's something in this for you, too.

I'll close the loop on Cooper's story by saying it has a happier trajectory, one nowhere near its ending. CS is continuing forward. So is the transformational relationship-based work in direct support of Black lives that Cooper is plugged into with a community of humans also creating belonging with one another as a constant practice.

Mapping our spheres of influence doesn't yield magical results. But it's a practice that can be so grounding. It's a practice that makes us notice what, where, and when we are involved (or not).

Most important, it's a practice that can help us bring our commitment to racial justice and white antiracism out of the realm of the abstract. From the internal realm of our hearts and minds, and beyond the teachings and principles we've learned, our spheres of influence are the places where we materialize our values in concrete action in the world, in local contexts, in our daily lives. How am I, how are we, practicing Black lives matter . . . here?

TAKE A NEXT STEP

1. List your spheres of influence. Use the table below to identify your formal and informal power. (The president of your school's PTA, a decision-maker over some aspect of your organization at work, or a parent—formal power. Member of a church community, a volunteer coach for your kid's soccer team, a neighbor in an apartment building or a suburban development—informal power.) Consider the overall racial dynamics in this sphere and the role you play.

2. Focus on at least one sphere of influence in which you want to grow your influence for antiracism and racial justice in that space or place. You may have no idea where to start or what that means. *Yet.* That's okay! Identify what you need to learn. Start a list of skills you need to develop to grow your capacity to influence antiracism in that specific space.

3. Commit. Find people within that sphere of influence and outside of it! Who do I need to talk to, be in relationship with, try to grow a relationship with? How can I participate with as much accountability as possible and in a spirit of collaboration and connection? Because, regardless of who is in the room, white antiracism is always a multiracial and a collective project.

Spheres of Influence Reflection Exercise

PHASE 1

STEP ONE	STEP TWO	STEP THREE
What are the spheres of influence in my life right now? (List as many as possible.)	What is my role in or relationship to this sphere of influence? What kind of formal and/or informal power do I have?	What kind of role do I play in terms of racial learning and antiracist learning or change in each of these spheres? What kind of role might I play or change might I want to see?

PHASE 2

STEP ONE	STEP TWO	STEP THREE
What kind of educational work do I need to do to build my capacity to be an antiracist change maker in this sphere? What do I need to read, listen to, learn about? Who do I need to talk to? What kind of commitment am I making to be intentional in this sphere of influence?	What racial justice or antiracist initiatives are underway here? How can I support them? What initiatives need to be created or generated? What skills and tools do I need to be part of that? What questions do I need to ask, explore, and seek to understand to move in that direction both clearly and responsibly?	What does my community of accountability look like? Who can I count on to support me by holding me to my commitments? What relationships do I need to focus on and nourish to grow an accountability network for myself?

How Do We Change Our (Predominantly White) X?

As we start to make meaningful movement toward antiracism in organizations or in other collective spaces, racial differentials in experience, knowledge, and capacity pose a significant challenge. The challenge is especially powerful in settings that are predominantly white.

The school that Lisa Johnston, the white parent we met in the introduction, is affiliated with was not unique. Following the massive outpouring of justice-focused resistance in 2020, parent-teacher associations all over the country began to take up the question more seriously than they had before: How can we make this school more antiracist, more equitable, a place where the well-being and educational experience of all students of color and their families are given the focus they need and deserve?

This question may have seemed long overdue to parents of color whose children were attending predominantly white schools. Perhaps such parents welcomed the salience of that question finally being acknowledged. Perhaps, even knowing the question was vital, they also experienced some trepidation at the thought of white parents (or staff and teachers) rushing in to make efforts in this direction. Black parents and other parents of color, even in schools where some rapport, trust, and multiracial initiatives were already underway, didn't need a podcast like *Nice White Parents* to know that "yes, we must do this work, and wow can it go sideways with all these white folks leading the charge."

Some PTAs may have been engaged in equity work for some time. Many were focusing on the question for the first time. But wherever they were and however long they'd been at it, the different levels of knowledge about and experience responding to racism that existed between parents of color and white parents created remarkably similar challenges. And these aren't unique to schools.

(By the way, if excellent work and meaningful connection with others trying to work through such thorny issues in public schools are something you need, the organization Integrated Schools is worth checking out! See Further Resources at the back of this book.)

We need models that can help us be thoughtful and strategic. We need to design strategies and structures. I find it really helpful in the context of predominantly white entities to think in terms of two concentric circles.

The center circle is the priority. We start by figuring out how to invest most deeply there. Which is to say, the needs and concerns of people of color in spaces come first. Resources, attention, support for self-determination, and programming to strengthen and nourish the center are where predominantly white organizations need to begin.

The outer circle is where we resource the education of white constituencies to help them learn to do better. This is vital to strengthening antiracism in organizations, because what white people are doing or not doing directly affects people of color. Growing white capacity for equitable behavior and practices not only contributes directly to the well-being of people of color but also moves the organization as a whole farther down the road to transformation.

In fact, if we don't grow white capacity, not only will various forms of racially harmful impact persist, but they can worsen. There is always risk of white backlash. So as an entity or organization invests in the center, an ongoing commitment to trainings, dialogues, and advocacy partnership opportunities in the outer circle is just as important.

Below are three examples of how we can approach the challenges of racial justice in predominantly white spaces. My hope is that they will stoke ideas about what concrete steps toward racially just change could look like in the entities or organizations that you are part of.

Example One: A School Building

Every day in buildings across the country Black and Brown students and all students of color walk into classrooms with mostly white teachers. In so many contexts, they sit at desks next to white students who bring whatever racial culture or conversations are happening at home into the classroom with them.

Of course, the experiences and needs of parents of color whose children are students in those buildings, as well as the experience of teaching staff and administrators of color, are connected to the experiences of students as well.

This was the case in the school Lisa Johnston was affiliated with.

As she worked through the trepidation *Nice White Parents* had raised, the small group of parent leaders Johnston was working with decided to organize a series of small groups focused on building the capacity for antiracism. The focus was whiteness. The goal was to influence the school culture by focusing on the white parents. Parent leaders knew they would have to clearly explain to everyone in the school community the reasoning behind such an experience. Namely, that white socialization affects everyone—not only white children, but children of color at school, as well as parents of color.

At Johnston's school, a small multiracial team kicked off this work. But in a context where such an idea is generated by a group of white parents, it is so important that parent leaders engage parents of color as early as possible. Certainly long before any idea is fully developed, let alone pushed into the broader school environment. In ideal circumstances it's not just white parents initiating and/or sponsoring such efforts. Still, if white leadership is the only option, it's better to do it this way than to not do it at all. But here again, high levels of transparent communication with parents of color are vital to ensure clarity, as well as genuine opportunities for any ideas or concerns parents of color have to influence and change the direction, timing, or some other aspect of programming.

Before the white antiracism workshops got underway, the team helped create an affinity group for parents of color. A direct relationship was established with the principal. The purpose was to proactively nurture relationships between administrative leadership and families of color, ensuring the experiences, knowledge, and needs of families of color in the building had the most direct route possible to be heard.

As the parent leadership group got ready to announce the white antiracism conversations to the entire school, they made clear the six-week online workshop was open to anyone who wanted to attend. But they also made clear that the focus was *white* antiracism and explained the "why" behind such a focus. They secured the principal's willingness to endorse the project. He made a short video they included in the email invitation in which he said why this workshop was important for the climate of the whole school and encouraged folks to attend. The parents also planned with the principal for what kind of support he would need if critical questions or even harsh pushback came.

The white antiracism workshop was free. But the leadership group team created an invitation for white parents who took part to donate. The funds raised would be used to hire a professional educator of color who would work with teachers to develop skills, resources, and abilities to teach in more culturally and racially responsive and inclusive ways.

Resourcing teacher development is obviously vital to the well-being of students of color. And the invitation to create white parental investment in the well-being of children by raising funds, as well as connecting this initiative to the antiracism work on whiteness, created a shared effort in the school.

The model I've just described could be developed even beyond what the parent leaders in Johnston's school did. For example, a parent or parents from the families of color affinity group might sit in on the PTA as liaisons. (This is not to suggest there might not also be additional parents of color in the PTA.) This structure would open a collaborative communication channel between parents so often underrepresented in the PTA. A PTA officer could serve as a liaison in the spaces where parents of color gather with administrators, or perhaps a white parent whom parents of color identify as a good candidate—someone who has learned to practice listening to the experiences of people of color with care—could serve in that role.

In this way a PTA would hopefully end up supporting events and planning school initiatives more reflective of the needs of all families in the school. Over time, the strength of the perennial question "Why aren't more parents of color active in my school's PTA?" might dissipate. As the work of a PTA becomes more relevant and meaningful to everyone, a culture of genuine openness to the leadership and vision of parents of color is established—not to mention healthier interracial relationships among parents. More parents of color might just decide the PTA is a place where they want to share their time, energy, and expertise.

By building intentional structures, being clear how they interact and making sure there are folks tasked with supporting consistent interaction and relationship-tending, as well as by creating communication channels between administration, parents of color, white parents, and official school bodies like the PTA, white families making antiracist commitments are more likely to remain aligned with and mobilized in ways that strengthen, support, and amplify what families of color need and deserve in a school. And if or when our efforts do go sideways, we will also be better prepared to respond or change course quickly and in meaningful ways.

Example Two: The Crew Scholars Program[1]

The Crew Scholars Program at Drake University began in 2013. Black and Latinx students came to campus as ready to excel as did their white peers. They had the same high school grade-point averages and entrance exam scores. But as is true with most predominantly white universities in the United States, racial disparities existed in rates of retention, graduation rates, and GPA gaps.

The Crew model vigorously rejected the deficit thinking, pervasive in higher education, that presumes racial disparities exist because students of color just aren't "college ready." Any existing deficits were in the institution, not in the students.

Attending college while experiencing various forms of racism gets in students' way; that's the problem. Crew was built to respond to the specific ways racial harm manifested on campus. The goal, in a sense, was to run as much interference as possible between racism and students, so Crew Scholars could thrive the way they came to college prepared to do.

It's worked. Within a couple of years, the gaps closed. Students in Crew began to demonstrate graduation rates higher than any other constituency of Drake students. Retention rates among Crew Scholars also quickly increased. They became, on average, on par with or higher than retention rates for their white peers.

That doesn't mean racism is gone at Drake. There is ever more work to do. But Crew has been remarkably successful. And the success of Crew students, as well as their increasing numbers, continues to dramatically change the university as a whole. When increasing numbers of students of color come to a school, stay at a school, and *thrive* at a school (which often translates into campus leadership, greater visibility, creativity more generously shared with the broader campus community, and more), the entire campus becomes a better, more educationally excellent environment for everyone.

Students of color are at the center of the Crew model. Crew places a particular, but not exclusive, focus on Black and Latino/a/x students. The program is laser-focused on resourcing this student constituency. The resourcing is not in the form of extra academic support, which so many predominantly white institutions presume students of color need (following deficit theory logic, which assumes something is lacking in the students or else, "why wouldn't they be doing better here?"). The resourcing is tethered directly to specific harms racism causes—both within the campus environment and resulting from structural injustices that create inequal access to higher education prior to arrival. It is a model based on redress and repair.

Perhaps the most important form of resourcing is the creation of a formal space for students of color to build community with one another. They do so with the direct and sustained institutional support of at least two Drake employees (one a professor and one a staff person).

This community-building takes place in programming that begins three days before the first day of entering first-year student orientation. It continues formally for the first four semesters in the form of a weekly class.

Even when the larger racial climate creates challenges for students of color, a community of mutual support increases thriving in a powerful way. Community provides an anchored space where students who are underrepresented can be seen, acknowledged, and relieved from the burden of needing to explain themselves. Students can walk into a room less "armored up" because they aren't having to anticipate the possibility of racial harm—which is something students (and staff and faculty) have to constantly scan for on a predominantly white campus.

Crew students are also invited to live with and near one another in the residence halls if they want to. This is another way to center their experiences and mitigate harm. Students of color often find themselves the subjects of curiosity or unwelcome questions or comments by their white peers, who arrive on campus with uneven prior experiences and levels of racial literacy and competency. If Crew students live near one another, this decreases the number of such interactions and the experience of isolation that comes when they do happen.

It's also a way for the institution to signal clearly that "your job isn't to educate your white peers." Instead, the message is "You have the same job as every other student at this school: to focus on getting a great education." Students of color are more able to do precisely this the more they have spaces in which they experience safety and can be seen and valued for who they are in their full authentic selves.

There are other components in Crew that support the well-being of students of color by investing in the growth and development of white antiracism among white people on campus. For example, Crew students are all assigned committed mentors (of diverse racial identities, including many who are white). Mentors undergo training to better understand the challenges predominantly white university settings place in the way of students of color.

Students in Crew have regular contact with someone outside the program and their major. This mentor's only role in their educational journey is to be a listening ear and an advocate when necessary—a human being they know is in their corner and is specifically charged with accompanying them as they move through their university experience.

Meanwhile, the mentor aspect of the program improves collective interracial relating on campus. Dozens of students of color every year (hundreds of students, by this point) and nearly a dozen staff and faculty mentors every year are supported in building relationships with one another. This alone improves the overall campus climate and community.

Mentors—especially the white ones—end up changed by their relationships with Crew students, which come only after the mentors have also received antiracism training. In a strong mentor/mentee relationship, mentors often end up learning more about the racial climate at Drake and the day-to-day racial challenges students of color navigate than they ever have before.

They begin to show up differently in their other roles: more equity- and justice-minded on hiring committees; clearer about why diversity matters, and more willing to go to bat for it in all kinds of places; more courageous in responding if they hear a colleague resistant to growing their own commitment and skills for equity. Over time the community of mentors become ambassadors who are emboldened and skilled at changing the overall racial climate of the campus.

The design of Crew is multitiered and longitudinal. The well-being of students of color is directly affected by the faculty teaching skills, the posture toward equity and inclusion white students develop, the policies and processes through which the institution grows demographic diversity, and the climate for inclusion in staff and faculty spaces as well.

So, various investments in transformation among white communities on campus overlap with resourcing students of color—for example, professional development (both required and/or incentivized) for faculty to develop their ability to teach in ways more responsive to a diverse student body, and workshops in which staff and faculty explore the history of racism in higher education and strive to better understand the larger forces still at work affecting the environment in which we're all teaching, learning, and—in some cases—living.

A required course introduces Drake's publicly stated commitment to equity and inclusion to all first-year students. Here they become enculturated into an intellectual understanding of campus values. Another required course later in students' programs focuses on racial justice in the United States. These courses are educationally vital for all students.

The more diverse the campus becomes, the more ably we can recognize where we continue to have gaps in policies and processes—whether at the level of hiring, bias-reporting, alumni relations, or in other places. The more we are able to recognize these gaps and build stronger multiracial teams to address them, the more the institution changes again, becoming more attractive to and able to support the thriving of students, staff, and faculty of color.

Crew has proven to be a powerful model to intervene in what can sometimes be a chicken-or-egg problem: institutional desires for more diversity, but a climate that makes it difficult to sustain and risky for people of color to be part of.

This model is also one that might be used in many different businesses or organizational contexts, far beyond higher education.

Example Three: SURJ, Community Organizing

Showing Up for Racial Justice (SURJ) is a national organization with local affiliates. The purpose of SURJ, as they state it, is to get more white people off the sidelines and into the struggle against white supremacy. By definition, then, SURJ is a predominantly white organization. But SURJ explicitly understands itself as part of the multiracial movement for justice and was established by longtime white antiracist organizers who were in long-term and publicly accountable relationships with organizers of color.

The organizational model we use in our local chapter in Des Moines draws directly from the principles and structures advocated by the national SURJ (not all local SURJ chapters necessarily follow this model).

Des Moines SURJ is committed to supporting and amplifying the work and growth of racial justice in Iowa by supporting and amplifying the agendas and leadership of organizations that are led by people of color and activists of color. (To be clear, those organizations are not part of SURJ.)

A primary orientation of SURJ is to invest in the center by working closely with up to four or five BIPOC-led groups. We call these groups our accountability partners. The process of identifying and growing the connections with the particular groups we've come into partnership with was—and continues to be—more art than science.

Sometimes partnerships have resulted because some member of SURJ had already been involved with a particular group. As this person became consistently active in SURJ as well, increasing contact and connection unfolded into a more formal partnership. Sometimes a group has come to SURJ and made some kind of ask related to increasing white support for an event, an initiative, or even a whole organization. Over time, as such engagement continued, relationships were built and accountability partnership began to be an obvious next step.

However the partnership has come to be, each has been preceded by meaningful relationship, typically some kind of action or work together. In other words, we don't just march in cold and just say, "Hey! Do you want to be our accountability partner?!"

What the relationship between accountability partners and SURJ means is multifold. Des Moines SURJ makes a formal commitment to amplify and support the work of that partner. When we receive requests for support, our accountability partners are the priority if (or when) our resources of time, energy, or funds are limited.

This support means many different things. It means getting the word out to our members to write letters or make calls to a public official in response to a problem or organizing goal a people of color–led group has identified. It means asking members to show up to events at the request of our accountability partners. It might mean we engage in fundraising on behalf of a partner—doing a direct ask, putting on a fundraising event—

simply funneling resources that have come our way back out to our accountability partners. (Other than minimal dues to national SURJ or occasional needs for flyers or tabling signs, we don't hold on to any resources for our own organizational support. Also, we're completely volunteer.)

In addition to supporting a particular organization, we engage in regular work to grow the capacity for activism, antiracism, and racial justice among white people in Des Moines (white people, do work in your own communities!). This might look like a session on how to write a letter to the editor. Then when the session is done, we ask those who attended the session to write such a letter around an issue or campaign one of our accountability partners is working on.

For many years we've facilitated a session on how to engage our state legislature and identified specific racial justice concerns and aspirations that will come up during the legislative cycle. We support our membership in remaining active and activated around legislative priorities our accountability partners see as priorities.

It might be a session on white racial identity development— a reflective workshop designed to invite growth in antiracist capacity through processing one's life experiences with the tools of social psychology (looking at the roles of shame and guilt in white life, for example). It might be a presentation on the history of redlining in Des Moines so we can better understand our own context or, as I described earlier, a hands-on practice session on how to have conversations with our white families.

Over the course of each year, some of these educational sessions are led by white people. Sometimes they're led by an interracial team. Some are led by people of color, including people who are leaders in the organizations we're in accountable relationships with.

Sometimes, simultaneously with these sessions, we also sponsor a book group. This space and format can attract a different type of person who may not be inclined to come to an activist meeting. But it isn't unusual for people to end up getting involved in SURJ after participating in a book group. Even if they don't, we grow our network.

Much like the example of the school building, we've tried to develop clear structures to support good communication and invite relationship-building. So, for example, we've identified within SURJ a small group of folks who agree to serve as liaisons with our accountability partners. These people attend the meetings convened by our accountability partners and otherwise take responsibility for cultivating an intergroup relationship.

Liaisons are not just any white person who might express an interest or desire in volunteering in this way. Liaisons are people who have been and continue to be on an intentional journey to grow their skills for humble and careful listening, relating with authenticity, being reliable, and otherwise showing up well when and as they share space with people of color.

The SURJ model is an example of a more informal and less clearly defined entity. It might be applied to other contexts that are also more volunteer- or movement-based than structured—for example, a neighborhood association!

We've heard from so many people and voices that it's well past time: White people, do work on your own communities!

Knowing what to do, knowing how to do it well, and *supporting other white people in learning to do it well, too* are anything but easy.

So we just have to start. And when we do, it's always safe to assume we need to start at the center.

TAKE A NEXT STEP

1. Identify what constituencies are most harmed by racial inequity and racism in your predominantly white organization. Work with others to identify policies, programs, and structures that need to be prioritized for resourcing and supporting such groups.

2. Engage in a similar strategizing exercise: Ask what programs and actions white people need to increase their skills and capacity for antiracism and just inclusion.

3. Depending on the kinds of relationships and leadership that exist, engage people in constituencies at the center, as well as white people who are the most likely to be enthusiastic about interracial and cross-racial relationship-building. Create mechanisms for discussion, programming, and connection that strengthen these relationships on the foundation of a shared commitment to equity and justice.

Conclusion

Let the Real Dance Party Begin

My colleague's eyes got wide after he glanced down to look at the message on his phone. "I have to take this," he whispered. Something seemed wrong. I nodded at him. "I'll be right back," he said and slipped quietly out of the room.

A few minutes later I would find myself planted in a doorway blocking an entrance to the back reading room of our campus library. My arms would be crossed tightly, partially covering the Black Lives Matter logo blazoned on the T-shirt I was wearing. I'd be floating outside my body; watching myself more than actually being myself. The floating version of me would have to prod the actual version of me along into doing whatever the chaotic situation next required of a faculty member.

It wouldn't ever have occurred to me as I left home that night that I might later end up standing in a doorway—as if I actually could stop someone from barging in if they wanted to (especially if they had a gun). A dizzying elixir of adrenaline, cortisol, and who knows what else was released into my veins after our university president came back into the library (he'd left when my colleague did) and addressed the group.

"Sorry, but I need to interrupt." He held his hands up, signaling the person at the microphone to stop talking. "We're not quite sure what's going on, but phones all over campus are ringing. And someone on the other end—we're not sure who; well, it's a recording—speaks some of the most vile, racist things I've ever heard." He went on to tell us campus security was already outside the room and officers from our local police department were on their way.

It was at that moment that I'd gotten up out of my chair and walked over to block the doorway.

As has happened on so many college campuses across the nation, we'd discovered a swastika scratched into the elevator in our main student building, the N-word scrawled on the eraser board outside a Black student's room, notes taped to the door of the room a Latina student lived in that read "make a wall" and "make america [*sic*] great again." But as much as I'd walked with students through all kinds of racist incidents before, nothing in my fourteen years had been like the ten terrible days in November of 2018 that had eventually landed us all in the library.

Someone had slipped a note under a first-year student's residence hall door. It contained repugnant racist and threatening language.

You had to have an ID to get inside the residence halls. So we knew the person who did it was part of our community.

Each day that passed without a suspect being caught found

students of color more wary. Nowhere felt safe. I started to feel on edge, too. I'd peer around the edge of my office door every time I opened it before going in.

There would be more notes and a more complicated story would entangle us all in devastating plotlines over three weeks. But that night at the library we didn't know that yet. We just knew people were scared and angry.

And that's why we were in the library. Together.

When news of that first note sent waves through the campus nervous system, students of color started organizing. They had a goal and began letting everyone know they expected a public show of solidarity in the form of #paintitblack.

Every spring, before the nationally renowned Drake Relays, students paint fifty-four squares on the path that sprawls in front of the library. Each square celebrates a student organization, and together, the squares create a tapestry of color and creativity showcasing the spirit of our community. For the next twelve months after the daylong painting event is over—until the street gets painted again—"painted street" greets each of us as we walk along to whatever building we may be heading toward.

Painted street is Drake's brand. It even has its own Instagram account.

So "since racism impacts our daily lives," said Black students, "solidarity has to be as daily." Solidarity has to be visible. Sustained. The minimum requirement before we dare approach use of a word like *solidarity* is that we find a way for everyone to bear at least some of the cost. In this case, the cost needed to include an interruption of the peace of white mind that too quickly re-blankets campus life after the initial shock of an incident wears off.

"Paint it black!" students said. "So no one can look away." "Paint it black in protest." "Paint it black to defy hate." "Paint the street black in a *celebration of blackness*!" students said.

These same students quickly convinced the student senate to support the plan. Over four more days, they mounted a massive social media pressure campaign. Faculty and staff covered our office doors. "#paintitblack!" we wrote with white chalk on black construction paper in buildings across the campus.

Our collective resolve grew as folks got behind this expression of grief and resistance. It became a shout of defiance. It was also a response to more than just our campus. We were defying the hate and fear that had been emboldened across the country since 2016. We were saying, "Enough! We won't shrink. We won't cower. Even if we're afraid, we aren't going anywhere!"

So there we were in the library on a Monday night so students of color could rage and present to upper-level administrators their demand that we paint the whole street black.

That was the meeting we planned, anyway. That was the meeting barely underway when phones all across campus began to ring.

The rest of that night is seared into my mind but also hazy.

Words scrawled first on paper are now being spoken. Someone is upping the ante. Who are they? How do they know we are here? And—a breathless thought—are they coming in?

"Please, if your phone rings, don't answer it," our president said. The room got chaotic as students talked all at once, some shrieking. A few doubled over sobbing, afraid. Other students sat in their chairs staring straight ahead, looking like they've been turned to stone. "Why is this happening?" I heard an occasional voice cry.

I'm consumed with a longing for a world, a future, a today where all of us flourish. And I cannot let go of the question of where white people choose to stand and how we show it.

Our collective future depends on many things in this country. One is that more white folks learn to show up in rooms like the one nearly two hundred of us were in *together* that night. That we do so in particular kinds of postures and stances.

I believe more of us finding our way into such rooms is crucial to our collective survival. I also believe more white people than ever before want to know how to get inside those rooms.

And that's why I wrote this book.

When I finally went home after hours in the library that night, my insides were still heaving as adrenaline and cortisol slowly drained from my system. I left with cellular knowledge of the flesh-and-blood stakes we're all facing. Hate is close and personal. Its reach is intimate.

That night it was in our library.

But I also knew something else. We were in there together. And in that togetherness we were powerful.

Systems of racism have had their way with us for so long and their logic is so powerful that choosing against them is difficult. But the hardest part is this: These systems make it hard for us to imagine *why* we would do so. The violence and denial of violence, passed down to us, have hidden portals of possibility that are right here. Portals that could open into joy, celebration, the beauty of pluralism and difference, collectivity, healing.

Community. Community. Community. White supremacy has denied us the possibility of the most gorgeous kinds of community. In so doing, it has left those of us who are white mostly bereft of real awareness of how incredible true community would be. I want us to learn to long for it.

In that sense, doorways like the one I stood in that night in the library are thresholds. Thresholds mark the boundaries and borders of human living and lives; they keep us apart from some and push us together with others.

It's the unknown of what lies on the other side of those thresholds that keeps so many of us from taking the risk to walk on through.

But here's what I know. I know from firsthand experience that when we do, we come into spaces with the possibility of life-giving, love-lifting, liberation-insisting celebration. There's no way to go there that avoids grief and pain and anger. No way to get there that circumvents the hard work of acknowledging our complicity. The past cannot be undone.

But depth and joy and freedom (real freedom) become a possibility when we walk on through. When we decide to notice the parts of ourselves that are whispering, "This isn't all there is. It isn't supposed to be like this. Something isn't quite right. I want more and I want different." And then when we muster the courage to listen. Then take a next step.

I don't know how long it was before I saw the university president conferring with police. Thirty minutes? Maybe only twenty? He waved at all of us to come back into the dark-paneled room where some students still sat like stone.

He had word.

Later, news reports would say a neo-Nazi group called Stormfront had hacked Drake University's phone lines. They would explain the group was based in Idaho. The word *Nazi* understandably made many students panic when the president said this. But I've never been so happy to hear the word *Idaho* come out of someone's mouth in my life. (For those of you for whom the

Midwest is flyover land, Idaho is nowhere near Iowa. We weren't in any real danger—not physical danger anyway. Not this time.)

After the initial eruption of sobs in response to this update had slowly ebbed and died down, and once it sunk in there was no physical threat to our safety that night, a student senior stood up. "Okay, y'all." She took the mic. "This is all well and good, we're okay. But we had a reason we came here tonight. Are we going to paint the fucking street black or not?"

And, in response to that, the collective and determined rumble of voices and nods of assent were instantly reconvened. We refocused on our purpose.

We painted the street black.

Together.

As in, all of us.

Later that week, I was in the library again. This time all the students in Crew were gathered for a celebratory meal we'd planned long before the incident involving a series of racist notes had taken place. This meant, of course, we arrived to the meal in a state of mind and heart very different from what we'd been in when we'd planned it. There was a sense of exhaustion in the room. Grief.

But we sat together still. In that same room. And we ate. The food was good. We checked on each other. We complained and sighed. We vented.

Students loved up on each other. And we faculty and staff loved up on everyone.

Then, as we sat there, someone said something funny. Told a joke. It was the kind of joke stand-up comics tell—when the best of them skirt just the right line of inappropriate and hilarious and use humor to process grief. The kind of joke that's cathartic if perfectly timed and perfectly delivered and told by the perfectly right person.

Then students began to laugh.

Then someone went over to their bag and pulled out a speaker. Turned the music on. Then turned the music up.

Then this community of people began to get out of their chairs. And they began to dance (we began to dance). To be playful with one another. To metabolize the rage. To soften just a little bit, from the necessary show of defiance and resolve that had carried us all thus far into some expressions of joy and tenderness—the joy of their connection and the tenderness of their way of being with one another. The joy of their knowledge of their utter beauty.

I write with caution about this sacred experience. This is not an "all's well that ends well" story.

But that community of students did reconsecrate that room. That space. They did reclaim the very ground that violence and threat had dared tread on only days before.

And it was quite a sacred privilege to be allowed to be there. One I didn't take for granted then, nor do I to this day. And all I could think (even though I totally screwed up the double dutch ropes that, yes, students brought into the library) was *My god, if more of my people knew, felt, and could acknowledge our need for such authentic connection, and if more of us experienced such full-throttled celebration of life and living, we'd never again ask, "Why would white people want to do antiracist journey?"*

The question of why any white person would give up privilege quit making sense to me a very long time ago. This is not to say I don't still have it—if you've hung in there with me this long, please don't mishear me now! I do. I have a lot of white privilege.

But it is to say this: the "good party" Patricia Williams wants us to be willing to ruin? That party *isn't even good*.

A totally different kind of dance party is just waiting to be thrown.

That's the party I want to be part of every day of the week. And I hope you want to come, too.

Acknowledgments

Anyone who's ever written a book knows no *one* writes a book. That's especially true for a book like this. I am deeply grateful for the institutional support of Drake University where I worked during most of the writing. The Louisville Institute provided me valuable sabbatical resources to write just as a global pandemic rendered the word *sabbatical* meaningless (so it had to wait a long time and, as a result, supported what became a very different book). Garrett-Evangelical Theological Seminary celebrated with me, as it invited me to join its community of educators right before the book actually came out.

But people make institutions. From the bottom of my heart I want to specifically thank Crew students and alumni, the fantastic Jazlin Coley who now leads that program so beautifully, and the many colleague-friends at Drake who encouraged and supported me; these humans were deeply generous as I wrote, but were also partners in creating relationships of accountability and belonging during periods of time I was learning lessons I had to learn to become able to do so. Craig Owens and Melissa Sturm-Smith deserve specific mention and thanks.

The writers convened, supported, and loved by the amazing Jen Louden listened to early versions of this book two years in a row. They bore witness to my process in ways that grounded me and made me feel safe—I'm so grateful.

Roger Freet, my agent, has stuck with me and believed in my work since long before it was clear I was writing books people would want to read. And working with Elisabeth Dyssegaard and her team at St. Martin's, including Jamilah Lewis-Horton, has been a gift. I must say here: Elisabeth's ability to provide direct and clear feedback that there is simply more revision to be done, combined with her kindness of clarity that there's a book in there if you'll faithfully revise, has made me a much better writer.

Finally, I need to acknowledge and thank my most beloveds. Queer people create such beautiful, complex webs of connection, relationships as unique and stunning as glass in a kaleidoscope and not easily captured by the mainstream categories that define friendship or family. I am so grateful to be no exception.

So many such humans have cheerled and cared for me in immeasurable ways over the last three years. In particular Aaron Agne, Renée Cramer, Melanie Harris, Janée Harvey, EJ McGaughy, Melanie Morrison, Jaime Nevins, Tobi Parks, Lucy Suros, and Aana Vigen each and all provided me so many different kinds of necessary and deep support and love while I was writing this book. Words fall short, but I need not write out the details of the what and the how. They know who they are and I know I am most blessed.

Chris, Harper, and Emery Patterson remain at the center of my universe. They are like gravity. They exert just the right amount of force to keep me, on the one hand, grounded and, on the other, free to create my own patterns of orbit (I hope I always do the same for them). I am because we are. Thank you.

Further Resources

DEEPENING RACIAL AWARENESS

Centering the voices and analyses of journalists of color can deepen our everyday understanding of how "race affects every part of society" (Code Switch).

ARRAY 101, https://array101.org
Founded by Ava DuVernay, ARRAY 101 is an online educational initiative that provides free learning guides to accompany films and other storytelling created by "Black artists, people of color and women directors of all kinds."

Code Switch, https://www.npr.org/sections/codeswitch/
A National Public Radio podcast and blog offering "fearless conversations about race. . . . Hosted by journalists of color, [their] podcast tackles the subject of race with empathy and humor."

Color of Change, https://colorofchange.org/about/
This online organization supports various campaigns for growing "real power for Black communities." Their email subscription does a fantastic job of keeping their base informed about racial justice momentum and challenges.

Colorlines, https://colorlines.com
A digital multimedia platform, Colorlines has provided "quality, race-focused

journalism that centers people of color and marginalized voices" for more than twenty years.

It's Been a Minute, **https://www.npr.org/podcasts/510317/its-been-a-minute**
Hosted by Brittany Luse, this NPR radio program and podcast engages weekly news and "people in the culture who deserve your attention."

BOOKS FOR MORE NEXT STEPS

The Antiracism Handbook: Practical Tools to Shift Your Mindset and Uproot Racism in Your Life and Community by Thema Bryant and Edith G. Arrington (Oakland, CA: New Harbinger Publications, 2022).

Do the Work!: An Antiracist Activity Book by W. Kamau Bell and Kate Schatz (New York: Workman Publishing, 2022).

Doing Nothing Is No Longer an Option: One Woman's Journey into Everyday Antiracism by Jenny Booth Potter (Downers Grove, IL: InterVarsity Press, 2022).

How to Be an Antiracist by Ibram X. Kendi (New York: One World, 2019).

It's Time to Talk About Race at Work: Every Leader's Guide to Making Progress on Diversity, Equity, and Inclusion by Kelly McDonald (Hoboken, NJ: Wiley, 2021).

Me and White Supremacy: Combat Racism, Change the World, and Become a Good Ancestor by Layla F. Saad (Naperville, IL: Sourcebooks, 2020).

Me and White Supremacy: A Guided Journal by Layla F. Saad (Naperville, IL: Sourcebooks, 2020).

The Quaking of America: An Embodied Guide to Navigating Our Nation's Upheaval and Racial Reckoning by Resmaa Menakem (Las Vegas, NV: Central Recovery Press, 2022).

The Racial Healing Handbook: Practical Activities to Help You Challenge Privilege, Confront Systemic Racism, and Engage in Collective Healing by Anneliese A. Singh (Oakland, CA: New Harbinger Publications, 2019).

SKILL-BUILDING AND COMMUNITY INITIATIVES

This list of organizations and recognized leaders in transformative justice work offers various kinds of opportunities to connect, learn, and access tools to help us collectively move the needle for justice—while also taking seriously the need to heal ourselves.

Acts of Reparation, **a documentary film by Selina Lewis Davidson and Macky Alston, https://www.actsofreparation.com/**
In addition to being a film highlighting community-engaged reparative justice projects from different parts of the country, *Acts of Reparation* also has impact campaigns and ways to support those inspired to get involved with the work of repair in their own lives and communities.

America & Moore Diversity Education, Research & Consulting, https://www.eddiemoorejr.com
Eddie Moore Jr., who founded the White Privilege Conference, offers a variety of twenty-one-day equity challenges for different contexts, and for both individuals and organizations.

The Catalyst Project, https://collectiveliberation.org
Working to "build powerful multiracial movements that can win collective liberation," this organization provides many resources to support white people in participating in this vision.

The Community Remembrance Project of the Equal Justice Initiative, https://eji.org/projects/community-remembrance-project/
A project that works with community coalitions to memorialize local racial violence and foster dialogue about race and justice, out of the conviction that creating a just future requires that we tell the truth about our past together.

CTZNWELL, https://www.ctznwell.org
An organization that creates content and facilitates dialogue and action in support of creating a culture of radical wellness.

Integrated Schools, https://integratedschools.org
A grassroots movement of families committed to integrated educations while working to keep antiracist principles and humility among white parents central to how integration happens.

White Awake, https://whiteawake.org
This organization creates content, courses, and practices especially focused on those of us "who've been social categorized as 'white' in the creation of a just and sustainable society."

PODCASTS AND PRACTITIONERS FOCUSED ON CONNECTIONS BETWEEN HEALING SELF AND SYSTEMS

Chris Crass, http://www.chriscrass.org
An organizer who helped found SURJ (Showing Up for Racial Justice), Chris Crass leads workshops supporting white people in their work for racial justice, increasing their capacity to be "awesome" for collective liberation.

Prentis Hemphill, https://prentishemphill.com
Prentis Hemphill is the founder of the Embodiment Institute (https://www.theembodimentinstitute.org), which is focused on embodiment and

healing and offers courses and other kinds of trainings. They are also the host of the podcast *Finding Our Way*.

Resmaa Menakem, https://www.resmaa.com

In addition to his books, Resmaa Menakem offers courses online and training on embodied antiracism; he also hosts a podcast called *Guerrilla Muse*.

Mia Mingus, https://leavingevidence.wordpress.com/about-2/

Focused on transformative justice and disability justice, Mia Mingus writes and teaches. She also founded SOIL: A Transformative Justice Project (https://www.soiltjp.org/home), which focuses on ending generational cycles of harm and violence by helping all of us build our skills for such work.

Notes

1. Where Are We?

1. Fabiola Cineas, "Ibram X. Kendi on Anti-racism, Juneteenth, and the Reckoning That Wasn't," *Vox*, June 17, 2021, https://www.vox.com/22538592 /ibram-x-kendi-juneteenth-racial-reckoning-antiracism.

2. See Pew Research Center. The 53 percent of white women is complicated; later reports showed that the number was 47 percent—slightly lower but still more white women who voted for Donald Trump than for Hillary Clinton. I leave 53 percent here, however, because that initial number still resonated with people of color despite it having been later slightly revised down. Also, it wasn't just evangelical Christians (81 percent), even though they get most of the press. Fifty-eight percent of white Protestants did it. So did 60 percent of white Catholics (https://www.pewresearch.org /short-reads/2016/11/09/how-the-faithful-voted-a-preliminary-2016 -analysis/). The 2020 numbers were about the same among white mainline Protestants (57 percent), worse among white evangelicals (84 percent), and slightly better among Catholics (57 percent) (https://www .pewresearch.org/short-reads/2021/08/30/most-white-americans-who -regularly-attend-worship-services-voted-for-trump-in-2020/#:~:text =In%202020%2C%20White%20non%2Devangelical,Trump%20and%20 48%25%20favoring%20Biden).

3. adrienne maree brown, *Pleasure Activism: The Politics of Feeling Good* (Chico, CA: AK Press, 2019).

4. See Corinne Shutack, "106 Things White People Can Do for Racial Justice,"

last updated on February 5, 2022, https://medium.com/equality-includes -you/what-white-people-can-do-for-racial-justice-f2d18b0e0234.

2. Why Is This So Hard?

1. Rebecca Solnit, "Old Conflicts, New Chapters," in *Whose Story Is This? Old Conflicts, New Chapters* (Chicago: Haymarket Books, 2019), 1.
2. Alicia Garza, "Our Cynicism Will Not Build a Movement. Collaboration Will," *MIC*, January 26, 2017, https://www.mic.com/articles/166720 /blm-co-founder-protesting-isnt-about-who-can-be-the-most-radical-its -about-winning.

3. Let's Run Around the Block!

1. Prentis Hemphill, *Finding Our Way* (podcast), "Building Power with Alicia Garza," August 29, 2022, https://www.findingourwaypodcast.com /individual-episodes/s3e6.
2. Rebecca Solnit, "Old Conflicts, New Chapters," in *Whose Story Is This? Old Conflicts, New Chapters* (Chicago: Haymarket Books, 2019), 1.
3. Solnit, "Old Conflicts, New Chapters," 8.
4. Solnit, "Old Conflicts, New Chapters," 9.

4. The Freedom of a Ruined Party

1. Patricia J. Williams, *The Alchemy of Race and Rights: Diary of a Law Professor*, rev. ed. (Cambridge, MA: Harvard University Press, 1992).
2. My friend Rachel was not white, though she did live in my neighborhood, had white parents, and was as economically secure as I was.
3. Chase Strangio, "No One Can Take Away Our Joy," *The Nation*, November 25, 2022, https://www.thenation.com/article/society/colorado-shootings -trans-joy/.

5. Beyond White Fragility

1. Peggy McIntosh initially coined this term in the now-famous essay "White Privilege: Unpacking the Invisible Knapsack," first published in *Peace and Freedom*, July/August 1989, https://psychology.umbc.edu/wp -content/uploads/sites/57/2016/10/White-Privilege_McIntosh-1989.pdf.
2. George Yancy, "Tarrying Together," *Educational Philosophy and Theory* 47, no. 1 (2015): 26–35, https://www.tandfonline.com/doi/abs/10.1080/00131857 .2013.861197?journalCode=rept20.
3. See "What Is White Supremacy Culture?" at https://www.whitesupremacy culture.info/what-is-it.html.
4. Ezra Klein, *The Ezra Klein Show* (podcast), "What 'Drained-Pool' Politics Cost America," with Heather McGhee, February 16, 2021, https://www.nytimes .com/2021/02/16/opinion/ezra-klein-podcast-heather-mcghee.html.
5. Lucy Duncan, "What's at Stake for White People in the Struggle for

Racial Justice? A Conversation with Chris Crass pt. 4," by Lucy Duncan, American Friends Service Committee Blog, October 20, 2017, https://www.afsc.org/blogs/acting-in-faith/what's-stake-white-people-struggle-racial-justice-conversation-chris-crass-pt.

6. See Resmaa Menakem, *My Grandmother's Hands: Racialized Trauma and the Pathway to Mending Our Hearts and Bodies* (Las Vegas, NV: Central Recovery Press, 2017).

7. See https://www.resmaa.com.

8. Beverly Wildung Harrison, *Making the Connections: Essays in Feminist Social Ethics,* edited by Carol S. Robb (Boston: Beacon Press, 1985), 13 and 14.

9. See https://anniesfoundation.com.

6. Finding Our Way Through Paradox

1. See "Ava DuVernay: 'Not Our Job to Explain to White Folk' How to Combat Racism," CBS News, May 28, 2020, https://www.cbsnews.com/news/ava-duvernay-array-101-when-they-see-us/.

7. Accountability as Belonging

1. Prentis Hemphill, *Finding Our Way* (podcast), "Questioning Culture with Richie Reseda," July 18, 2020, https://www.findingourwaypodcast.com/individual-episodes/s3s3.

2. Hemphill, "Questioning Culture with Richie Reseda."

3. Prentis Hemphill, *Finding Our Way* (podcast), "Building Power with Alicia Garza," https://www.findingourwaypodcast.com/individual-episodes/s3e6.

4. See https://www.ctznwell.org/about.

5. See https://www.resmaa.com/movement.

6. See https://eji.org/projects/community-remembrance-project.

7. See https://www.actsofreparation.com.

8. So, What *Do* We Do with Our Families?

1. Christine Sleeter, "White Racism," *Multicultural Education* 1, no. 4 (Spring 1994): 5–8.

2. See Beverly Daniel Tatum, *Why Are All the Black Kids Sitting Together in the Cafeteria? And Other Conversations on Race,* 20th anniversary ed. (New York: Basic Books, 2017).

3. Patricia J. Williams, *Seeing a Color-Blind Future: The Paradox of Race* (New York: Farrar, Straus and Giroux, 1998).

4. George Goehl, "How We Got Trump Voters to Change Their Minds," *The Atlantic,* October 26, 2020, https://www.theatlantic.com/ideas/archive/2020/10/how-we-got-voters-to-change-their-mind/616851/.

5. Goehl, "How We Got Trump Voters to Change Their Minds."

6. See Daniel Cox, Juhem Navarro-Rivera, and Robert P. Jones, "Race, Reli-

gion and Political Affiliation of Americans' Core Social Networks," Public Religion Research Institute, August 3, 2016, https://www.prri.org/research /poll-race-religion-politics-americans-social-networks.
7. Rebecca Solnit, "Old Conflicts, New Chapters," in *Whose Story Is This? Old Conflicts, New Chapters* (Chicago: Haymarket Books, 2019), 9.
8. Layla F. Saad, *Me and White Supremacy: Combat Racism, Change the World, and Become a Good Ancestor* (Naperville, IL: Sourcebooks, 2020).

9. Mapping Our Spheres of Influence
1. A concept that originated with community organizer L.F.
2. See https://leavingevidence.wordpress.com/about-2/.

10. How Do We Change Our (Predominantly White) X?
1. Very similar implementation of this model could be used in a number of different organizational or entrepreneurial settings.

About the Author

Keesha Ward, Ward Creative Studios

Dr. Jennifer Harvey is a writer and educator long engaged in racial justice. Her books include the *New York Times* bestseller *Raising White Kids*. She has written for *The New York Times* and CNN and has been a guest on NPR's *All Things Considered*. Dr. Harvey served nearly twenty years at Drake University as both professor and associate provost for campus equity and inclusion. She is now the vice president of academic affairs at Garrett-Evangelical Theological Seminary in Evanston, Illinois.